RELIGIOUS AND SOCIAL RITUAL

Religious and Social Ritual

INTERDISCIPLINARY EXPLORATIONS

Edited by
Michael B. Aune
and
Valerie DeMarinis

STATE UNIVERSITY OF NEW YORK PRESS

Published by
State University of New York Press, Albany

Printed in the United States of America

For information, address State University of New York
Press, State University Plaza, Albany, N.Y., 12246

Production by Cathleen Collins
Marketing by Theresa Abad Swierzowski

Library of Congress Cataloging-in-Publication Data

Religious and social ritual : interdisciplinary explorations / edited
    by Michael B. Aune and Valerie DeMarinis.
            p.   cm.
    Includes bibliographical references and index.
    ISBN 0–7914–2825–7 (alk. paper). — ISBN 0–7914–2826–5 (pbk. :
alk. paper)
    1. Ritual—Comparative studies.   I. Aune, Michael Bjerknes.
II. DeMarinis, Valerie M.
BL600.R44   1996
291.3′8—dc20   95–17022
                                                                      CIP

10 9 8 7 6 5 4 3 2 1

Contents

Acknowledgments

As the organizers of the Graduate Theolgical Union Workshop on Ritual and the editors of this volume, we wish to acknowledge with gratitude the financial support we have received from our Dean, Judith A. Berling, and our Faculty Grants and Projects Office. Thanks are also due to the American Academy of Religion for awarding us a collaborative grant that enabled the project to continue into a second year.

Acknowledgments and gratitude are also extended to those who helped us with numerous prepublication tasks: Barbara Anderson, Audrey Englert, Yvonne Vowels, and Carol Jacobson.

Michael B. Aune
Pacific Lutheran Theological Seminary
Graduate Theological Union, Berkeley, CA

Valerie DeMarinis
Department of Theology
Uppsala Universitet, Sweden

Introduction

BACKGROUND OF THIS VOLUME

Ritual continues to be an important topic, if not a fashionable interest, in the contemporary study of religion and culture. Whether it is understood as a certain kind of symbolic action, a form of stylized behavior, a self-contained dramatic frame, or a distinctive sort of cultural practice, ritual is increasingly regarded as playing a salient role in the meaningful construction of personal and social worlds. Once upon a time, however, this way of acting and speaking was regarded as a relic of the past, attributable to superstition, magic, or simply weird, if not obsessive, behavior. Somehow this has all changed. Nowadays, it seems, ritual is everywhere and doing practically everything. It can be powerful, dramatic, transformative, good, and healthy. Ritual experiments and workshops abound that purport to offer intense, authentic experiences. Yet, we have also become more aware of ritual's capacity to abuse, to terrorize, to dominate, or to repress.

The veritable explosion of scholarly and popular literature on the topic of ritual has spawned new sets of questions about its role and nature in collective and personal life. Historians of religion, anthropologists, psychologists, theologians—to name only a few—have eagerly set themselves to the task of discussing, analyzing, and interpreting ritual processes in order to account more fully for their purpose and power. But whereas there is keen interest in various scholarly disciplines about what ritual is and does, there has been little conversation or discussion to determine whether we might be able to learn something from one another.[1] For if ritual is being studied and interpretations are being proposed from sometimes convergent and sometimes incompatible perspectives, why not bring together a group of people who are concerned, in their teaching and research, with advancing crit-

1

ical understanding of this particular phenomenon in order to see what
might happen?

In the lively, imaginative, and challenging milieu of the Graduate
Theological Union (GTU)[2] and the University of California, Berkeley
(UCB), we often converse with one another on topics of mutual interest that are being explored across disciplinary boundaries. Someone
says, for example, "You know, so-and-so is working on ritual. You
should go and talk to her." One such conversation between the editors
of this volume—one a teacher and researcher in the area of psychology
and religion (DeMarinis), and the other a liturgical scholar with a wide
range of interests (Aune)—prompted the idea of organizing and con-
vening a workshop on the study of ritual that would include persons
from a variety of disciplines. We had noticed that although there was a
good deal of interest in this topic among our multi-denominational
faculty colleagues, discussions of what ritual is and does (usually
termed "liturgy" or "worship") were often limited or shaped by our
respective institutional agendas or by the perceived normative interests of theology and doctrine. We also noticed that the scholarly investigation of ritual that was taking place "across the street" at UCB
tended to be of the sort that eschewed what we at the GTU called the
"committed study of religion." The preference in university disciplines was for description and analysis that we thought overmystified
and even looked critically askance at certain modes of ritual behavior
and sensibility.

Nonetheless, it seemed clear to us that if we at the GTU were to
continue working toward a balance between the "committed study of
religion" and the "critical disciplines and perspectives" of the university, a collaborative inquiry with ritual as a common focus might be a
good way to explore together an issue that mattered on both sides of
the street. Since our Dean, Judith A. Berling, and the Director of our
Faculty Grants and Projects Office, Cheryl Tupper, were envisioning
such collaborative inquiry on an intellectual theme or issue that
would cut across the lines of GTU areas of doctoral study and also
would include faculty members from UCB, we were able to propose
such a workshop. At that time we wrote:

> Religious ritual, both awesome and austere, provides mem-
> bers of a community of faith with an occasion and a set of
> symbols to either reinforce or to transform the ways in which
> they think and feel about themselves and the world in which
> they live. Study and reflection upon this "transaction of con-
> sequence," as ritual has been called in one recent discussion,
> are currently carried out in a wide variety of disciplines in

both the humanities and the social sciences. Once in a while interdisciplinary conversations occur on the topic of ritual, especially religious ritual, as the recent volume *Violent Origins* attests. Moreover, recent scholarship in such diverse fields as feminist psychology, transcultural psychology, medical anthropology, neo-analytic psychotherapy, and liturgical studies has recognized the vital importance of religious ritual and its constitutive role in offering answers to, or at least perspectives on, the fundamental question of what it means to be a human being, whole and healthy or diseased and distressed.

In an ecumenical and inter-religious setting such as the Graduate Theological Union, questions about ritual's cultural, theological, and psychosocial dimensions emerge with particular forcefulness and urgency. Yet discussions of these questions tend to be limited to our individual seminaries with their respective denominational agendas or to those areas which have certain methods and approaches for addressing the role and function of religious ritual in a pluralistic, ecumenical, and inter-religious context. Given the increasing interdisciplinary interest and ferment in discussions of certain fundamental issues in ritual theory and practice, however, it is certainly timely, if not urgent, that such discussions begin to occur among GTU and UCB faculty and some of our doctoral students.

Thus, in the fall of 1989 we received a grant to begin formal exploration under the rubric of "ritual as mediator of memory and meaning."

The scholars who were invited to participate represented divergent methodological interests and fields of study. There were those whose focus was on cross-cultural and historical themes and whose scholarship and teaching sought to advance critical understanding of interreligious, multicultural, and contextual religious experience. There were others whose field of study centered on the theological and pastoral examination of various traditions of Christian worship in relation to particular institutions and communities of faith. A third group of participants represented the interface between contemporary psychological disciplines and different religious traditions of pastoral care. In short, the members of our working group each had a discipline of reference—the comparative study of religion and religious experience (which included history and anthropology), liturgical studies, and religion and psychology.

In addition to this GTU and UCB faculty component of the project, two other features or dimensions need to be mentioned. First, there was also a doctoral seminar involving eleven GTU students who were working in a variety of areas including historical studies, systematic theology, religion and psychology, liturgical studies, and the history of Christian spirituality. The second feature was that we invited two speakers from outside the GTU/UCB communities. Ronald Grimes of Wilfrid Laurier University, Waterloo, Ontario, who is credited with the development of "ritual studies" as a distinct focus, presented a public lecture entitled "Ritualizing: Tradition and Culture, Meaning and Memory."[3] Volney Gay of Vanderbilt University, an author and researcher in ritual studies in religion and psychology, presented a lecture with the title "The Role of the Despised" (revised for this volume under the title "Ritual and Psychotherapy: Some Similarities and Differences").

OUR THEME AND ITS CONTESTATIONS

Although we thought that our organizing theme, "Ritual as Mediator of Memory and Meaning," suggested a theory that we thought applicable to a wide range of ritual activities, we invited each participant, in preparation for our first meeting, to provide an initial working definition of ritual. Or, at least, some argued that certain matters needed to be taken into account when attempting to delimit the range of our inquiry. For example, one noted that ritual and religious ritual should be distinguished from the merely customary and habitual. Another observed that ritual has a social and normative context that assumes the seriousness of "performatory action." Almost all the participants emphasized that ritual is a particular kind of forceful or charged activity. We also asked the participants to suggest a reading list that could assist us in developing a common vocabulary for our conversations. As one might expect, the suggested readings covered a broad range of studies—theoretical as well as ethnographic. We were reminded of the contentious debates about the meaning and definition of ritual, as well as the continuing lack of agreement about how to define it. In spite of this definitional warfare, there was a general assumption—both in the scholarly literature and among the participants—that whatever ritual might be, it is the kind of activity in which certain things happen or signify complex realities in particular ways.

Once we had assembled the participants for this project, our initial task was to exegete the theme that the coeditors presented in the original grant proposal: "Religious Ritual as Mediator of Memory and

Meaning." Our primary purpose was not to assert a univocal viewpoint, but to surface issues of method, theory, and interpretation within a larger contemporary epistemological landscape. This was really the challenge of our interaction and engagement across disciplines and perspectives.

We spent a great deal of time trying to clarify and to explain the "memory and meaning" theme. For some, it seemed hopelessly decontextualized and already reflective of both methodological/conceptual commitments and a certain stance toward ritual theory. We were reminded, however, that the theme had emerged from a particular context, in this instance a psychotherapeutic one, and was simply being offered as an entree into a characteristic or dynamic of ritual—its capacity or special ability to create much-needed continuity in people's lives by linking the past to the present and the present to the future. This particular characteristic proved to be more evident in some of the rituals that we explored and, consequently, certain essays in this volume refer to that perspective.

Over the long haul of the project, however, the organizing theme was variously employed, modified, criticized, re-defined, and even discarded. What seems to have emerged early on in our discussions was the necessity of probing further the nature of ritual activities themselves as we recognized the pluralism embedded in the study of ritual, both methodologically and religiously. Moreover, most participants understood both their respective study and the common work to have meaning while, at the same time, raising more questions than answers.

In our work together, we also realized the necessity of paying close attention to the very acts we were purporting to describe and to interpret. We needed to articulate our own respective awarenesses and multiple judgments regarding the rituals under study. For the question that was continually provoking and challenging us was this: "Whose meaning are we constructing when rituals are interpreted: our informants' or our own?"[4]

The unity of our group was in attending to and contesting the assumptions and "truth claims" as they are operative in our disciplines, as well as in acknowledging that our own experiences of ritual were at work as we went about our tasks of description and interpretation. Our sense was and is that if we did not include such matters we would be guilty of exemplifying the sort of thing recently commented upon by Stephen A. Tyler in his book, *The Unspeakable: Discourse, Dialogue, and Rhetoric in the Postmodern World*:

The ethnographer suppresses the experience of ritual, its fits and starts, movements from center to periphery, its plurivocalism, and substitutes for it the smooth, uninterrupted flow of a univocal narrative in which the sequentialized action builds logically to its climax and moves unfalteringly to its conclusion. Both ethnographer and reader suppress their experience of ritual and know it only as literature, as a text of a ritual which can be understood only by comparing it to texts of other rituals, seeing it finally as part of the ultimate "how to" book of magic, or as a preliminary, though hesitant, step on the road to science.[5]

Among the lively questions to emerge from this portion of our work was whether any privileged or articulated role of the influence of the personal experience of the respective workshop participants (or perhaps lack thereof) needed to be acknowledged. We realized that this was the case these days in certain forms of cultural and social analysis where the notion of the "positioned subject" is invoked or when it is argued that the role of subjectivity in ritual studies must be expanded.[6] One of our colleagues stated this issue well:

When it is the ritual of "my" tradition [there is] familiar pattern with subtle variations which express the cycles of the sacred year and/or personal or communal experience; a sense of belonging; best when multivalent (when [it] contains layers and levels of meaning); breaks the race of profane time to a different rhythm and thus helps to stimulate a certain level of reflection/prayer/contemplation/focus. . . .

When it is "their" rituals: the pattern is both powerful and communicative even though I am not "within" the community; [there is] a sense of connectedness to others; [there is] the power of the dramatic structure (rituals have a plot); roles and relationships are defined; conveys more deeply than any other mode (except perhaps art) the vitality of the tradition.[7]

We were very aware that to describe such vitality and veracity as "meaning" or "meaning-making" might ensnare us in the nasty debate over whether ritual "means" anything or whether instead it should be regarded as "pure activity without meaning or goal."[8] With the demise of referential theories of meaning at least since the time of Gottlob Frege, however, there has been a corresponding broadening and deepening of "meaning" as involving much more than "signifying to the intellect."[9] While ritual may not or need not have *intellectual content*, this is not at all to say or to suggest that it is meaningless. Rather, as has been observed and argued recently,

> Meaning is meaning, in the vague and wonderful sense we use the word when we talk to each other. . . . We have to learn that when we ask "What does ritual mean?", we must immediately qualify our query: "To whom?", "When?", "Why?", and, importantly, "How?"[10]

Moreover, ritual, in the final analysis, is

> a matter of human culture, enacted by men and women, sometimes alone, more often in community. It is therefore a question of subjective experience. As we describe it, soberly, and as objectively as we can, we are describing the real experience of a real person or group of people.[11]

Thus, the essays collected here have sought to describe ritual experiences of a real person or groups of persons.

Our descriptive and interpretive efforts, while trying to avoid the contentious and often nasty discussions of how to define the term *ritual*, nonetheless have been influenced by implicit or explicit definitions. For example, some of us found the recent shift from the concern with formal definition to an approach in terms of "qualities of ritual" or "ritualization" to be useful, if not more advantageous.[12] This shift allowed exploration of certain dimensions of the experience of ritual such as cognition and emotion that, say, more theological investigations would not consider or be willing to consider at all. For example, in liturgical studies, a primary concern has been with "official" and "normative" meaning—"the things the experts say that a rite means" and "the structure of signification that ritual affixes upon the non-ritualized world that the ritual participants re-enter when the rite has been concluded."[13]

Yet other essayists, particularly those writing from comparativist or clinical points of view, found it necessary to be more definitionally specific. As Volney Gay has observed, "The way in which one defines the term 'ritual' directly influences the development of one's subsequent analysis of the phenomenon."[14] But it also needs to be noted that the theoretical debate in the study of ritual has yet to produce a precise way of specifying what this sort of human activity is. It just might be that precise definitions are neither possible nor are they necessary. In fact, most definitions, as Don Handelman has pointed out, are "unremarkable, noncommittal, and innocuous. . . ."[15] Moreover,

> they really tell us almost nothing, apart from some vague sort
> of instruction, perhaps akin to: PAY ATTENTION—SOME-
> THING SPECIAL GOING ON HERE AND NOW. [16]

THEORETICAL INTERESTS AND CONCERNS

Paying attention to something important going on here and now (or, then and there) does involve, however, an awareness of or responsiveness to theoretical interests and concerns. "Theory," of course, has many meanings, but here we need be concerned only with its meanings in the context of the study of ritual. By "ritual theory" we mean the debate over the nature and function of this sort of activity. The focus is on the problematic of how to understand or explain appropriately just what is being done and said. Throughout our discussions and in the essays in this volume, we strove to be as clear and forthright as we could about what were our operative theoretical interests and concerns. Yet a crucial question that surfaced, particularly during the writing of the essays, was whether we were using theory applicatively or critically.

For example, it is rather easy to think of theory in the applicative sense. That is, we bring to our inquiry a systematic statement of rules or principles to be followed. For the study of ritual, this usually means that there is a thing that can be generally labelled "ritual" and that it exhibits certain distinctive features. In the early work of our project, it was clear that most of us operated with this notion of theory. We assumed, often without testing, that there is some sort of universal construct—i.e., "ritual"—and the task is to figure out how it works and why. So, we would employ our favorite theorists—Ron Grimes, Victor Turner, Theodore Jennings, Catherine Bell, Evan Zuesse, Mircea Eliade, Clifford Geertz, Stanley Tambiah, Arnold van Gennep—because we thought they best helped us to illuminate a particular ritual or ritualizing situation.

What is fascinating is that even though we began to find the formulation "ritual as mediator of memory and meaning" to be problematic because it did not work as a satisfying explanation for some of the expressions we were exploring,[17] we found it difficult to proceed to the realization that our inquiry into particular ritual instances could challenge and reformulate the theorists' positions. This may have been due to a naive understanding of how theory and practice are related—that is, we think that theory is applied to a ritual expression rather than formulated from it. But once some of us interrogated theoretical positions from the perspective of our examples and cases, theory began to emerge as having a great deal to do with the very basic questions that any serious student of ritual must face. These include: How did they do that? How did they make sense of that ritual? Where are they coming from? Why does ritual still have the power to do what it does? This can be, of course, very unsettling, because assumptions are questioned and more problems are created.

Often, for example, it is assumed that ritual has to do with order, structure, unity, identity, transformation—to name just a few characteristics and dynamics that a dominant theoretical discourse might claim. But is it always the case that such activity is about or actually doing these things? Some of our colleagues discovered otherwise. In their research and writing, they found very different characteristics and dynamics. Resistance, subversion, as well as redefinitions of power and performativity, began to surface. Others of us became uncomfortable with notions of "meaning" because they overshadowed or displaced "knowing" or did not account for "embodiment," which were emerging as salient features of the rituals under investigation. What these discoveries indicated is that ritual and ritualizing are "inherently historical"[18] or radically contextualized with "context" requiring as much interpretation as the ritual activities themselves. Any theoretical insights needed to emerge from the specificity of the activity being explored.

This specificity includes the "frame" in which the ritual occurs, its cultural history, and its universe of morphological significance (i.e., relating to form, structure, pattern).[19] To accomplish this, at least the following sets of issues need to be addressed:

- meanings and meaningfulness
- time, place, and the participant's perceptions
- recent *and* older history of the ritual and of its interpretations
- role of pattern, indigenous structure, particularity
- relation between "interpreter" and "interpreted"

Theoretically, we believe that it is our attention to these sets of issues that has made our collaborative endeavor both significant and worthy of further discussion.

ORGANIZATION OF THIS VOLUME

The provision of "case studies" across a wide range of cultures and historical instances is exactly what has been suggested by recent ritual studies.[20] More important, each of our contributors has sought to incorporate his or her historical, methodological, and autobiographical situations in responsible and graceful ways.

The volume is divided into three parts: comparative explorations, liturgical explorations, and clinical explorations. Our choice of "explorations," both for the title of the volume and for its three parts, is deliberate. As noted earlier, this project began as an "exploration" of the topic of religious ritual and its relation to memory and meaning-making. During our process of discussion and exchange, this relation was explored, criticized, modified, and utilized in a variety of ways—some more explicit than others. In particular, the presentations of Ronald L. Grimes and Volney Gay challenged us to reconsider the commonly accepted views of ritual as "traditional," "collective," and "meaningful."

The "exploratory" nature of these essays means that they can be also "hypothesis generating." That is, they raise critical questions for further cooperative exploration *beyond* the liturgical, comparative, and clinical areas. And, finally, the essays can be considered "explorations" in the sense of undertaking the theoretical and methodological challenges present in the study of ritual in the 1990s.[21]

Each part of the volume has its own introductory essay, which provides a point of entry to and thematic overview of the essays. The three-part structure of the volume is intentional. The comparative, liturgical, and clinical explorations reflect the three broad disciplines of the scholars involved in our project. Our placement of the comparative explorations first grew out of the realization that the rituals we were investigating seemed to proceed from those embedded in particular religious or belief structures to those which were located within certain ecclesial communities to those which emphasized ritual and the individual. The progression, of course, is not terribly neat or tidy since there are overlaps as well as tensions between and among the comparative, liturgical, and clinical. But, in terms of matters of emphasis, our triadic structure reflects, we think, the push-and-pull that exists between belief systems, institutions, and individuals.

Also, the placement of the comparative explorations first is reflective of a historical progression in the study of ritual. Comparative studies have been the most traditional and have tended to be the dominant mode of explanation. Liturgical and clinical studies have only recently begun to utilize and to take advantage of the breaching of scholarly boundaries. What we wanted to know about particular instances of ritualizing—whether in church or in the clinic—was being restructured by interpretive paradigms that one might think belong more to the comparative enterprise. Yet we also think that our triadic organization of this volume testifies to how the disciplinary can give way to the interdisciplinary because changes in interpretive approaches actually ensue in changes in what can be seen and then thought about with respect to the rituals being explored. We began to realize that formulations of the question also change—and this is what has happened in this book.

Finally, our triple focus represents a movement in the relation between "interpreter" and "interpreted." That is, those writing in the comparative section are outsiders to the rituals they investigated. The question which their "outsider" position raises is whether we can really understand a culture other than our own. Such a question has been at the forefront of so-called postmodernist culture writing and theorizing.[22] The essayists in the liturgical section of this volume are insiders. They stand within the particular traditions they explore. Such a vantage point allows for exploration of ritual activity, experience, and impact at both the individual participant and group levels. Although this vantage point permits discussion and analysis of normative claims as well as descriptive matters of empowerment and identification, it may also blind the essayists to certain issues, such as the private or the political. The clinical essayists write as professionals concerned with articulating and exploring the consequences of ritual experience and ritual memory at the following levels of meaning-making: cognitive, behavioral, and symbolic.

The interpreter—interpreted relationship thus raises the larger issue of "integrity": how to be present in the face of radical difference. Anthropologist Bruce Kapferer's observation is useful here. He has written, "For the worlds of others to realize their critical force, their schemes of thought and practice must be explored systematically and, further, must be given equivalent ontological and epistemological status."[23] A brief glance at our triple focus will begin to make this concern with integrity clearer.

THE ESSAYS

The essays in Part I are "comparative explorations" of a wide range of ritual behavior—Aboriginal, Javanese, Shingon Buddhist and Shaker (Martin, Fischer, Payne, and Stortz). These authors have isolated key issues and themes such as bodies, knowing, power, authority, gender, person, and status and, at the same time, have historicized and contextualized them. In so doing, they reflect the multiple ways complex cultures require decoding, recognizing how treacherous is the terrain of comparison whether across time or geographical boundary.

What these diverse essays offer, even generate, is an enhanced understanding of the multiple levels of ritual experience and function. In some cultural and meaning-making contexts, these levels work to personally or communally transform. Investigations of other contexts, however, challenge traditional theories of ritual that emphasize the conservative or transformative function of this way of acting and speaking. Sometimes, what is found instead is an understanding and experience of ritual that embraces chaos and resistance or confronts various kinds of power and authority.

In every case, however, the dimensions of social identification and social consequence of each ritual expression are undertaken. The essays also raise insights and questions regarding recognition and appreciation of the category of space, both internal and external, in ritual experience and analysis.

The essays in Part II are primarily "liturgical explorations" of certain rituals or ritualizing activities in several Christian traditions (Aune and Slough). They are "liturgical" in the disciplinary sense of the authors' training in the investigation of church or synagogue activity enshrined principally in texts but now expanded to go beyond them in order to discover the ways that liturgy might actually be said to work in particular communities. The activities investigated in these essays include a Communion service and hymn singing. The essayists have in common the "insider" position of participant-observer. They each stand within the particular traditions which they explore, using a variety of theoretical and methodological approaches, especially those where ritual is regarded as a distinctive kind of strategic action that embraces social and (inter)subjective dynamics of knowing and feeling.

The essays in Part III involve "clinical explorations" of the nature and function of ritual (Gay, DeMarinis, Driskill, and Noonan). There is a consideration of the similarities and differences between ritual and psychotherapy, followed by two case presentations of the therapeutic efficacy of religious ritual in clinical settings, and an exploration of the commonalities of the experience of surgery with the phenomena usually associated with rites of passage.

The interactions are investigated from different clinical vantage points. Yet, each does so with attention to intrapersonal and interpersonal consequences. Each author employs an approach to ritual activity and experience by way of phenomenological and functional categories. These essays are located within the broad field of the psychology of religion, with special emphasis on psychotherapeutic contexts.

In this part of the volume, the focus shifts from an analysis of religious or social rituals within particular cultures or ecclesial traditions to the use and application of ritual categories in various clinical contexts. This shift is significant, for it necessitates experimenting and a broadening of understandings of ritual. The essays in this section deal the most explicitly with the interactions among ritual, memory, and meaning. Hypotheses concerning these interactions are generated for the clinical arena and beyond. First, the essayists emphasize both the positive and negative dimensions and consequences of the power of ritual experience. Second, ritual experience affects behavioral, cognitive, and symbolic levels of development. It generates ritual memory, which is itself of an order and magnitude that requires carefully constructed containment systems. Third, the memory of ritual makes a conscious and unconscious impact in ways that other experiences do not. It cannot be restricted to cognition because what occurs is both bodily and affective. The involvement of the body in ritual understanding and reconstruction in the therapeutic context is essential.

TOWARD FURTHER DISCUSSION

These explorations of ritual expression and experience raise further questions concerning the kind of *work* ritual does. Is it "transformative"? That is, are there reorganizations or reinterpretations of cultural and personal experience that produce newly meaningful wholes—one being or state has become another being or state? Or is the work of ritual less tidy and less dramatic, achieving not so much a shift in consciousness or status but rather a reinvigorating and sustaining of an already existing awareness of the way things are, have been, and will be? Is ritual "humanizing" in its use of shared symbols and communal affirmations? Have some of us "romanced ritual" or mystified it into a central socio-cultural process that is source and shaper of values and beliefs? Or is it something else altogether?

Along with raising these questions, the essays also suggest directions for further explorations of the nature and function of ritual. These directions include analysis of the special power in ritual acts; the influence of ritual upon behavioral, cognitive, and symbolic levels of development; the role that structure and history play in conserving or resisting hegemonic order; and the impact upon conscious and unconscious levels of meaning-making. It is clear that ritual experience cannot be restricted to cognitive categories alone but involves the body as well as the mind. Continued inquiry into ritual practice is, perhaps, not so much for the sake of presenting a new or grand theory of how it works and why. Rather, these essays point to a kind of attentiveness and engagement with those activities that just might leave us with more complicated and more unsettling questions. We have noted some of them—performance, sense-making, cultural location, and power. As these questions are posed, so the horizon enlarges, habits of simplification and reduction are challenged, and more conversation with a plurality of voices is invited.

NOTES

1. Exceptions might be the papers and conversations collected in *Violent Origins: Walter Burkert, René Girard, and Jonathan Z. Smith on Ritual Killing and Cultural Formation*, ed. Robert G. Hamerton-Kelly with an Introduction by Burton Mack and a Commentary by Renato Rosaldo (Stanford: Stanford University Press, 1987) and *Understanding Rituals*, ed. Daniel de Coppet (London and New York: Routledge, 1992). The issue of *Journal of Ritual Studies* 4/2 (Summer 1990) devoted to the topic of "Ritual and Power" and the ongoing "Ritual Studies" group of the American Academy of Religion should also be mentioned.

2. The Graduate Theological Union, located in Berkeley, California, is a consortium of nine seminaries representing various Roman Catholic orders, Protestant denominations, and faculty in Jewish, Orthodox, and Buddhist studies.

3. This essay was subsequently published as "Reinventing Ritual" in *Soundings* 75/1 (Spring 1992), pp. 21–41.

4. James L. Watson, "The Structure of Chinese Funerary Rites: Elementary Forms, Ritual Sequence, and the Primacy of Performance," *Death Ritual in Late Imperial and Modern China*, ed. James L. Watson and Evelyn S. Rawski (Berkeley, CA: University of California Press, 1988), p. 5.

5. (Madison, WI: The University of Wisconsin Press, 1987), pp. 93–94.

6. See Renato Rosaldo, *Culture and Truth: The Remaking of Social Analysis* (Boston: Beacon Press, 1989); S. Michael Price, "Ritual, Meaning, and Subjectivity: Studying Ritual as Human Religious Expression," *Epoche: UCLA Journal for the History of Religions* 16 (1988), pp. 11–32.

7. Judith A. Berling, discussion paper prepared for the GTU Interdisciplinary Project on Religious Ritual as Mediator of Memory and Meaning, March 22, 1990, p. 2.

8. Frits Staal, *Rules Without Meaning: Ritual, Mantras and the Human Sciences*, Toronto Studies in Religion, vol. 4, (New York: Peter Lang, 1989), p. 131.

9. S. Michael Price, "Ritual, Meaning, and Subjectivity," p. 23.

10. Ibid., p. 29.

11. Ibid., p. 31.

12. E.g., Ronald L. Grimes, *Ritual Criticism: Case Studies in Its Practice, Essays on Its Theory* (Columbia, SC: University of South Carolina Press, 1990), p. 13ff; Catherine Bell, *Ritual Theory, Ritual Practice* (New York: Oxford University Press, 1992), pp. 7–8, 73–74, 88–89, 140–41, 205, 209, 218.

13. Lawrence A. Hoffman, "How Ritual Means: Ritual Circumcision in Rabbibic Culture and Today," *Studia Liturgica* 23 (1993), pp. 80, 82.

14. *Freud on Ritual: Reconstruction and Critique*, (Missoula, MT: Scholars Press, 1979), p. 40.

15. *Models and Mirrors: Towards an Anthropology of Public Events* (Cambridge: Cambridge University Press, 1990), p. 11.

16. Ibid.

17. See, for example, the essays by Fischer, Payne, Stortz, Aune and Slough in this volume.

18. John D. Kelly and Martha Kaplan, "History, Structure, and Ritual," *Annual Review of Anthropology* 19 (1990), pp. 119–150; *Modernity and Its Malcontents: Ritual and Power in Postcolonial Africa*, ed. Jean Comaroff and John Comaroff (Chicago: University of Chicago Press, 1993).

19. What follows is based on Fred W. Clothey, "Toward a Comprehensive Interpretation of Ritual," *Journal of Ritual Studies* 2/2 (1988), pp. 147–161.

20. E.g., Grimes, *Ritual Criticism*, and Bell, *Ritual Theory, Ritual Practice*.

21. See the challenges raised by ritual studies as a field as well as the study of ritual in general: for example, Bell, *Ritual Theory, Ritual Practice*; Grimes, *Ritual Criticism*; and *Violent Origins: Walter Burkert, René Girard, and Jonathan Z. Smith on Ritual Killing and Cultural Formation*.

22. See, for example, James Clifford's introductory essay, "Partial Truths," in Clifford and George E. Marcus, eds., *Writing Culture: The*

Poetics and Politics of Ethnography (Berkeley, CA: The University of California Press, 1986), pp. 1–26.

23. Bruce Kapferer, "The Anthropologist as Hero: Three Exponents of Post-Modernist Anthropology," *Critique of Anthropology* 8/2 (1988), p. 95.

Part I

Comparative Explorations

Introductory Essay

JOHN HILARY MARTIN

Comparing religious rituals, like comparing anything touching the subject of religion, involves many imponderables. Do we know the tradition from which the ritual springs? Do we know it in sufficient depth to make judgments about it? Even when we have reason to think that we know the lineaments of a ritual quite well because we have seen it performed many times and have talked extensively to well-informed participants, do we know enough about the religious and cultural setting out of which it grew? Is the emphasis that *we* put on a specific ritual (because we have learned to know or cherish it) consonant with the emphasis put on it in that religion itself? When we have answered all these questions to our satisfaction we are not finished with the problem of making fair comparison. We next need to ask ourselves, What are we comparing the ritual with? Are we comparing it, whether consciously or not, with rituals from other religions? Comparisons between isolated fragments of religious material, as we well know, are of dubious validity at best. Or are we comparing a ritual with other aspects of the same culture where it originated, or at least where it is now usually found? Chanting of tantric mantras juxtaposed with other forms of rhythmic singing in India would be an example of such infracultural comparison. Or are we looking at a ritual as it has become associated with questions of political authority, legitimacy, charisma, and power? In the case of the latter, we need to keep in mind that rituals have a different value. Finally, are we comparing rituals against the backdrop of some general theory of ritual that we would like to put forward? Every student is familiar with the perils of that course. It can lead to judgment of a ritual by the standards of a predetermined methodology. Nineteenth and early twentieth century scholarship is littered with examples of the reductionism produced by such an approach.

The authors of the comparative essays presented in this section are well aware of these issues, all of which were raised at one time or

19

another in our collaborative effort. Mercifully, no attempt has been made here to draw up yet another methodology that tries to answer all questions about all rituals for all time. Religious symbolism is too complex and operates on too many levels for that to be very successful. On the other hand, the essays presented are more than scattered views of personal experience of rituals taken from different traditions. Certain common themes did emerge, and we believe that they are worth taking note of.

First of all, it seems clear that rituals, at least those presented here, offer a symbolic expression of religious attitudes. Among other things, rituals teach, they form identity, they draw a community together, they transform the psyche of individuals and of individuals within a community. Few rituals ever get around to doing *all* these things, of course. Some rituals, for example, produce a strong binding force in a society. Clare Fischer has shown in her essay that the ritual of investiture for the Sultan of Yogyakarta (Indonesia), which was once a significant political event, has now become an event of cultural importance. Whereas the investiture ceremony creates greater coherence in a highly diverse religious cotnmunity, the sacred and the secular aspects of Javanese life are not expressed as separate realities. The power that is focused in the palace and conveyed by the Sultan through this ritual of investiture points to tradition in transition and the adaptation of a regional palace to modern democratizing life.

Richard Payne discusses something very different in his essay on the self-transformation ceremony, the *shido kegyō*, or Training in Four Stages, of Shingon Buddhism (Japan). It deals with the disciplined performance of the rituals that aim at the transformation of the psyche. It was only reasonable to use the tools of analytic psychology to try to interpret to Western readers what was happening to the personality during the course of the ritual performance. As Richard Payne himself points out, the emphasis of this ritual is upon personal transformation with little reference to collective aspects of ritual such as a Westerner might expect. And yet the Training in Four Stages stands within a tradition. A Westerner, or even the average Japanese, would hardly be expected to secure its results by simply plodding through the steps of the ritual. Clearly, ritual must be more than a mechanical technique (such as simple breathing exercises might be). Westerners and other non-Japanese who successfully undertake the shido kegyo after careful preparation in Buddhist traditions find that the ritual evokes for them a reality carefully crafted over many generations.

Martha Ellen Stortz finds that rituals not only conserve, but can be used to regenerate. She describes ritual innovations among American

Shakers in the mid-nineteenth century that served to refocus the Shaker movement at a time when it was faltering under the influence of the secularism of that day. Newly created ceremonies like the Midnight Cry and the Annual Mountain Feast, which were introduced by the leadership of the Shaker community, enabled individuals to reposition themselves and regain touch with their own bodiliness, an ideal harking back to the original impetus of the Shaker elan. They are an example, not uncommon in America, of ritual serving individualism so that reformed individuals can then return and recreate their community.

In a study of Aboriginal rituals (Northern Australia) John Hilary Martin draws a profile of the elements of ritual that he has found there. He describes ceremonies in use among the Murrinh-patha and local groups that grant to an individual a new and different status relative to members of the community and at the same time to its *Dreaming* ancestors. These rituals could be said to be performatory because they enable laws laid down by ancestral beings in the all-creative period known as The Dreaming to intrude on the present. Rather than drawing individuals into a mythic past (as is often suggested), rituals allow the past to be brought to bear upon the present, a slightly different relation. Martin has come to recognize that Aboriginal rituals are not static, but rather reflect a dialogue between past and present.

The studies in this section suggest that rituals have diverse functions and that some rituals do several things simultaneously. In a given ritual some functions are clearly more important than others, and it is worth highlighting them as these studies do, but what may capture one's imagination on first reading is not likely to tell their whole story. In addition to their interest in mediating between the past and present, a common thread found among these rituals was their transformative character. They can be described as effective provided we do not look for the same kind of effects in every case.

In the Shingon rituals investigated by Richard Payne it is the individual who is transformed through his or her own personal efforts while working under the principle of enlightenment that is a part of every sentient nature. The investiture of the Sultan of Yogyakarta presented by Clare Fischer also shows the transformation of a single individual, not *intrinsically* as in the case of a ritual designed to procure personal Enlightenment, but rather as an individual acquiring a new public value. Through the investiture ceremony someone is designated as ruler, not in the familiar sense of becoming a governing monarch, but rather as the figure within a vibrant center who gives focus to religious and cultural life of the people.

In the Shaker rituals reported on by Martha Stortz, again it is individuals who are transformed, but she finds that another important result is their transformation of leadership. Without generalizing on ritual in Aboriginal Australia Hilary Martin finds that with initiation individuals are assigned and receive a new Dreaming identity. This fact changes a person's relations to other members of the community enabling all to play their proper role in the social and ritual life of the community. Through ritual they are opened to the power of The Dreaming in a new way and more deeply associated with their country.

Another theme that has appeared in these essays, one which was not expected at the outset of the project, was the importance of space in ritual. As the essays took shape discussion often turned to physical land, to landscapes and to those spatial relations which are interiorized as structure. In the investiture ceremony and in the events surrounding it Clare Fischer's account of ritual indicated a movement through space along the north-south axis that had symbolically rich significance for the *kraton* (palace). Martha Stortz writes of the importance of moving through a variety of spaces as well as the tension between two centers of Shaker life. Aboriginal religions are closely associated with land, lands not sought out and chosen by the Aboriginal peoples themselves but rather handed down to them by the various ancestral beings who formed and shaped the land in the creative period known as The Dreaming. Among the Murrinh-patha, as with other Aboriginal peoples, there is a powerful sense of obligation to perform rituals at appropriate locations, that is, at the proper sacred sites. As Martin notes, the element of *scene* is important, for it provides ritual participants with access to communal memory. Finally, ritual can also depend upon interior space. In his discussion of the Training in Four Stages, Richard Payne points out that the training process requires the participant to visualize in the mind's eye elaborate imagery of the Buddha. Projecting the image in internal space is an important part of the ritual and absolutely required if transformation is to occur.

Of the educative function of ritual little has been said. This is somewhat surprising because ritual and liturgy are so often regarded as vehicles for reinforcing what a religion teaches. Perhaps the lack of emphasis is due to the fact that the didactic aspect, so prominent in the formal instruction associated with Western religions, was less in evidence in these rituals. Rituals make their effects felt in non-cognitive ways, and so much of their meaning lies below the surface. A fair conclusion from our collaborative discussions would seem to be that whereas rituals affect both the cognitive and noncognitive part of the personality, they make their greatest effects in the noncognitive part of the psyche.

1

Bringing the Power of the Past into the Present

Murrinh-patha Ritual

JOHN HILARY MARTIN

I

In the spring of 1994 eight Aboriginal artists from the outback community of Wadeye-Port Keats in Australia's Northern Territory were invited to exhibit their art and dancing in the San Francisco Bay Area.[1] Their paintings traditionally depict scenes from *The Dreaming*, both their personal Dreamings and those situated in their *countries*.[2] The schedule of their visit, which was heavy, included an afternoon appointment where the artists had promised to paint a bark or canvas painting in order to give observers a chance to see how they went about producing their work and to give them an opportunity to ask questions about the meaning of their stories. As the session began in a back yard under some trees, it quickly became obvious that this was a time when the artists could relax and feel a bit more at home. The painting began with the application of a coat of red ocher to each bark or canvas.[3] After that had dried each artist set down first the major symbols that would illustrate the chosen Dreaming story and then started to decorate and illustrate that story with further symbols and with the circular strings of dots that are a peculiar stylistic feature of the painting of the area. At each stage of the artistic process there seemed to be small surprises as the painting took shape. As the painting progressed the Dreaming symbols were articulated bit by bit and were outlined by the dot sequences that illustrate power and movement. The symbols then began to exercise their power and attraction. The artists worked steadily at their craft with care and diligence, chatting to themselves in their own languages or in English to field the odd question from the watching audience. Part of the fascination of the afternoon, something unexpected, was the involvement of the audience. People who had intended to drop by just for a moment or two out of courtesy, became caught up in the process and stayed on for the two hours, watching mostly in silence or chatting quietly with each other. Some of the paintings were executed in what we might call the *old style,* that is, purely abstract and requiring a great deal of verbal explanation because none of the symbols used are part of a Western repertoire. Others conceded more to our imaginations showing totem animals, such as the crocodile, in recognizable form although still heavily embedded in an abstract symbol system. A few presented their local landscape in a pictorial fashion that was immediately accessible. What the artists were doing by means of these different styles, whether consciously or unconsciously, was to bring their past into the present and, a more tricky task, to bring it into the presence of an alien community. In each case they were providing a glimpse into their eternal Dreaming. They were happy to shift styles to do this, but—as they vigorously insisted—they had left their stories intact.

Painting is not ritual (although watching the process under the trees seemed to take on almost a ritual flavor), but it helps throw light on the problem of what ritual should bring into the present. Something of the past surely, but not everything. The study of Australian Aboriginal religions was once the great preserve of the timeless. Eliade left a generation of students with the impression that what happened at the beginning of time, *in illo tempore* as he put it, was somehow a self-repeating pattern.[4] Aboriginals seemed to agree. They themselves told us they had participated in rituals of The Dreaming in their isolated continent for over 40,000 years. The literally minded among us sometimes jumped to the conclusion that this meant that the ceremonies observed today could have been found 10,000, 20,000, perhaps 40,000 years ago, conducted by the same sort of tribal leaders and for the same purposes. The Aboriginal elders would have smiled at such a naïve conception. They knew better. Their presentation of Dreaming was far more subtle, far more plastic. The first caution they give is that The Dreaming should not be called "Dreamtime" as if it were some static period that we had to learn about. Nor were its rituals static reenactments of what was done long ago. It was better to think of The Dreaming as a creative period in which all important things happened. It was an epoch when the Dreaming *Ancestors* shaped and formed the earth as we know it today and gave the law still to be obeyed. The Dreaming was not something that was repeated now; rather, it was something that was still actively present. Because this time was the source of all value, stories needed to be told about what happened in The Dreaming and rituals had to be performed that remembered the activities of the ancestral beings. There must be *remembrance* of them or The Dreaming would be lost (that is, it would become inaccessible) and with that loss would follow the loss of all meaning. Yet, paradoxically, not everyone in the community needed to know everything. Aboriginal religion is also a religion of secrets. The ancestral beings that shaped a local landscape, giving it its hills, valleys, and watercourses, and which produced the flora and the fauna that populate it, had also endowed the land with a particular set of people who were to be responsible for a country's upkeep and welfare. They taught the people the songs they needed to know and the appropriate ceremonies that needed to be performed. From the outset, then, in Aboriginal thought there is a certain private character, a personal relationship to a particular land, to one's own *country*. This privacy was extended to the stories and ceremonies associated with it. If the country has not been entrusted to you, it is inappropriate to know too much about the secrets of a place and dangerous to report on it indiscriminately.

As the elders knew, rituals both create and recreate. They always transformed people, and we will return to that aspect, but their rituals did more. They cared for the land itself as the Dreaming Ancestors had made it. If the rituals were not performed, if the law were not kept, the power of the ancestral beings would no longer be available to maintain the features of the place. The land and its people would return to chaos. This in turn implied that the power of the ancestors would no longer be accessible to help shape and order the people of the land; they would be cut off from the land even when occupying it. The shape of the land did change over time, however. There was no denying that. In the course of centuries the sea rose and the Australian coasts were inundated. The land bridges between the continent and the rest of Asia fell. The continent dried out so that the ancient flora and fauna gave way to new forms that could adjust to the new climatic conditions.[5] Last of all, the whitefolks came and profoundly changed the ordering and management of the land. Along the way the ancient rituals also had to change, of course, but change in a way that did not deny what they were supposed to do. This posed a problem that Aboriginal elders and all ritualists continually have to face—how to bring the past to bear on the present without either abandoning the past or denying the validity of the present. If we want to phrase the Aboriginal problem more precisely we might say, "How can ritual bring the *present* into the past so the past can become the standard by which the present will be measured?" As Martha Stortz might have asked of the Shakers' leaders, 'How can an older ethos tame and configure the ongoing experiences of the present?'"[6]

II

Before proceeding further it might be well to summarize briefly the ways in which Aboriginal peoples look on ritual.[7] At one level Aboriginals of Australia, like most ritualists, assume that participation in ceremonies will do something to educate tribal members about the verities of life and will cement tribal unity. Whereas participation in rituals helps ensure social cohesion and disseminates information about The Dreaming, what the ceremonies ultimately focus on is procuring what might be called *cosmic effects*. Ritual activity is designed to conserve the correct order on the land, the order that was given initially by ancestral beings in The Dreaming. Contrary to what is sometimes said, Aboriginal rituals are not performed solely for the immediate benefit of tribal members, but rather reflect a more abstract desire to care for the long-term health of the land, for its plants and animals. This is not to deny that they elicit feelings of tribal solidarity and help construct self-identity, factors made much of by Western observers, but their more important job, however, is to *follow up* The Dreaming. To follow up The Dreaming means to expend oneself in keeping it alive. Whereas the ritual action may keep The Dreaming going and so enable each new generation to gain access to it, that is not the only matter at stake. Participation in ritual action opens up each generation, making it, shall we say, *vulnerable* to the powers of The Dreaming. Through ritual The Dreaming gains effective access to the minds and hearts of the upcoming tribal members. [8]

This brings forward again the way in which rituals are vehicles for transformation. There can scarcely be any doubt that they are transformative, but to what extent and in whose favor? Not all rituals accomplish the same things, nor are they even designed to. At Wadeye-Port Keats there is a ceremony called *Kanthirra* that is, literally speaking, a namesake ceremony that usually involves a child and an adult. It is transformative, but, as we shall see, only to a minor degree, at least from the point of view of the personal ego. A Kanthirra ceremony can be as modest or as elaborate as the participants want, and on the whole is a happy occasion. If the child is a boy a name is assigned by the paternal grandfather; if a girl, the honor falls to maternal uncles. Clap sticks call participants and observers to the ceremony and they continue to be used throughout. During the ceremony the infant (or even a toddler) is held in the arms of his or her sponsor. The pair is surrounded by a circle of dancers, with more participants simply looking on. Participants dance in an ever-tightening ring while carrying and displaying signs of their Dreamings. At the conclusion of the ceremony gifts are cheerfully given to the child (through the parent), either of food or the ever-present modern substitute, money. The ceremony seems to be found in only some of the clans at Wadeye-Port Keats and is performed only occasionally when need arises. That occurs when two individuals of a different clan are found with either a birth trait (usually a mark) or a personal name in common. These factors would normally generate an aversion relationship between them that would continue throughout life. What Kanthirra does is regularize the ritual avoidance relation by transfering their classification. The effect of the ceremony is to reattach an individual to his or her land; in the process another Dreaming may be assigned to them or be recognized. Kanthirra is not designed to change the inner individual, who is normally an infant or a small child, but inasmuch as no one in an Aboriginal community is an isolate, effects will follow as the child grows up. The ceremony establishes a set of relationships to clan and family members and severs others. The ritual is certainly transformative because it resituates the subject through ritual action. Although the transformation is external, and may seem quite trivial, it will carry weight since, like everything else, it is guaranteed by the context of The Dreaming. [9]

Kanthirra is not the only status-changing ceremony at Wadeye-Port Keats. There is another important set of ceremonies, here and throughout the continent, generally called rituals of initiation, or, to use Van Gennep's phrase, *rites of passage.* They have attracted a great deal of attention among ritualists, because similar ceremonies appear so commonly elsewhere. Rites of passage are clearly transformative because they confer on an individual new legal relationships and because they are designed to generate in the initiates an inner experience that strengthens their personal identity and their attachment to the community.[10] When considering initiation it should be kept in mind that for many religious traditions initiation is in a quite literal sense the first incorporation of the initiate into, shall we say, *a sacral order of being.* Among the Murrinh-patha, and the Aboriginals of Australia generally, the situation is not parallel. All individuals at

birth are already people of The Dreaming. It is the obligations of the
law that overtake them during their initiation. In this sense initiation
is for both men and women, and is conducted in separate ceremonies
by adult men for males and by women for females.[11] The rite among
the Murrinh-patha among males has been described by W. E. H.
Stanner, and it will not be necessary to go into detail here.[12] It will be
enough to note that classically it involves a long period of indoctrination, lasting a month or more. This is a time of continuous intensive
ritual activity involving a good percent of the adult community. The
rituals are carefully prepared beforehand, and a good deal of thought
goes into the nuance of their performance. The physical rite of circumcision, the cutting of the male member, is a major focus of the rituals,
but it is followed by a number of other important ceremonies designed
to reintroduce the successful initiate into the tribe as a new person,
one who is fully adult. The common expression among the Murrinh-
patha that it *makes a boy into a man* seems absolutely apt. On completion of the ritual the new person takes his full place in the
community, being able to marry legally and to foster children.

The effects noted are external and legal, but the ceremony was
clearly designed to produce internal psychological changes that are not
so easy to judge. The intense mental and physical exertions extended
over many months gave ample opportunity for the young boy to interiorize the transformation. The physical ordeal, traditionally associated
with the rite, certainly tested the inner strength of an individual. Some
elders (although by no means all) have gone so far as to insist that circumcision is all about pain. An informant told me that for many years
the ceremony [circumcision] had been conducted by their own elders
within the sterile conditions of a health clinic. This implies the use of
anesthetics, suturing, and general white man medicine. In 1990 an
elder, who lives outside the community but was related by kinship ties
insisted upon returning to the old way of doing things, that is, without
the support of the clinic. His position was, there is trouble with the
young men [would-be initiates] these days because they are *not connected in the right way* [my informant's phrase; he felt it fit the elder's
mind] . . . *This ceremony is about pain and unless the young boys
experience this pain, then they are not really connected. . . . This
health clinic way stops the young boys from being connected.* A contrary view was expressed by others: *In the past we lost many young
boys from infection. . . . This new way is much better.* The issue
remained unresolved. In the same year a few months apart an "old
way" ceremony and a "new way" ceremony took place, each with its
own set of initiates. Either way seemed to be sufficient, however, for

no repeat performance was on anyone's agenda. The initiation had occurred, both the old and the new ceremonies seemed to make The Dreaming accessible and that was enough.

Initiation of young boys is not the only ceremony that can be classed as an initiation. There is a further ceremony of *punj*, again described by Stanner, who thought of it as a more religious experience.[13] Unlike circumcision, where the preparatory dancing is often public and the elements of the rite fairly well known, punj is conducted with far greater secrecy. It is a ritual that is said to make an circumcised adult into *a man of mystical understanding.* Whereas both rites incorporate the individual into the life of a community, the purpose of punj appears to be one of incorporating an association with the life of an ancestor. A program of initiation, as we would expect, socializes individuals and produces psychological changes. There is no lack of evidence that fully initiated men are expected to be more self-confident, less likely to be passive in following directions, but at the same time more under control by the elders. Perhaps this is what missionaries and other white administrators were seeing when they said that after an individual had gone through a tribal experience they became disinterested in Western modes of religion and culture. Punj conferred power and influence on the initiate within the community but it also strengthened power of another sort, the ability to approach and make use of the power of the ancestral beings residing in the earth. This latter power was to be found most intensely in specific geographical areas along the trek followed by a Dreaming ancestor which are popularly referred to as sacred sites. Here the focus was in favor of The Dreaming itself, ensuring its accessibility to the land. Rituals were central experiences in shaping individuals and in renewing ties both to the tribe and to The Dreaming. They are even more central, however, in making the creative powers of The Dreaming that past which is always present to be active on the earth.[14]

III

As these examples suggest, rituals are complex phenomena that accomplish many things at once. Perhaps that is why a certain ambivalence always clings to our descriptions when we try to analyze ritual. When generalizing we usually begin by saying that they are a form of communication, but we take "communication" in a broad and not in a didactic sense. They affect the conscious mind, of course, some rituals more than others, but they affect the unconscious part of the psyche, perhaps to an even greater degree. Speaking again in general terms, we say that rituals are performances, for it is difficult to think of a ritual conducted entirely within the isolation of one's own mind.[15] On the other hand, mere performance (going through the motions) does not constitute ritual. We have only to think of wedding or coronation rehearsals. Every step of the forthcoming ceremony may be executed to flawless perfection together with the appropriate regalia, dress and music, but no ritual takes place at rehearsals. At the end of the wedding or coronation rehearsal the couple remain as unmarried as before, and the sultan is still merely a prince. Again, speaking generally, rituals can be said to be patterned activity. This is true enough, but patterned activity by itself is not ritual. We have only to think of the daily walk up and down a flight of stairs, swimming or riding a bike, tapping on a drum, all of which are patterned actions, but they are not meaningful in themselves. Patterned actions become ritualized only when it communicates meaning, when the repetitive actions of the ritual are set in a wider context.[16] This brings us to the point that ritual will involve reference to memory, as both the long memory of the tribe and the short memory of the individual participants. Through memory past experience is recalled, or better, is returned to the *ego* to be contemplated there over and over again.[17] This is not to say that rituals are solely or even predominantly cerebral events. Among the Murrinh-patha rituals invoke an awareness of the land which is simultaneously a visual object of beauty, a place to gain sustenance and to live out one's life, and housing a set of symbols that can only be talked about in analogous terms. Not every aspect of the personality need be explicitly rational. There is much else there that is merely imaginative and would not stand logic's close scrutiny. There is plenty of room in the ego for the memory of physical sensations and for bodily awareness. It is generally recognized that ritual somehow simultaneously engages the imagination, the emotions, and even the biological side of our nature. Rituals put the ego in a context that is both cognitive and affective.[18]

Good rituals, the kind that have successfully retained their vitality over the generations, are a record of many experiences and, as a consequence, gain objective value in the sense that they are not simply the reflections of personal subjectivity, nor even the subjectivity of one's own generation. What they say stands, if not over and against, at least aside from the individual and the community and the transient aspects of its culture. A good description is to say that rituals are dialogic. When they change successfully, to anticipate our conclusion a bit, we find they have addressed a new situation and have evoked a context that is new but one which is, nonetheless, faithful to their origins. Rituals accomplish their task by operating at many levels at once, making an impact on individuals and on society, in the public forum and one hidden in the unconscious. As we might expect, within ritual we find many elements tightly bound together. Attempts to discuss ritual in oversimplified terms without taking into account their complexity did much to impoverish appreciation of them in the last century. This has left behind a legacy of reductionisms and false problems that is only recently being overcome. Exclusive concentration, for example, on what rituals taught, especially when what they supposedly taught was reduced to statements found in prayers or ritual texts, was a one-sided approach that ultimately broke up the unity of ritual experience. It gave an opening to false questions that ask whether it is possible to have a true ritual without an accompanying ritual formula, or whether it is possible to have ritual without preaching something or whether there is need for any meaning at all.[19] On the other hand, examination of rituals without reference to what they might have to say did little better. The truly bizarre meanings assigned to rituals by field workers who observed dances and ceremonies before fully understanding the language or the history of the community performing them should put us on our guard about interpreting rituals as if they were the products of movement alone.[20] Let us now turn to a brief overview of some of these elements that are found in ritual and along the way see something of how they accomplish transformation.

IV

Without exhausting all the possible headings we can class the more significant elements of ritual under *gesture, [musical] score, scene,* and *story line.* This is not to say that other elements besides these four might not be isolated, only that these seem to be the most prominent. Let us begin with the element that seems to be the most indispensable and most characteristic of ritual—*gesture.*

Gesture

Under the general heading of *gesture* we lump together all the various body movements that go on during ritual. Gesture embraces the movement of individual or solo performers up to the full panoply of processions and communal dancing that may involve virtually everyone in the community. Under gesture we can place the stylized, unchanging (or relatively unchanging) movements that are traditionally demanded of a performer together with what is often left out, the more original movements that flow from a performer's artistic abilities and from personal attitudes and feelings.

We should also include here the type of recurring and patterned activity carried on by performers at the semiconscious and habitual level. In all cases the gestures are made in order to communicate the meaning that belongs to the ritual. If it should appear, for example, that performers are using a ceremonial occasion simply as a backdrop to display their own skills and accomplishments (a bit of human vanity not unknown in many cultures), they are usually criticized and accused of letting themselves get in the way of the ritual. Ritual performances may entertain, but they are not viewed as entertainment. But what sort of meaning is supposed to be communicated through gesture? How is the ego engaged? A certain caution is required here because gesture can communicate meaning in two very different ways.

In one sense gestures are little more than language without the benefit of words. Stylized gestures can be, and often are, simply a kind of code that communicates a precise meaning which is dutifully recognized by observers as the ritual unfolds. In the context of a given ritual, for example, the laterally descending movement of the hand may communicate the idea of a dove flying to its nest. The gesture can make the point as effectively as if words had been sung or spoken. In such a case the gesture is conventional and the observers are simply asked to decode its conceptual meaning. This is *gesture as language* and, like any language, it is designed to communicate a conceptual understanding. Although this may be an effective way of reporting information, gesture as language is an impoverishment of what ritual gestures are best able to do. Gestures can communicate in quite another way because they have the subtle ability to draw forth emotional shifts of mood and changes in attitude. Within the conventions of ritual some latitude is almost always allowed for individual artistry and interpretation. If the descending, lateral movement representing the dove is nuanced by a performer on a particular day—with a bit of hesitation, perhaps, or an extra flutter of the hand—a perceptive observer will unconsciously note the variation and begin to feel that not all is well today. The ritual flight of the dove to its nest is made to seem less easy by the performer; perhaps there is a hint of danger in the air, perhaps the salvation, the safety or whatever, promised in the ritual, is going to be more difficult to secure. This is where the ritual character of *gesture* comes into play.

Gestures are not so much designed to communicate information (texts can do that in a much better way) as to mediate mood and feeling. Ritual gestures make their impact in the context of a particular ritual. The repetition of a well-known gesture establishes contact with the past (the flight of the dove is well remembered from past ritual performances), whereas the breaking of that repetition in controlled and recognized ways (in the slight hesitation of the hand movement in our example) recaptures the attention of participants to the past as situated in the present context. *Gesture* moves below the surface of consciousness to mold and modify our emotional life to be in line with the flow of ritual events and to graft our personal and idiosyncratic interpretation of life onto the ongoing life of the ritual community. In this way a gesture reinforces the purpose of the ritual, which is to carry meaning forward from the past in order to create a new meaning here and now.

Can gestures change without generating a changed meaning? This question deserves a very long answer, but we can make only one or two suggestions here. We have already pointed out how performances may differ. A certain amount of latitude is allowed when making a gesture, and that will influence the impact which a ritual will make on different occasions. If and when a gesture begins to add to the initial meaning (that is to say, enriches an older meaning as it contextualizes it) the total ritual will also change as it adapts new moods appropriate to the new meaning. Aboriginal tradition does allow an elder to create or Dream new ritual, but more often older gestures and meanings are retained.[21] The change of gesture more commonly will be successful and be accepted only to the extent that its former self remains recognizable within its new ritual meaning.[22] Aboriginal rituals change, but Aboriginals have been careful to conceal their own creativity. They seek to highlight continuity with the past. *Creative* rituals tend to lose popularity and die out after a time for the simple reason that their creative elements are seen as not in dialogue with the past, but as simply discontinuous with it.

Scene

Perhaps it is the close interplay between gesture and meaning that has called forth the definition of ritual as *gestures with meaning*, that is to say, *gestures with a story line*. (This enables us to add the corollary that religious rituals are gestures with a religious story line.) These descriptions are acceptable provided we do not forget the contributions that *scene* and *musical score* make to the ultimate viability of ritual.

Location has a great deal to do with what can be described as the shaping and the tempo of ritual action. If a ritual is assigned to be held in a cave with a long, narrow, and restricted entrance, we can expect that the audience will feel a constriction that will increase the tension of the rites performed there. Wall paintings were sometimes drawn in underground chambers that were difficult to reach, and it has been suggested, plausibly enough, that a sense of ordeal was part of the original purpose. Aboriginal dancing grounds are located in open places where the surrounding rock facings form a natural echo chamber that will enhance the volume and resonance of the chanting. The decoration of a site, the use of vestments or masks by performers, all reflect what a particular ritual is about and add to its intensity. The setting of the scene can also involve a factor like time, with dusk, daybreak, and midnight themes.[23] The presence of candlelight, the use of smoke and incense, all have meaningful associations and make a psychological impact that is much more than peripheral extras. The participants in the Kanthirra ceremony must needs carry their proper Dreaming symbols, after all. The same gesture can even have different meanings in different settings. In the West, for example, the smoke of incense is usually understood as a sign of the presence of the deity; in Aboriginal rituals of Australia smoke signals purification and separation instead. Perhaps the most common mistake made by those unfamiliar with requirements of ritual is to assume that materials to set a ritual scene can be gathered at random and changed around at will, something like furniture in a living room. Ritual space is not so easily detachable from ritual meaning. A scene must accord with the needs of the ritual itself if appropriate meaning is to be conveyed.

Scene like gesture creates mood, but it does much more. It is often the scene that establishes continuity with the past. The values of a past scene can bring crushing weight to bear upon the present. Musical groups soon discover this reality when they try to carry on popularized rituals replete with guitars and modern folk tunes in the formal setting of a Gothic cathedral. Architecture makes its statement long after the builders have left. Major ritual events are communal events that are designed to be conducted in designated locations. They occur in sacred places, like temples, churches, dancing grounds, caves, and the like. They have social significance for the community looking to the past and to the future. Here rituals act as mediators of past as they put flesh on the bones of bare literary remembrance, and they are designed to carry the community into the future.

The element of *scene* acquires overriding priority with religions that are attached to the land and to their sacred sites far beyond what appears in worldwide religions such as Christianity.[24] With Aboriginal religions location involves more than an enhancement of meaning; it is central. If a sacred site becomes unavailable through conquest or destruction, some substitute place can occasionally be pressed into service, but if one cannot be found the ritual has to be abandoned. This is why Aboriginal communities continually plead that seemingly insignificant bits of land be returned to them for ritual purposes since, for them, substitute places can never make The Dreaming accessible.

More than any other element of ritual *scene* seems to generate depth to meaning because it forwards the communal associations of past ages. For this reason adjustment of scene is the most delicate, but perhaps the most necessary, adjustment that needs to be made when a community is forced to look to the future. The vitality of its rituals will depend on how well past associations of a group are integrated with its present scene.

Musical Score

If *scene* seems important because of its ability to evoke communal associations, *musical score* has significance because it is intimately linked with interiorization of *meaning*. Curiously enough, musical score is the one element that is often overlooked in academic discussions of ritual (with the possible exception of students of liturgical performance). Perhaps the common use of the phrase *musical accompaniment* is to blame. It inevitably suggests that the musical score is some sort of optional extra that can be dispensed with easily enough. To think of *score* simply as accompaniment is in fact misleading. When we move beyond the strictly cerebral level it is music that bears much of the burden of generating meaning. Without music the patterned movements of ballet dancers seem ridiculous.

If the relation of *gesture* and *score* may be recognized readily enough, the more intimate relation of *score* to *text* is often slighted. There is a stubborn expectation that the text will have the lion's share in transmitting meaning. Ritualists have been all too slow to recognize that whatever is being communicated by texts will be modified in significant ways by the music, that is, by *score*. On many occasions the mood that should accompany an event is presented through its music rather than the story line or even gesture.

In the contemporary culture the impact of music is more easily recognized in films rather than in rituals. In films the so-called background music is often charged with the task of telling the audience of all sorts of things. When certain chords of music are struck audiences have now become conditioned to pick out their significance and change their attitude toward what is going on accordingly. A shift of cadence, for example, alerts the audience to the danger that is lurking for the hero just around the door. A swelling of sober tones is enough to sound an inner alarm that prepares the audience for the coming earthquake that will soon demolish that unsavory town where so much wicked revelry had been going on. Bright intervals of music assure everyone that, despite appearances, the sick child in the hospital bed will soon get well again and all the family's problems will have a happy resolution. Sweet violin notes at the same sickbed, on the other hand, prepare us for a sad end. Without a word being spoken music disposes participants to expect a specific kind of thing to happen and prepares their reaction.[25] If the music should happen to mislead, we feel cheated and let down somehow. In the hands of a genius musical themes can be developed that powerfully reinforce a plot and give depth to the characterization of a figure in the story.

It is no accident that the love arias of Mozart were routinely written in E flat major.[26] The sensitive ears of musical greats like Mozart and Verdi made them acutely aware of the possibilities of key and the power of melody to affect physically the human psyche. They made full use of it. By following their music we participate in their genius, although most of us could not create such music ourselves. A shift from C major to E major leads us to expect the character in question to sing of courage and strength, or at least that he or she will be courageous and strong in future actions. Music with repeated perfect fifths (made familiar by the popularity of the fifths favored by Steven Spielberg) exudes confidence, strength, and optimism. Music had a great deal to do with the popularity of films like *Star Wars* and *E.T.*, which overcame the bareness of pedestrian scripts that were otherwise unlikely to capture the popular imagination. People leaving the theatre often felt confident and, on the whole, happy about life in the universe, not because of the story they had followed, but because of the music they had heard. It moved below cerebral consciousness to reach their emotions and possibly even reached down to change physical blood pressure and metabolic processes. It would be foolish to think that the rhythm of clapsticks and drone pipe (the *marluk*) do not have similar transforming effects.

Catherine Ellis has shown how the recounting of Aboriginal stories depends on an extremely sophisticated use of music. She argues that training and tradition have made Aboriginal peoples extremely sensitive to pitch and to rhythmic forms.[27] The inversion of notes, melodic retrogressions, and the like not only add richness to the mood of a ritual music, but they also add a cerebral dimension, if we know what to look for. Traditional Aboriginal music is characterized by narrow ranges of melodic and rhythmic variations, by bursts of notes followed by silences. This usually leaves an impression of flatness and tonelessness (although a powerfully insistent one) when first encountered by untrained ears, but the range of variation has been skillfully put to work in ritual performances. Gestures assisted by musical score and combined with a few words of text are regularly used to charge mood and attitude, as we might expect with all music, but they are also employed to convey the meaning of the ritual. Rhythmic, melodic, even harmonic variations function as a kind of code that carries a portion of the message. Even something relatively simple, such as whether a sacred ancestor stayed on in a place or moved on with others somewhere else, Ellis believes, is expressed by the tonal variation that accompanies the words concerned. The song burst accompanying the words forms a part of their meaning. In a curious way score helps bind Aboriginal ceremonies together, giving them internal coherence as well as ordering the way in which clusters of ceremonies will be performed over a period of time at different locations along a Dreaming tract. Score can make an inadequate story come to life and sometimes adds meanings to what is already there.

Story Line

Students of ritual often assume that the *real* meaning of a ritual will be found in the texts that accompany them. If the meaning is going to be found anywhere, it will be found here. In one sense they are correct. The texts used in ritual are often taken from the sacred writings that have been read, reread, and analyzed for centuries until they become virtually inseparable from the experience of a community. The function of such texts is to express in myth and story form the ideas and beliefs that hold a community together. Through the repetition of stories and myths in a ceremonial context its religious symbolism was reduced to a conversational level.

In many religious traditions, especially those of the West, decisions have been arrived at, policies formed, and worldviews constructed through arguments that appealed to reason. By selecting texts and sermonizing (or meditating) on them during the course of ritual the power they contained was opened up to the mind of individuals and communities. Texts of a ritual are undoubtedly important is presenting its story line, but story line cannot be limited to texts or to sermonizing on them. This approach is an impoverishment of ritual because it reduces ritual to a cerebral exercise, something on the order of a dramatic reading.

Story line cannot be limited to what is found in ritual texts. What formulas, prayers, and hymns that accompany ritual gestures do is to

encapsulate the essence of a ritual's meaning and present it to participants in a conceptual manner, but whether they be long texts or short
texts they do not convey, nor are they designed to convey, the full
meaning. Aboriginal practice is instructive here. At performances of
Aboriginal rituals visitors often ask for a translation of the words that
were sung during the ceremonies in order to acquire a deeper understanding of what they just witnessed. They are often nonplussed by
meager replies they receive. As few as three or four words are given to
them, words that seem to mean virtually nothing at all. There is a natural tendency for observers to believe that they have not been told the
whole truth or else that their Aboriginal translator had only an imper-
fect command of English. Reticence is certainly present at times
among Aboriginals, since the meaning of the ceremonies not in the
public domain is kept profoundly secret and would certainly not be
shared with a chance visitor. Reticence is not always the issue, however. Friendly visitors are usually given a tolerably correct translation
of what was being said or sung at public events, but without an appreciation of the music and dancing accompanying them very little of that
message comes across. Whenever words are separated from *gesture* and
score they leave a cryptic impression.[28]

Before we dismiss Aboriginal practices as simply exotic, we might
take note that limited texts are not so foreign as one might assume. In
other traditions, Western included, it is not uncommon to find words
and simple phrases repeated over and over again in what seems to the
unsympathetic ear to be a bit of mindless repetition. If the truth be told
the meaning of the words recited at ceremonies is often far from the
minds of the participants, even pious participants, during the actual
performance. Aboriginal communities are more tolerant of this kind of
lapse, or perhaps they have made a better accommodation for it.

In Aboriginal communities many important stories are never
made public at all but are imparted selectively to the few trusted and
mature individuals who have an inherited right to know them.
Younger adults and children are not expected to know everything; in
fact, they are forbidden to know too much. They can listen to the songs
and watch the movements of the dance at corroborees even if their
knowledge is fragmentary. Later, as these same children proceed to
maturity, their knowledge is filled in as stanzas are added to the songs
and with extended elements in the ritual dancing. The elders know
that symbolic values are not easy to communicate. Even adults do not
always take away from a ritual the same things, or *read* it in the same
way.[29]

But rituals do not have to make sense, or better, do not have to make complete sense to everyone. It is enough that *someone* in the tribe is expert about them. Simple possession of the text, even a well-translated text, does not necessarily mean that a reader has interiorized what the ritual implies. The words and phrases repeated during rituals are not, after all, written for the purpose of giving information to an uninformed audience, or for purposes of intellectual review by those who are informed. A classroom situation or even a discussion in a circle with an elder would be a far more efficient way of achieving that kind of goal. This has led some to talk of rituals as being essentially meaningless, or as arising from the activities of pre-logical people. But we need not draw this type of conclusion either.

The meaning of a ritual is to be found embedded in the whole experience of the people. Its *story line* is not carried fully by the texts, it is possible in some cases for a ritual to be without a text in the ordinary sense, yet it still has story line. A *story line* it is drawn from the memories and the understandings of the community, which always has a fuller version of what is at stake. Meaning is formed in significant ways by the symbolism filtered through the texts. This symbolism has many roots flowing at once from nature symbolism recognized by much of the human race, from specialized myths that have been interiorized in a particular community from time out of mind, as well as from historically based symbols that arise out of the experiences which have shaped the political and social life of a people.

In ritual the *story line* draws on many sources that are, in turn, enhanced and enriched in the setting provided by *score, scene*, and *gesture*. Without adopting all the views of Jung, we can safely say that meaning is contained in the archetypal patterns embedded in whatever it is that carries forward the collective unconscious of a community. Rituals, therefore, are never really isolated from the general understandings of a religion even when they are not expressed explicitly in a given ritual text. In any healthy ritual the myths, the natural and historic symbols, the archetypes of the collective unconscious, all fold together in a meaningful and straightforward way.[30]

V

Participation in a ritual normally involves an experience of unity. It is always possible, of course, to replay the music performed at a ritual and enjoy it later as an orchestral score; it is also possible to look at prehistoric cave paintings to try to learn something of the type of worship that went on there; it is even possible to catalog the gestures observed during a performance to help other dancers reproduce them in the future. It is possible to do all these things separately, in isolation, but they will not recreate the ritual. Each of them deals with only one aspect of a ceremony and not the ritual itself. If there is a diminution or attenuation to any of them in practice, whether of *story line, score, scene,* or *gesture* the ritual will speak in an impoverished and perhaps in a distorted voice.

To the first of the questions we asked at the beginning, "How *do rituals transform,"* one answer is that ideally they provide a context where the ego can grow and mature, where it can gain a religious identity and join into a community. But that answer is only partial. Rituals have a certain Janus-like quality. They look both ways. They provide a context for the ego to develop its potential, but they also open the personality to accepting what the ritual represents. This can be a powerful experience, for a healthy ritual affects all parts of the personality at once. But even seemingly impoverished rituals often have a significant role to play. Whether healthy or not, a ritual will always intrude upon the individual and community, communicating to them an experience of that object which ritual is talking about. In the case of Aboriginal rituals, there is no doubt it will be about the power of the Dreaming Ancestors.

The existing ceremonies of Aboriginal communities, which must stem from what is surely the oldest surviving culture, possess a richness and a complexity that clearly bears the stamp of genius. Who, then, was at their beginning? The members of an Aboriginal community will always conceal their own creativity. Whatever of genius may exist, or whatever may be found that is new, whatever they adopt from other traditions, will always be said to have originated in that creative epoch. We can rest assured, even as a matter of polite form, that we will be told that their sacred ceremonies have been handed down from the time of The Dreaming. Aboriginal understanding of religious values—not unlike the symbol systems in all great religions—is a seamless continuum. We will never be able to find out how far back historically their genius extends. In that sense they represent what is old, new, and timeless.

If the ceremonies attached to The Dreaming are so ancient, can they ever really be brought into the present? More significantly, in line with the second question asked at the beginning, can contemporary Aboriginal experience be brought into the past so that The Dreaming can act upon it? Although said to be timeless, their genius should not be regarded as frozen, "way back in the past somewhere," still less should it be regarded as a flame that is now extinct. If nothing else, The

Dreaming serves as a standard for conduct and belief. That standard is seen as very objective, being identified with the land and the ancestral powers that shaped that land. Within traditional lines Aboriginal rituals have survived (assurances that they are dying out always seem to be premature) and the insights of The Dreaming continue to make themselves felt. This is because their interpretation of what constitutes a life remains unchanged in its essentials. As with a number of other religions Aboriginals see that interpretation of life as entering into human experience from outside (from the ancestral gift) and as an interpretation that is simply to be accepted. Present reality is to be grafted onto it, and not the other way about. To what extent can that interpretation, or indeed any meaning from the past, be brought to bear upon an ego formed in the context of the present? There will be adjustments on both sides, for The Dreaming is also creative. Human experience, like the land, does change over the generations. There can be no denying that. But this fact does not require that Dreaming interpretations remain discreetly in the shadows and be incapable of having realities of the present grafted onto them. Those rituals which last and which retain vitality, even while they change in form, are a witness that such a grafting is taking place.

NOTES

1. The Wadeye-Port Keats reserve is located about 150 km southwest of Darwin in Australia's Northern Territory. The reserve is occupied by many different Aboriginal groups (*mobs* in the more familiar vernacular) with the Murrinh-patha being the largest and the traditional owners of land about Wadeye. Other linguistic and cultural groups include the Murrinh-Ke, the Murri-Jabin, and the Marringarr. There are in all five distinct groups with differing languages, customs, stories and totems. Little has been written about them since the extensive work done by the Australian anthropologist W. E. H. Stanner, who lived with them in 1935 and again in the 1950s. For his acute analysis cf. *On Aboriginal Religion* (Sydney: University of Sydney, 1963, 1966); reprinted as Oceania Monograph, no. 11, 1989. [N.B.: page numbers will be taken from the 1989 facsimile edition.] Sister Teresa Ward, *The Peoples and Their Land About Wadeye* (Wadeye, Australia: Wadeye Press, 1983) is very helpful, especially for people who have visited the area. I first visited this community in early 1987 and have returned five or six times in the following years, remaining for some months on each occasion. The community, which is one of the largest in the Northern Territory, had a Roman Catholic mission from 1935.

This is important for any study, since the sacramentalism of Catholicism can serve as a window on Aboriginal ways of thinking and ritualizing.

2. The term *country*, like the term *community*, has to be handled carefully here. It can refer to the whole Reserve, and the people about Wadeye do live as a unified, cooperating unit within it. Families and individuals, however, relate to a particular locale that was given, *i.e.*, assigned them by their Dreaming ancestors. This land with its religious history is what is, properly speaking, *one's country*.

3. Acrylics and not traditional earth paints were used to avoid possible difficulties with U.S. Customs regulations, which frown on bringing in samples of foreign soil. Acrylics posed no major problem, however. The artists were accustomed to using them, since they are now in wide use among Aboriginal artists.

4. *The Sacred and the Profane* is his most popular account of the notion, which appears throughout his work. More recently J. Z. Smith has shown that there are difficulties with Eliade's interpretation of the Arrernte (Arunda) myth he chose as his example. Cf., *To Take Place* (Chicago: University of Chicago Press, 1987), pp. 3–10. Aboriginal elders would probably answer that Eliade, in choosing the Arrernte story, did indeed choose a nontypical example, and that they themselves have little awareness of the *axis mundi* theory that Eliade was trying to illustrate, but they would agree that Eliade was correct enough in seeing the whole of The Dreaming as a paradigm for the present and not just a collection of etiological tales.

5. This has been investigated by Josephine Flood, *The Archaeology of the Dreaming* (Honolulu: University of Honolulu Press, 1983).

6. In her chapter on the ritual among the Shakers, Martha Stortz has shown how the Central Ministry during the Era of Manifestations was able to use ritual to reconfigure a current situation while at the same time regaining its leadership role ("Ritual Power, Ritual Authority: Configurations and Reconfigurations in the Era of Manifestations"). Following Diane Bell, who has made intensive study of Aboriginal ritual among women, Stortz argues that a dialectical understanding of ritual and ritualization is necessary if we are truly to understand the ritual process. This would fit in with some suggestions made by Peter Willis, *Riders in the Chariot: Aboriginal Conversion to Christianity in Remote Australia* (Charles Strong Memorial Lecture, 1985), and Stanner, *On Aboriginal Religion*, bears further investigation.

7. Aboriginals are concerned primarily with their own ritual life, but in a curious way their interest also extends to non-Aboriginal ritualizing. Aboriginal peoples have expressed sympathy for all spiritual manifestations, which they expect will appear in various ways in every place. Albert Muta's (a Murrinh-patha elder of the 1950s) statement, *White man has no Dreaming, him go 'nother way, . . . Him got a road belong himself,* reflects a puzzlement rather than anything else. Aboriginals have accepted and happily taken part in Christian rituals both Catholic and Protestant, which were *'nother way. Cf.,* W. E. H. Stanner, *White Man Got No Dreaming,* (Canberra: Australian National University Press, 1979). In a perceptive analysis Peter Willis argues that Aboriginals were happy to take on another ritual system [*i.e.,* Christian] to enrich their ritual repertoire and were happy to accept affiliation into the church . . . and still retain Aboriginal identity with its overlaid perspectives of self and relations, territory and dreaming. "Riders in the Chariot," p. 12.

8. The social origin of all religion was stated in classical form by Durkheim, using, as he supposed, Australian social models. *The Elementary Forms of Religious Life* (London: George Allen and Unwin, Ltd., 1915). After an extensive examination of the Murrinh-patha Stanner concluded, "(i) If any Australian aborigines . . . lived in a stationary state of society with a static culture, the Murinbata were certainly not among them . . . (ii) to identify [aboriginal] religion with totemic phenomena would be a mistake; (iii) The society was not the real source and object of the religion." *On Aboriginal Religion,* p. 154.

9. To change the external relations of a person may, of course, effect significant changes within an individual. Infant baptism does just this. To be told from one's early years, *You are a Catholic, or You are a Lutheran,* or even *You are a Christian* imposes a role on that person that is well nigh indelible. In the secular realm, being told *You are an American* or *You are an Australian* has much the same effect. No one nowadays wishes to be told when they are twenty that they are a *stateless person.* One is left unprotected and without a political community. To be without a religion can produce similar lack of ease. Individuals in our present society often make great efforts to find their cultural roots or their religious identity.

10. As a result of his researches among the Murrinh-patha Stanner felt able to identify a number of such rituals, some currently in use, some vaguely remembered but by then discontinued. He notes *Karamala* (for boys about 8–10), circumcision (for youths approaching puberty) and *Punj* (for adults, c. 16 or older). There are also rites of initiation for women, but this Stanner does not discuss. As a man he

would not have had easy access to informants and would certainly not have been taken to any ceremonies. *On Aboriginal Religion*, 6, for women pp. 140–43, 147–48. Diane Bell warns that authors such as Roheim and Warner have seriously underreported and badly reported the activities of Aboriginal women in Australia, especially their ritual role. Stanner was given the impression by his informants that women were held in low regard ritually as well as in other ways. It is possible that the ritual practices of women were not being observed when Stanner was there in the 1930s and 1950s. D. Bell, "Aboriginal Women and the Religious Experience," *Traditional Aboriginal Society, A Reader*, ed. W. H. Edwards (Melbourne: Macmillan Co. of Australia, 1987), pp. 243–246, 252. Since Aboriginal life is motivated, before all, by an attempt to secure an equilibrium of checks and balances in human affairs, it stands to reason that the gender roles would also be carefully balanced and intrarelated.

11. To avoid any possible confusion it should be said that physical circumcision is practiced here among males only. There are no mutilating ceremonies for women here such as occur in some African situations.

12. Details can be examined in *On Aboriginal Religion*, Chapter 5, pp. 108–117. The ceremony is only partially in the public domain, and important aspects of it were kept secret. Deborah Rose gives a lively account of a contemporary initiation conducted in an area adjoining Port Keats involving several clans. We are reminded that ceremonies are events that do not always proceed according to the script and where disruptions can be generated by factors external to the ritual itself. D. B. Rose, *Dingo Makes Us Human* (Cambridge: Cambridge University Press, 1992) pp. 145–149.

13. This has been described by Stanner in as much detail as we can expect in *On Aboriginal Religion*, Chapter 1 p. 4 ff. and Chapter 5 p. 109 ff. Stanner sees circumcision as expressing the highest secular values, punj as expressing the highest religious values. He also knew of another initiation rite, *Tjimburki*, said to be greater than punj, but it was displaced, he thought, by the end of the nineteenth century. (Chapter 6, pp. 41.) Stanner was of the view that there were many such.

14. As Stanner remarked in 1962 in his talk "Religion, Totemism and Symbolism," "*[T]he end of Aboriginal religion was in Confucian terms 'to unite hearts and establish order' . . . the yearly round of rites let the aborigines renew both the sources and bonds of life . . . religion was not the mirage of society, and society was not the consequence of religion. Each pervaded the other within a larger process.*" In *White Man Got No Dreaming* (Canberra, Australia: ANU Press, 1979), p. 143.

15. The rituals described by Richard Payne in this volume might seem to be an exception, and indeed as enacted by an individual on a given day this is no doubt the case. But as Payne points out, the fictional world of rituals a monk enters is one that has been crafted over centuries by Tantric Buddhist practitioners . . . we open ourselves to discovering something beyond our own powers of imagination" ("Realizing Inherent Enlightenment,").

16. This is the reason why we have felt that animal behavior is not really ritual, although we may find elaborate patterned behavior among animals during the time of mating, for example. Animal activity of this kind is communicative—animals do respond to one another; birds answer calls—but it lacks meaning. The patterns animals use are fixed and instinctual. They engender response, but not understanding. The fact that patterned behavior over the course of generations or at geographical distances can be assigned different meanings in different cultures reinforces the point. Similar gestures can figure in two or even more rituals, but with different meanings. (Animals never seem to do this.) Ritual includes patterned behavior, but patterned behavior of itself is not ritual.

17. The word *ego* will not be taken in any technical sense. A discussion of ritual in tandem with a personality theory (as, for example, the ego over and against the self, as Jungians would have it) would take us far afield. Ego will refer here simply to the personality in general terms, which obviously embraces conscious and preconscious as well as subconscious strata.

18. This is a point made by V. Turner and criticized by Aune. Aune wishes to avoid false dichotomies, as I do too, that would see ritual as problem solving. Ritual's function is more dialogic; it mediates between the person and his or her community. Cf., "The Subject of Ritual." Stortz, commenting on D. Bell, makes the same point in "Ritual Power, Ritual Authority." Later on we will examine the elements in ritual and how each contributes to the dialogic process.

19. Stanner, in dealing with Murrinh-patha, titles Chapter 4, "The Design Plan of a Mythless Rite" and Chapter 5, "The Design Plans of Mythless Rites." Earlier, he suggests *"[T]he symbolic [ritual] accompaniments of the ceremonies become loved, not for their recondite import, for their own sake. Many of the songs* [i.e., the texts] *have no meaning, and the fact signifies nothing: but they are not sung less lovingly."* . . . *On Aboriginal Religion,* 1, p. 20.

20. Isolating text or gesture was not the only font of misinterpretation. Falsifications can also occur when *scene* or *score* is taken out of context. Comparisons between the shapes of temples from diverse

centuries or the paintings found in caves from widely separated regions cannot when taken by themselves be trusted to tell us much, if anything, about the rituals that may have gone on in them. The very function of *place* itself is problematic. In some religions one location is as good as another for holding a ritual; with others, such as Aboriginal religions, location is so interlocked with the requirements of myth that it is quite impossible to perform a ritual outside of its sacred place. No amount of *going through the motions* will be of any value. J. Z. Smith discusses this in To *Take Place.*

21. Willis, *Riders in the Chariot*, p. 11.

22. An example of the opposite comes from the Reformation in the sixteenth century. The gesture of offering both bread *and* wine to the congregation at Communion was introduced, replacing the older gesture of offering the host alone. This change reflected the new understanding of the Eucharist by the Reformers, who no longer saw it as a sacrificial Mass, but as the Lord's Supper, a communion rite. The change of gesture was quickly recognized by Unreformed and Reformed alike as making a new statement about the meaning of the Eucharist. It quickly became a touchstone dividing the two groups.

23. The evening darkness at the beginning of the Christian ceremony of the Easter vigil, which is penetrated by light as the ritual progresses in remembrance of the Resurrection, holds a powerful attraction for a Christian community. A sunrise service at dawn also uses light to herald the Resurrection and is popular for the same reason.

24. There is some interest in place even in Christianity, as a study of Christian pilgrimage or even a glance at the elan behind the Crusades makes clear. Christians, however, do not look to any Holy Land as a place where rituals absolutely must occur, nor does its parent Judaism (although place is more important in the latter case).

25. In the cheaply made B movies, such as cowboy westerns of the 1950s and early '60s, musical chords and themes were used so often that they gradually became clichés, exciting the children, who were still naive, while at the same time being a source of amusement for the adults, who recognized the double messages. The sound tracks of TV programs are replete with musical cues.

26. One of Mozart's major works, *The Magic Flute,* has been analyzed by Moberley with this in mind.

27. Ellis has discovered that many Aboriginals, especially their song leaders, have what is called perfect pitch, which attests to a very sensitive ear. Perfect pitch gives the ability to sing a precise note (i.e., to imitate the same vibrations per minute) whenever asked to do so

without the use of a pitch pipe or other instrumental help. It is an extraordinary ability, and rare in the West. Relative pitch, which involves the ability to sing a note in the same octave when a note has once been given out (i.e., the ability to sing E when G has been given) is an ability that most of us possess. Ellis argues that pitch in ceremonies can function as an imprinting device. In the context of a ceremony (music, dancing, verses, etc.) and especially in association with the ordeal of initiation, the pitch of a note is sometimes equated with totemic ancestor or some other aspect of The Dreaming. The effect of the imprint can remain with an individual throughout life and elicit a set of emotional responses when particular music is heard. Cf., *Aboriginal Music*, pp. 65–67.

28. This gives the Aboriginal communities, of course, a distinct advantage in maintaining the private, or rather the secret character of their rituals. They can politely permit outsiders (even Europeans) to be present and to witness the whole of a ceremony without, on that account, surrendering the inner meaning, which is kept secret from profane ears (*i.e.*, uncircumcised ears). It also enables children to be present and witness and share in the ritual life of the people without being prematurely exposed to its inner mysteries. These can be revealed later, in good time, when children are mature enough to understand.

29. Michael Aune gives the example, taken from Ole Rölvaag's *Giants in the Earth*, of the pastor who thought he had failed, that his words had been halting and his execution of the Communion service impoverished, yet members of his congregation found the ritual as powerful as any they had experienced, see "The Subject of Ritual: Ideology and Experience in Action."

30. Needless to say, not every ritual is in such a happy state. Because rituals are complex phenomena there is ample room for them to break up and to speak at cross purposes, to set up false expectations, to lead astray. Rituals can cause an individual or a people to rehearse moral and psychological mistakes. It is hardly a discovery to say that rituals can be harmful as well as healthy and that there is need for a therapeutic framework for approaching religious ritual. Cf., Valerie DeMarinis, who, although speaking more in terms of an individual's appropriation of ritual than we have been, shows how ritual can both open a person to memories of the past and also find ways of containing unwanted ones. She has some valuable insights on the dialogic character of ritual. See "A Psychotherapeutic Exploration of Religious Ritual as Mediator of Memory and Meaning."

2

Power in the Palace

The Investiture of a Javanese Sultan

CLARE B. FISCHER

Is there any meaning to installing a sultan within an independent country and during this development era?[1]

In March, 1989, five months after the death of the ninth sultan of Yogyakarta (Hamengkubuwono IX), a new sultan was invested with elaborate preparation and enthusiastic celebration. Forty-nine years had passed since the former sultan was installed, and the political life of the citizens of this central Javanese district had dramatically changed. No longer subjects of a complex political arrangement, involving both the authority of the sultanate and the colonial administration of the Dutch, the people of the special district of Yogyakarta had good reason to speculate about the role of their newly invested sultan. Perhaps, echoing the words of the epigraph, the citizenry of Yogyakarta asked themselves about the function of a sultan in the context of a national political life; how would his authority be defined in light of the central government in Jakarta?[2]

Both the language and symbolic gestures of the newly installed sultan offer an excellent introduction into the study of ritual in the context of modernization. A multitude of questions emerge from the study of investiture, not least of which is the character of power. In what measure is a traditional court understanding of authority shaped by current political practices and bureaucratic values originating at the nation's center? Has the status of the palace *(kraton)* and its king diminished? For my purposes, the most salient inquiry involves the practice of investiture itself and the degree to which it can be said merely to repeat traditional rites of elevation or whether this event is an example of ritual understood as historically unique. I am persuaded of the latter, especially by interpreting the investiture materials through the lens offered by Kelly and Kaplan in their groundbreaking essay on ritual and history.[3] Given that the ritual occurs at a particular time and in a historically shaped site, how accurate is the Kelly and Kaplan assertion that "ritual plays a crucial role in practice, as a vehicle for all forms of authority"?

Upon close analysis of the investiture material I have assembled, it is clear that no aspect of the event was a mere matter of form in spite of the outward appearance of a traditional installation of the sultan. In the first place, there had been speculation that with the demise of the ninth sultan, there would be an end to the sultanate of Yogyakarta. Clearly, this was not to be the case, and the failure of the new sultan's predecessor to name his choice for this position required that the inner court members (presumably uncles and brothers of the sultan) make a selection. Four centuries of continuous rule were unbroken by this decision, but the event itself created precedents that could not have been anticipated in earlier installation rites. The communications revolution had made it possible to invite millions of Javanese into the solemn event simultaneously, allowing the television screen to be an immediate source of information and assurance that the new sultan's prestige would be embraced by the constituents of this central Javanese special district. Although I cannot be certain that the media presence helped to construct a popular leader, I suspect that the tenth sultan became instantaneously a familiar and household figure. As I will indicate in a later section of this essay, such accessibility departs from the traditional sense of the sultan as both distant yet generous in his blessings.

Along the same lines, the immediacy of the press' dispatches to all parts of the globe most decidedly engaged a larger audience than any that had known of the sultanate and its leadership in previous generations. The international corps of reporters as well as the making of a film of the investiture ensured coverage that would eventually become archival, documents of a historical moment. In effect, the possibilities introduced by the diverse forms of modern reportage guaranteed that the 1989 installation would be both noticed and observed by a highly diversified audience compared to those witnesses of the former investiture rites.

The two sultans who preceded the current one were extraordinary figures in their own right. Sultan Hamengkubuwono VIII was committed to extensive cultural development, undertaking extensive architectural and musical improvements within the palace. His children were sent to Western schools within Java and in the Netherlands. In 1939, as he lay dying, his eldest son returned from his doctoral studies abroad to assume responsibility for the court. Many stories are told of Sultan Hamengkubuwono IX's charismatic and mystical character, but he is best remembered as a determined, independent leader of strong social consciousness, spiritually adept and politically tough.[4] Committed to the independence cause, he refused the offers of the Dutch administration to cooperate in exchange for the guarantee of an expanded territory. His firm resolve to aid in independence was continued after the national government declared itself. The sultan offered Yogyakarta as the seat of the new republic, and so it was that the first capital was located in what later was to become a special district. Obviously as a reward for his leadership, the new government created Yogyakarta a semiautonomous district, assuring the kraton of some political authority in spite of the centralization attendant to the new nation-state.

National service marked the ninth sultan's postindependence efforts, wherein he functioned as a cabinet minister for some years (1945–53) as well as vice president for a five-year term under President Suharto (1973–78). Two of his sons also worked within the national administration, one, the tenth sultan, as a member of the national legislature. Clearly, the establishment of a centralized government in Jakarta required massive adjustment to the concept of political authority in the kraton, raising the question of dualism in the determination of power. One commentator observes that in "an increasingly centralized and modern society," where functioning courts and had been effacious, they "may soon seem like an expensive anachronism—unless, perhaps, a new cultural and artistic role can be found for them."[5] Indeed, the tenth sultan recognized this tension and answered it with an assertion of distinctive authority. This clarification of function was made in his address before the assembled guests at his installation. More will be said of this text in the later section, which seeks to analyze "inaugural" speeches as specific historical communication.

FIELD AND LIBRARY RESEARCH

I had not come to Yogyakarta to study ritual activity, nor had I any interest in so-called elite studies. In the spring of 1989, however, the community was alive with discussion about the forthcoming installation and, many a day, I could hear the neighborhood school band practicing for its part in the festivities. When the invitation came to attend the "dress rehearsal" of the investiture at the kraton, my relative indifference turned to fascination about the court and its leadership. On that day, armed with camera and a mind that was tabula rasa with respect to the event, I asked questions, observed, and took photographs, wondering how I would decipher what proved to be a highly compelling event.[6]

Two days later, I had the good fortune to view the formal investiture before a television set in one of my Javanese neighbors. Not only did his running commentary inform me about what had earlier seemed thoroughly elusive, but the early moments of a research project emerged with my neighbor's critical assessment of the event. He pondered how the investiture departed from tradition, and why the new sultan spoke in the lingua franca of Indonesia (*Bahasa Indonesia*) rather than Javanese. Still dazzled by the symbolic splendor of the ritual, and unsure of what investiture meant given the changed status of the kraton post-independence, I returned to California determined to learn something about what I had observed.

I had in my possession copious field notes and a number of photographs that helped to guide my research in the library. After considerable reading, especially of history and ritual theory, I began to sort out what I believed to be a not-so-exotic event that could be useful in deepening the study of power in ritual life. Several return trips to Indonesia afforded me the opportunity to discuss my preliminary finding with Javanese friends, and my confidence grew as I began to draft one after another tentative approach to investiture at the kraton. In a relatively early version, I depended on the theoretical structuring of Turner, especially the analysis of liminality,[7] believing that the sultan's elevation could be seen as an instance of this between and betwixt process. This orientation truncated the really compelling dimensions of the investiture as I had come to know it and, soon enough, I set Turner aside, believing that what I was after was theory addressing the problem of order and cohesion. At this theoretical juncture I tapped the insights of Robert Bellah in the classic formulation of "civil religion."[8] What I thought might be helpful in this perspective would be a way of understanding how the sacred and secular merge, strengthening the traditional Javanese religious understanding of the sultan as a mystical/saintly being while appreciating the issues of polity within the kraton. This tack also proved unacceptable.

As I became clearer about the significance of the investiture rite, I sought an approach that would respect the question asked by the sultan at his installation. What elements of continuity and change can be decoded? As I have previously noted, the contribution of Kelly and Kaplan fostered a sense of history that acknowledged the unique character of the event and its location in the discussion of practice, rather than structure.[9] In their attempt to promote a view that contests the timeless character of ritual, the authors virtually prodded me to ask a set of different questions of my field materials and reading. What follows, then, is an examination of leadership indisputedly in transition and the part played by ritual in making history.

THE INVESTITURE OF SULTAN HAMENGKUBUWONO X

In human life, the nearest approximation of the perfect order depicted in dramas and texts was the ceremonial order re-created in the massive state ceremonies.[10]

Although the kraton, formally known as *Ngayoyakarto Hadingrat*, is the scene of a multiplicity of court celebrations, none compares with investiture, which follows a prescribed order, "complex codes of decorum" that defy a full description.[11] One approach is to understand that the ritual is constituted of many rituals that possess a chronological order, moving from preparatory activity, to status-changing gestures, and finally to the postinvestiture procession of the newly installed sultan around his palace.[12]

Preinvestiture Rites

Almost a week before the investiture, formal ritual activity commences with the pilgrimage of kraton officials to certain sites related to mythic history and the founding of the palace. With his entourage of court staff, the soon to be sultan traveled to royal burial sites believed to be sacred. After his full investiture, the new sultan will not be permitted to visit these holy cemeteries located at Imogiri and Kota Gede.

Prior to the cooking of a special pancake, *apem*, by female members of the court, all pots and utensils have been ritually purified by women retainers. This food will be brought to the South Sea as part of a postinvestiture offering to the Queen of the Indian Ocean, Nyai Ratu Kidul.[13]

It would be misleading to suggest that the activity around film and other commercial ventures represents ritual work, but there is no question that the arrangements with advertising companies and sponsors infused the preinvestiture period with a particularly modern feeling. Flags of the sponsors (including cosmetic and ice cream firms, officially endorsed for this occasion), lent a festive coloration to the kraton and its environs, offering all a vision of the new age of business connection between the palace and the everyday world of capitalism. I will develop this theme in my concluding observations.

Investiture

More than three thousand guests were assembled in the *Bangsal Witono* (public) section of the kraton to witness the investiture ritual, which embraced a variety of subritual events within the larger status-transforming one that elevated a prince to a sultan. In addition to the stately procession of the royal family, retainers, and the prince through the northern sector of the kraton, the court's heirlooms were carried by a select group of women (*manggung*), a spectacular display of symbolic artifacts of the court. The event began with chants from the Qur'an by officials from the court's mosque, followed by the invitation to the prince to come forward and be formally named crown prince. After a short period, the crown prince was again called forward and, with the pinning of the royal star upon the left side of his velvet jacket, a new sultan was created. At that moment a cacophony of sound filled the palace: a cannonade of rifle salvos, drumming, horn blasts. These next moments contrasted dramatically with the silence of all that followed. During this still time it was observed that the sultan was in deep meditation.

The final segments of this investiture ritual involved both secular and sacred expressions of the new sultancy. His Highness Sultan Hamengkubuwono X presented his thoughts about the function of the kraton, and as a first official action elevated his wife, daughters, and several princes to higher status. In naming his wife as queen, the new sultan departed from his predecessor, who had several wives but never appointed one to this prestigious rank. Formalities ended with prayers, calls from the mosque, and a dance-like exit from the throne room.

The sultan met with many of his invited guests directly after the ceremony in order to receive their good wishes. Then, following time-honored procedure, he met with the royal family in private quarters (the *Bangsal Kecono*), accepting their homage.

Postinvestiture

The day after the installation a number of ritual activities ensued, including further pilgrimages north and south of the kraton to bring special offerings to the guardians of the palace. Apem, the pancake baked several days earlier, and hair and nail clippings of the sultan were carried south to Parangkusomo; cigarettes and other offerings were given to the spirits inhabiting sites to the north (Mt. Merapi) and to the east, as well as at Dlepih, a royal burial site. During the morning, while these offerings were being made on his behalf, the sultan planted a new sapling banyon in the northern ground of the palace (*alun-alun lor*).

Later in the day, the much-anticipated procession of the sultan and his court took place in the form of a circumambulation by carriage around the perimeter of the kraton. It had been thought that the newly invested queen would accompany her husband in this procession (*kirab*), seated beside him in the royal carriage. However, although this would have represented a departure from tradition, it did not happen. In fact, the sultan rode a distance of some six kilometers, alone, with one brother accompanying him behind the carriage (on horseback), as well as six smaller carriages, eight platoons of soldiers from the kraton, and some seventy bands from local groups. During this procession, the newly installed sultan blessed the masses of people assembled on the streets of the kirab route.

Two days after these events, four of the brothers of Sultan Hamengkubuwono X were married in the kraton, thus marking completion of the ritual activities associated with investiture and resuming routine life at the palace.

THEORETICAL UNDERPINNINGS

"... rituals are always rhetorical and didactic."[14]

In the sketch of investiture that introduced the reader to the diverse aspects of the sultan's investiture, I failed to discuss either the symbolic dimensions of the event or the implications of this ritual for the study of ritual power. In this section I will attempt to provide such an elaboration, embracing the epigraphic assertion of Myerhoff regarding the instructive and persuasive aspects of ritual.

The installation of a new sultan served to dissipate doubts about the function of the kraton, in part through the new sultan's explicit assurances about the distinctive role to be played by the palace. However, with the assurance that there was to be meaning to the sul-

tan's activity, he did not substantially change the traditional understanding of the court's administration of power as potency at the
center.

In order to unpack these notions, I will approach the ritual of
investiture through a set of rubrics, allowing me to retrieve the historically constructed practices of investiture in the context of tradition
and change. Text, as Woodward notes, is fundamental to the contextual understanding of the kraton.[15] Accordingly, the mythohistorical
background of the sultanate of Yogyakarta requires notice, as does the
particular function of naming, which I consider a form of text.

The title held by the sultan is encompassing as it is impressive,
indicating manifold responsibilities and authorities. He is "The Royal
Feet, His Highness, the Most Noble Sultan, Hamengkubuwono,
Commander-in-Chief on the Field of Battle, Servant of the Merciful,
Lord of the Faith, Regulator of Religion, Caliph of God."[16] He is traditionally named royal sovereign and religious leader, and his position is
best understood in terms of court history, which formally begins in
1755 with the founding of the Yogyakarta kraton by Sultan Hamengkubuwono I. However, there is an earlier history that established the
sultanate within the lineage of a great dynasty, Mataram.[17] Both the
Surakarta and Yogyakarta courts are vestiges of this once powerful
military/political kingdom, which was reputedly founded at Kota
Gede in 1578. Although the dynasty was long besieged with both
external and internal strife associated with Dutch and British colonial
interference, both courts coexist today. Having once been united,
Surakarta (known as Solo) and Yogyakarta (Yogya) are located 60 kilometers apart and, to this day, deep kinship ties hold the two kratons in
close connection in spite of different modern histories.[18]

The chronicles that depict myth/history (*Babad Tanah Jawi*) from
the time of the founding of the Mataram dynasty amply demonstrate a
notion of the kraton as the center that contains power. In the narrative
of Sri Senopati, the founding figure of the dynasty, we learn that his
meditations provided prophetic visions of an empire that he would create. The same story tells of his continued *tapa* (meditation so powerful
that it effects climatic changes), the disturbance of the Southern Sea
and the encounter of Sri Senopati with the Queen of the Southern Sea,
who was angered by the harm his meditations caused to the life in the
sea. The Queen invited him to join her in her underwater palace, and a
liaison developed that was to implicate all sultans to follow in this lineage. The Queen, Nyai Ratu Kidul, promised protection and prosperity
to her lover and his heirs, as long as homage was paid to her thereafter.
This vow continues to be observed and had some consequences for the

investiture ritual in 1989. With the new sultan's decision to have his earthly queen ride with him in the kirab, there was some musing about the possible wrath of his spiritual bride; in fact, he rode alone in the carriage, with many a local Javanese speculating that Nyai Ratu Kidul accompanied him without any female competition.

The many titles held by the sultan are indicative of the highly descriptive sensibility of the Javanese court. His nomenclature refers to both functions and relationships that have been or remain essential to the kraton's leadership. In the palace there are many expressions of naming that identify both humans and objects with the potency of the center. All personnel receive new names when they enter the royal household. Each heirloom has a special name, and the objects that are perceived to be filled with cosmic energy carry honorific titles. Trees and roads within the palace grounds also bear special names that refer to symbolic meanings associated with the kraton understood as a mystical path.

There are two sites within the palace that possess chronographs. These are intricate representations of aminate figures or flora that date the founding and the reconstruction of the kraton. On the southern gate there are two pairs of entwined snakes, which are to be read as fixing the originating time of the palace's construction. On a northern gate, indicating extensive restoration work, is a representation of overlapping leaves. In this graphic representation, an alternate text points to the important dates of the kraton's physical presence, emphasizing in all instances the motif of two figures united. What these chronographs point to, in short, is the symbolic value of harmony/peace that the kraton represents through its leadership, a sultan who is centered, without internal tension, and capable of resolving differences that may lead to open strife.

The general position of Myerhoff and many of the contributors to the volume on secular ritual she coedited is useful in reference to the realities of the kraton. Specifically, Myerhoff rejects sharp dichotomization between sacred and secular ritual, urging, rather, that we look upon most ritualization along a continuum, being more or less one or another reality.[19] It is more likely the case, in the investiture ritual, that sacred and secular ritual resemble the entwined leaves and snakes of the chronographs; at one instant, both. Yet, there are elements within the event, for example the sultan's installation speech, that can be clearly classified as a secular expression.

In teaching courses on ritual, I have been experimenting with a typology that I find helpful for students who undertake ethnographic work. I label these the "five P's" of ritual analysis: place, personnel, paraphernalia, performance understood as an end, and perspective (which yields some information about interpretation). This classificatory approach enables me to tease out information about power in the investiture ritual. It should be noted, however, that the notion of the palace as center, as locus of cosmic power, involves some debate; a discussion of its contestation will follow in a later section. There are some parallels between my typology and that of Hilary Martin (this volume), although his rubrics are differently named and refer, in part, to other aspects of ritualization (score, gesture, and the like).

Place

There are two features of place as it pertains to the Yogyakarta palace that I want to emphasize: movement as an inside and outside activity, energizing a north/south axis; and the kraton grounds as symbolic body and a mystical movement between life, inspired life, and death. With respect to the first, it will be recalled that the preinvestiture and postinvestiture rituals involve considerable movement from the palace center to the outside—to relatively distant sites along a north/south axis that joins the mountains and the sea of the area. Pilgrimages by the sultan and his court to the holy burial sites of Kota Gede and Imogiri require travel to the south of the kraton, to places sacred because of their association with the founding of the Mataram dynasty and the burial of royal ancestors who require acts of homage. After investiture, offerings are brought by court officials to the mountains and to the sea (as well as to the sacred burial ground at Dlepih) at the same time that the sultan moves to the northern palace square in order to plant the new sapling that has been specially cut for this occasion.

I would suggest that the circumambulation around the palace, the kirab, is of a different order of movement; not of inside to outside so much as riding the perimeter of the palace. It seems to be a way of sealing off the boundaries of the kraton while, simultaneously, connecting with the citizens of the district. Perhaps this movement is like the entwined snakes of the chronograph, reconciling opposites in order to produce harmony.

When the kraton is perceived as a place of spiritual significance, as a mystical path derived from Sufi understanding, the human body and its growth becomes paramount. One of the Yogyakarta court members, author of a pamphlet about the kraton, writes:

Describing the building, roads, kinds of trees which are inten-
sionally (sic) planted, the situation and the architecture of the
buildings, we ought to think, that all much have a meaning. . . .
It symbolizes the genesis of a human.[20]

The kraton is reported to have twenty-two parts, a body with nine
holes (or entrances) that, when closed, ensure maximum achievement
in meditation. The southern section of the kraton refers to the lower
part of the body, with hairy flora and distinctive names of trees that
suggest sexuality, pregnancy, and expectancy. By contrast, the northern section represents the ideals and hopes of mature spiritual development. During the investiture, movement of the participants
occurred in the main, northerly section of the palace. In fact, the sultan sits enthroned in the most northern space and after his investiture
is said to be meditation out of the palace along a northern axis
through the city's monument (*tugu*) to Mount Merapi, the abode of
powerful spirits.[21]

Personnel

Obviously the pivotal person in the investiture ritual is the prince who
becomes sultan. There is a sizable cast of participants who demonstrate the hierarchical arrangement of a court once associated with feu-
dal authority. In the procession within the palace, en route to the locus
of the actual installation, royal family members lead the way, followed
by the women who are attired as Javanese brides and carry the regalia
of the court. Other women retainers carry the golden throne and footstool under a yellow umbrella. The prince follows.

In addition to these participants, nine platoons of soldiers parade,
and many other relatives as well as the invited guests are seated in the
main hall.

Two male relatives place a significant role in the ritual: The crown
prince's uncle and his youngest brother. Both stand near the throne
and officiate; another brother serves as announcer. There are representatives from the mosque who open and close the investiture event in
prayer.

Unlike earlier installations, there are no colonial officials looking
on and ensuring legitimacy. Moreover, the film crews and press representatives are discreetly placed but present throughout the official
event.

Paraphernalia

The display of court heirlooms and regalia infused with cosmic energy constitutes an important part of the traditional investiture rite. Those objects which contain *pusaka*, magical power, are removed from the places in the kraton where they are generally concealed and carried to the throne room. It is assumed that much danger can come from negligent display of these pusaka, lest they fall in the hands of ill-willed or foolish people. These particular items are returned to their repositories with dispatch after the installation has occurred and they have been blessed by the new sultan. In this public presentation of pusaka power is exuded, restoring and being restored in strength by the sultan's presence. Among these magical objects are the four hundred year old spear reputed to have belonged to Fri Senopati (*Kyai Hageng Plered*), the *kris* chosen by the sultan to wear on this auspicious occasion, the throne, footstool, spittoon, and golden umbrella—all essential paraphernalia for the investiture.[22] The *Bintang* (a diamond and gold pin) that is presented to the new sultan is another powerful object, as are the two *gamelan* ensembles (the percussion instruments played throughout Indonesia) said to have long connection with the court. Finally, the carriage and two saddles used for the kirab are regarded as pusaka but are not kept in a hidden place for safekeeping.

This lengthy inventory of power objects begins to reveal the way in which power is contained within the court. It is important to distinguish pusaka from the regalia carried by women in the installation procession. The latter refer to essential virtues that are believed to inhere in the court. Saturated with symbolic meaning, they are described by Woodward as objects representing the sultan's divine appointment.[23] Among the eight objects are a goose that symbolizes purity and watchfulness, a deer whose quickness of movement is perceived as a valuable quality for a successful reign, and a peacock, symbolizing pride and dignity.[24]

Performative Features

Having reviewed something about place, personnel, and paraphernalia attendant to the investiture ritual, I will summarize the last two rubrics of my typology by referring to the particular power of certain personnel, on the one hand, and the significance of the new sultan's speech, on the other. There is no question about the performance of the court retinue in this event, suggesting that investiture is, indeed, only a repetition of gestures and movements long prescribed and well rehearsed. The distinction drawn by Tambiah, and developed by Payne (this volume), is useful in presenting this material as evidence of ritual as historically salient.[25] In describing the manggung appearance, or the mannered way in which the procession moves, or how the newly installed sultan sits upon his throne and meditates to the north, illustrations of rule-bound behavior, there is an absence of spontaneity. All accords to expected normative conduct, and any departure would be considered an assault to notions of Javanese decorum.

But, if performative features of the ritual event can be distinguished from the actions so weighted with tradition, it is the presence of the human pusaka at the investiture that exemplifies ritual as "effective action" in itself. Physically different Javanese—albinos, dwarfs, others who might be regarded as anomalous—are called *punakawan* and appear to have some analogous relationship to the court jest and clown of other royal courts. However, these punakawan are perceived as important containers of cosmic energy and, on the day of the formal installation, lead the way into the section of the palace where the status of the prince will be elevated. I assert that their presence and the particular placement of this special group of court residents is performative. If effect, throwing an invisible light of magical power (*kaseketen*) over the whole environment, these pusaka beings ensure good fortune and protection.

Perspective

Although the investiture ritual does not end with the speech of the sultan, I have isolated this portion of the event to indicate how perspective is employed in the analysis of ritual action. Prior to the sultan's installation, signalled by the fastening of the eight-point star upon his jacket by his uncle, the prince has uttered no sound. At the completion of his meditation upon the throne, Sultan Hamengkubuwono X delivered a speech in Bahasa Indonesia, the language spoken by preindependence nationalists as well as the declared language of the new nation.[26] In assuring his listeners that there is a function for the kraton, Sultan Hamengkubuwono X embraced tradition in an explicit and implicit manner, but focused upon the kraton as a relevant center in a democratizing, modern republic.

Instructing his audience in the triple significance of his royal name, the sultan explained that it means that he must listen to and protect his constituents and redress inequity, especially in wealth. Suggesting that the sultan's purpose has always been for the benefit of the people, he added: "What is a sultan for if he does not give meaning to the society?"[27] In part, that meaning has been consistently held by the Yogyakarta court, to "*ngemong dan ngayom*" (to provide protection) as crucial to the sultan's religious leadership as a deputy of Allah. Developing his notion of the sultanate, Sultan Hamengkubuwono X addressed the issue of role within republican political setting, asserting that he was "someone aware of the nation."

Clearly rejecting that he was a mere figurehead, while recognizing that there was no political dualism in the relationship of the court to the nation, the sultan carved out his function in this way. Political authority belongs to the government, and cultural leadership to the kraton:

> Culture is a source of inspiration, creativity, and inspiration. Through culture, the voice and thought of the people can be expressed and heard as to what is right and wrong.[28]

In this seemingly bland statement of culture, the sultan envisioned a new understanding of the kraton as a place at the heart of tradition and modernity. No longer a kingdom defined by patrimonial notions of political sovereignty, the new kraton would find its place lodged within the national government's development ideology and commitment to large scale tourism as one of the leading Indonesian industries.

In addressing those who immediately witnessed his installation as well as countless viewers of the telecast, Sultan Hamengkubuwono X promoted a novel idea of centrality that could embrace a populist undergirding of participation and an enterprising base that might generate sufficient resources to guarantee the sustenance of the court's retinue and assure a way that would not dissipate a long held pride in the palace. Even those who, in future months and years, would listen to the sultan's speech (in rebroadcasts or in the film of the investiture) could be assured that the new leadership was earnest in endeavoring to make the kraton not a symbol of the past but a vital center for all times. His speech, in short, afforded a sense of adaptive strategy mixed with strong ties to the myths, symbols, and beliefs of past dynastic life.

THE POWER WITHIN

In a well-known essay published by the political theorist Benedict Anderson, a clear statement of Javanese power is given: ". . . the Javanese see power as something concrete, homogenous, constant in quality, and without inherent moral implications. . . .[29]"

Noting that these characteristics belong to an "ideal type" and refer most cogently to old Java before Western colonialism, the depiction nonetheless offers an excellent entree into the question of how power and ritual meet in the investiture ritual. It allows me to tease more from three of the rubrics I have already discussed: place—in this case as mystical center; personnel—the particular capacities of the sultan in manipulating power, and paraphernalia—objects as magical containers.

Power, understood as substance rather than willful engagement, is a point of departure.[30] In the Javanese case it refers to an invisible, suffusing, and originating energy that formlessly circulates and requires action to ensure its efficacy. In the Hindu-Buddhist Javanese understanding of cosmology, and to some extent in the mystical Muslim appropriation of the same, this energy is associated with a center that is ruled by an extraordinary leader who knows how to accumulate power and regulate its loss.

The center, in effect the kraton, is both a holy site and a vibrant locus that cannot be grasped as mere geographical locale. Although the Yogyakarta palace is situated in an auspicious place, midpoint between the Southern Sea and the active volcanic mountain, Merapi, its cosmological significance has more to do with the relationship between the inside of its grounds and the four quarters marking the powerful dynamics along a north-south axis. The Queen of the Sea, faithfully offering her guidance and force(s) to the sultan so long as he continues his fidelity, represents one such guardian of the axis. Semar, the clown figure of puppet theater and popular belief, resides in the northern boundary at Merapi; he, too, is provided offerings to ensure continued support for the kraton.

One might consider the metaphors deployed by writers about the cosmic energy that the kraton/sultan accumulate: the most focused beam of light in a cone of illumination; the navel of spiritual embodied power.[31] All these tropes suggest that there is little resemblance between the reality of court power and the understanding of political power that has dominated Western theory. Stortz' exploration of dominative and charismatic power in the case of Shaker experience (this volume) exemplifies this difference. Neither expansive volition from the inside, nor exceptional personal gift characterize the palace and the sultanate. He is vehicle, who is not without charismatic significance, a figure whose effort is not an exercise of power.

This elusive substance that originates in the cosmos becomes contained through exertion associated with ritual activity. The sultan is an adept who renders accumulation possible through his ability to concentrate and conform to rigorous ascetic practices. In the power-work of adding more power to the center, the sultan must both demonstrate his spiritual gift and manage the flow of energy such that it bestows maximum good fortune on the palace, its occupants, and the larger community of the Yogyakarta territory. From boyhood young princes are educated in both asceticism and spiritual concentration and the selection of the crown prince; in the final analysis, it has much to do with the care, display of ability, and discerning potential adjudged to be centered on one or another royal son. The current sultan appears to have been chosen because of his mystical skills and vocation. According, he is not without charismatic presence, but Anderson would argue that that concept serves more as a trope than a sociohistorical reality.[32]

With the kraton understood as center, it can be said to be understood as a "spiritual body of the sultanate." Earlier I identified the mystical notions of kraton as body, and noted that the installation occurred in the upper portion of the grounds—the sacred areas of mystical maturation. It is here that the sultan used his ability to concentrate and unite all opposition, here that the tugs and tensions of the mundane are transcended and true peace is achieved. The interior strength of the spiritual mediator constructs, through his power and the power accumulated at the center, a still space where all movement ceases. It will be remembered that directly after the crown prince is elevated to sultan that he sits motionless and appears to be looking into the distance, his inner self joining all the hustle and bustle of the busy streets of Yogyakarta, joining kraton to mountain in the furthermost corner of the district.

Ritual life entails the accumulation and deployment of power. The center has been likened to a stage for the "performance of royal rituals through which magical power . . . of the dynasty and the blessing of Allah are infused into the population and territory of the kingdom."[33] Yet there is movement during the weeklong investiture ritual along the axis outside the kraton walls as well as within. This activity enables power to be further accumulated by the sultan-to-be and vivifies history. Visitations to the royal burial ground ensure that the ancestor's power will be absorbed by the incoming ruler. At the same time the lineage is remembered and the dualism of past and present is overcome in this drama of homage. Errington's point about power as animating is entirely applicable to this ritualization, wherein dead things come to life. So, too, is Anderson's aside salient, indicating that Javanese power is the "ability to give life."[34]

The heirlooms that are perceived as power-filled are the sultan's responsibility. In effect, there seems to be a reciprocity that culminates in the addition of power, the objects absorbing power from the sultan and the other way around. Where display has been poorly regulated, power is likely to dissipate, and with this loss disorder enters the center, bringing poor fortune.

Exception has been taken to the theory presented in the foregoing pages by several commentators.[35] Three areas of contestation appear to be at stake: rationality, populism, and the hegemony of one religious tradition over all others. It is not possible, given the limits of this essay, to review the basic controversy arising from Anderson's analysis. However, the point should be made that each critic presents a concern that has implications for the understanding of the kraton within the context of modernization. If power is associated with cosmic energy and the sultan's mystical skills, does this advance the stereotype of Javanese irrationalism that Anderson sought to counter in his analysis?[36] If scholars concentrate on the court as center, how does this elite orientation preclude understanding of the general populace and the varieties of power that have been historically exercised in the rural areas? Finally, has Anderson's work represented a slighting of the role Islam has played in the spiritual life of the kraton? How has contemporary reform Muslim belief and practice encountered the mystical understanding of the traditional central Javanese?

CONCLUSION

Yogya has consolidated its position as the cultural centre of Java with, in its heart, a Kraton alive in tradition and close to the world famous temples of Borobudur and Prambanan.[37]

In the study of one pivotal ritual event in the history of a Javanese center I have attempted to probe the boundaries and qualities of power expressed in terms unfamiliar to the Western reader. In doing so, I have asked what is understood in the elevation of a prince to a sultan when political authority and legitimacy seem to have no meaning and cultural authority rises to the foreground. It is not possible for me to advance a general theory of transition, but I do believe that some preliminary conclusions would serve us well. Clearly, there is as much ambiguity in investiture ritual as there is order. Whereas continuity of a dynastic lineage must be recognized, is form the sole evidence of this persistent leadership?

I conclude by returning to the position of Kelly and Kaplan regarding ritual as history making. Through this lens investiture of a sultan without political or military responsibility is not a travesty, an empty ceremonial act, a spectacular moment without implications of further leadership. The promise of financial stability and the assurance of, at the very least, a thread of traditional coherence are tied to the way in which display has been transformed. Where display has been long associated with the controlling efforts of a divinely inspired king, it has assumed additional (but not dominant) presence through the modern demands of media and tourism. It is in response to these demands that the new sultanate found a viable path and resisted total absorption in the New Order of Jakarta.[38]

Departing from traditional practices, the court arranged to have some two hundred representatives from a host of media within the kraton for the purpose of providing a wide viewing of this historic event. In addition to the live telecast on local TV, closed-circuit viewing was made possible for those proximate to the kraton on some thirty sets. Most notably, the palace contracted with two large, Jakarta-based advertising companies to control the media event. Some press representatives charged that the monopoly worked against them, but the kraton was firm in its resolve to maintain maximum dignity and minimal loss of direct control over the film and photographs generated on that occasion. Copyright and royalty arrangements with the palace were part of the negotiation. One film director was quoted in the press with respect to the difficulty of the project. Allowing that there could be no re-takes, he asserted that the task "to be able to capture the sacred ritual mood" was paramount.[39]

The business of administering a spectacular media event did not end with the filming of investiture. Postcards, poster, and calendars are all available to the visitor to Yogyakarta, and these visual souvenirs of the sultan's elevation are routinely sold at the kraton in its small gift store. The impact of tourism on this city and the designation of the kraton as a main attraction cannot be understated. In one interview of a kraton dance teacher, we hear how vital tourism is the life of the center. Hesitant to disparage the material benefits of tourism, he admitted that the dance performances had to be adjusted to the schedule of tourists; to keep some tradition it appears necessary to adapt to the needs of those incalculable numbers of both foreign and Indonesian visitors who want only a superficial experience of Javanese tradition.[40]

In my depiction of the kraton as placed along an important spiritual axis I did not mention its location between two internationally known temples that draw thousands of tourists throughout the year and from all parts of the globe. Borobudur, an ancient Hindu-Buddhist pilgrimage site, has long interested travelers to Java, as has Prambanan, a Hindu temple built a century later. In today's world of "package tours" these temples and the palace are principal sites, and all have the full auxiliary support system to allow hasty exposure to traditional architecture, culture, and religious artifacts. Guides, taxis, buses, gift shops, and small restaurants, are essential factors in making tourism viable. Without doubt it is solid enterprise, and provides employment for hundreds of Yogyakarta residents who might otherwise move to Jakarta and other large cities.

The point is clear enough: the survival of tradition, ironically, depends on the massive infusion of tourist dollars.[41] How the motif of display embraces this adaptation is not altogether certain. Does the power of the pusaka remain contained and secure in the sultan's traditional practices? How is his part-time residence in Jakarta relevant to the pivotal function of the sultan within the kraton? Is the perfect stillness of the center ruptured by the busy movements of a fast-paced tourist industry?

It is reported that when the first sultan of Yogyakarta was about to found the kraton, he was given a choice of one of two symbolic objects, a container (*wadhah*) or a seed (*wiji*).[42] Sultan Hamengkubuwono I selected the former; thus the importance of the palace as a holder of tradition. However, a retelling is in order that understands Sultan Hamengkubuwono X as accepting both objects, recognizing that the palace is a dynamic center that must grow and accommodate long trusted practices to the specificities of historical life. This is what the ritual of investiture embraces and how it has ensured "life-empowering" survival.

NOTES

I wish to thank some of the people who contributed to the writing of this essay. Thanks to my friends in Yogyakarta who brought me to the kraton in the first place, to my neighbors in Bulak Sumur who opened their home to me and discussed the event with such good will and helpfulness, to my colleagues in Java and the United States who read and criticized this effort to communicate about the investiture. Finally, my thanks to the GTU and especially Dean Judith Berling, who has supported my studies of religion in Indonesia.

1. From the address given by Sultan Hamengkubuwono X, March 7, 1989; *Jakarta Post*, 3/9/89.

2. Indonesia became an independent republic in 1945 after centuries of domination under the Dutch. It is a country of 190 million people, with 30 percent of that number living on the island of Java. In addition to being the fourth largest population in the world, it is the largest Muslim nation. For the past thirty years it has been moving

through a massive development which has brought industry to the nation and a variety of consequences attendant to such rapid change.

3. See John Kelly and Martha Kaplan, "History, Structure and Ritual," in *Annual Review of Anthropology* 1990 (vol. 19: pp. 119–150).

4. An example of Sultan Hamengkubuwono IX's spiritual power is given in the now legendary story that when he returned to Yogyakarta to assume royal responsibility a thunderbolt sounded in a clear blue sky.

5. Peter Carey, "Yogyakarta: From Sultanate to Revolutionary Capital of Indonesia, The Politics of Cultural Survival," in *Culture Through Time*, ed. Emiko Ohnuki-Tierney (Stanford, CA: Stanford University Press, 1990), Chapter 9, p. 26.

6. I do not agree with my colleague, John Hilary Martin (this volume), who minimizes the ritual significance of the dress rehearsal. This ritualization was part of a weeklong activity that had powerful elements within it, even though the political-legal event was not formally marked on this occasion.

7. See Victor Turner, *The Ritual Process* (Ithaca, NY: Cornell University Press, 1969); I do regard his work on pilgrimage in later studies helpful for understanding something of the movement of the court's retinue during the investiture week.

8. Robert Bellah, "Civil Religion in America," *Daedalus*, 1967; also Robert Bellah and Phillip Hammond, *Varieties of Civil Religion* (San Francisco: Harper & Row, 1980).

9. Kelly and Kaplan, p. 41.

10. Shelly Errington, *Meaning and Power in a Southeast Asian Realm* (Princeton, NJ: Princeton University Press, 1989), p. 276.

11. Note that I have attempted to use Javanese spelling throughout this essay rather than follow the Indonesian orthography. See Aart Van Beek, *Life in the Javanese Kraton* (Singapore: Oxford University Press, 1990), p. 78.

12. See Martha Stortz (this volume) for a discussion of three stages of the Shaker ritual. I see some parallel between the multiphased activity of her subjects and the ritual work of the palace.

13. See Clare Fischer, "Ratu Kidul, the Queen of the Southern Sea," in Joseph Fischer, *The Folk Art of Java* (Kuala Lumpur, Malaysia: Oxford University Press, 1994). The presence of powerful female figures in both my study of the court and Stortz (this volume) is worthy of further development.

14. Barbara Myerhoff, "We Don't Wrap Herring in a Printed Page," in Sally Moore and Barbara Myerhoff, eds., *Secular Ritual* (Assen, The Netherlands: Van Gorcum, 1977), p. 200.

15.Note Mark Woodward, *Islam in Java: Normative Piety and Mysticism in the Sultanate of Yogyakarta* (Tucson, AZ: University of Arizona Press, 1989), pp. 49–50.

16. Merle Ricklefs, "Yogya's Crowning Glory," *Far Eastern Economic Review*, March 23, 1989, p. 5.

17. Much of this history is derived from Woodward, *Islam in Java*, passim.

18. The Surakarta (Solo) court is an equally compelling site for study of ritual, but I have chosen to keep a focus on the Yagyakarta kraton and avoid engaging in comparative effort.

19. Moore and Myerhoff, Introduction, *Secular Rituals*, and Barbara Holdrege, "Introduction: Towards a Phenomenology of Power," in *Journal of Ritual Studies* 4/2, (Summer 1990), pp. 5–35.

20.K. P. H. Brongtodiningrat, trans. R. Murdami Madiatmaja, *The Royal Palace Kraton of Yogyakarta: Its Architecture and Its Meaning* (Yogyakarta: Kraton Museum, 1975) (author's emphasis); see also Woodward, Ch. 6.

21. One reporter observed: ". . . his eyes looking straight ahead towards the *Tugu* or monument which is the mark of Yogyakarta . . . and further towards the peak of Mt. Merapi." From here, the report continues, "he could see throughout the centre of his realm which has survived more than two centuries." "Investiture of a Javanese Sultan," *Travel Indonesia*, April 1989, p. 22.

22. The *kris* is a small dagger that is worn ceremonially; every young man is given one at puberty.

23. Woodward, *Islam in Java*, p 164.

24. See Woodward, p. 165 for further discussion of these regalia.

25. Note the useful discussion of performative ritual in Richard Payne's essay (this volume) and his review of Stanley Tambiah's distinction.

26. When Sultan Hamengkubuwono IX was installed he spoke in Dutch; however, he expressed awareness of the tension between identity and education in Europe and proclaimed, "I am a Javanese!"

27. See *Jakarta Post*, March 9, 1989, for quoted text of speech.

28. Ibid.

29. See Benedict Anderson, "The Idea Of Power in Javanese Culture," *Language and Power: Exploring Political Cultures in Indonesia* (Ithaca, NY: Cornell University Press, 1990), pp. 17–77; p. 29.

30. In addition to relying upon Anderson for this discussion, I have integrated Van Beek, (see note 11), Errington, (see note 10), and Woodward, (see note 15).

31. Anderson, passim, and Errington, 13

32. See Benedict Anderson, "Further Adventures of Charisma," in *Language and Power*, Ch. 2.

33. Woodward, p. 200.

34. Errington, passim and Anderson, p. 34.

35. See R. M. Koentjaraningrat, "Javanese Terms for God and Supernatural Beings and the Idea of Power," in *Readings on Islam in Southeast Asia*, A. Ibrahim et al., eds. (Singapore: Institute of Southeast Asian Studies, 1985); Ina E. Slamet, *Cultural Strategies for Survival: The Plight of the Javanese*, Comparative Asian Studies Program Rotterdam: Erasmus University 5, (Rotterdam The Netherlands, 1982); and M. Woodward, passim.

36. See Anderson, "Introduction" and his review of research undertaken over a generation in Java.

37. Van Beek, p. 7.

38. I am reminded of the moving account of two sites in Stortz (this volume) wherein Watervliet, NY remains the heart and New Lebanon, the bureaucratic center; one might find some likeness between Yogyakarta as heart and Jakarta as administrative center of Indonesia.

39. From comments by film director, *Jakarta Post*, March 6, 1989.

40. From Walter L. Williams, *Javanese Lives: Women and Men in Modern Indonesian Society* (New Brunswick, NJ: Rutgers University Press, 1991), pp. 108–9. The dance teacher commented: "By paying attention to the traditions, I think people today can get important messages for how best to live their lives."

41. Kelly and Kaplan, p. 141.

42. From Carey, p. 19.

3

Realizing Inherent Enlightenment

Ritual and Self-Transformation in Shingon Buddhism

RICHARD K. PAYNE

INTRODUCTION

It is a widespread popular prejudice that, unlike science, ritual is not effective. This popular conception of ritual seems to be based on the acceptance of late nineteenth and early twentieth century theories[1] concerning the mutual exclusivity of magic, science, and religion.[2] Given the underlying Protestant prejudice against ritual assumed by many authors of the period, ritual tended to be assigned to the lower, more primitive level called magic.[3] The usual explanation is that magic's failure led on the one hand to science as a true technological mastery of the natural world, and on the other hand to religion as a true spiritual relation to the transcendent.

If such a view of ritual were true, the advance of science and secular institutions should have led to the disappearance of ritual. However, just as increasing secularization of society did not lead to the disappearance of religion, the successes of science did not lead to the disappearance of ritual. On the contrary, ritual remains a part of modern society, as seen in explicitly religious rituals (for example, marriage, baptism, and confirmation), and in secular rituals (for instance, graduation and the inauguration of a president).[4] One way in which the retention of ritual may be understood is that it is simply an irrational and atavistic habit. It seems to me, however, that people really are fundamentally pragmatic, that is, they retain only those cultural practices which serve some useful function.[5] If we do see people as fundamentally pragmatic, then the retention of ritual would indicate that ritual continues to serve some useful function in contemporary society, even if the function of ritual serves an emotional economy, rather than a material economy. I would propose that in modern society ritual remains an effective means of transformation, both personal and social.[6] The focus of this inquiry will be on the way in which ritual can provide for personal, that is, intrapsychic, transformation.

The question of ritual efficacy may be approached in two fashions, which in anthropological terms are called "etic" and "emic," that is, from outside the tradition or from inside the tradition. Whereas both kinds of explanations are needed to understand rituals, this essay will focus on an etic explanation, specifically, that which can be developed from the perspective of analytic psychology. Analytic psychology is not the only etic approach that can be taken. However, I believe that intellectual efforts should be driven by problems rather than by methodology, and that the methodology should follow the formulation of the problem. The question of ritual as an effective means of self-transformation, that is, as a means of intrapsychic change, leads me first to think in psychological terms.[7]

Of the variety of psychological approaches the analytic approach seems to me to be the most appropriate for three important reasons. First, analytic psychology includes more than a pathology model of human psychology. The concept of individuation provides a better model of self-transformation, as understood by religious traditions, than does any psychological theory that is limited to a pathology model.[8]

Second, analytic psychology has a well-developed hermeneutic for interpreting symbols, one that can be applied to the symbolic aspect of ritual. This hermeneutic is based on the concept of the archetype, which may be understood as a means of grouping symbols according to categories relevant to human experience.[9]

The third reason for employing the perspective of analytic psychology is the character of the rituals being studied. Familiarity with these rituals leads me to believe that analytic psychology provides a means of analyzing both the symbolic components of the ritual and the significance of the ritual sequence.

The rituals that will be examined here are the "Training in Four Stages" (Japanese: *shido kegyō*). The first of these, the "Eighteen Stages" (Japanese: *jūhachi dō*), is paradigmatic for the Shingon tradition. It is the first ritual a priest in training learns to perform, and the other rituals of the training sequence are structurally and symbolically related to it. A "syntactic" analysis of the organization of the rituals clearly shows that the later rituals are expansions of it.[10] As the paradigmatic ritual for the Shingon tradition, it is the Eighteen Stages that we will examine here.

A model of psychological growth found in analytic psychology will be employed to see what it may reveal about the process of ritual training as it is found in the Shingon tradition. Specifically, I will make use of the model of psychological growth found in Jungian analyst Edward Edinger's *Ego and Archetype: Individuation and the Religious Function of the Psyche.*[11]

Since the Shingon tradition may be unfamiliar to many readers, the balance of the introduction is devoted to a brief description of the tradition's history. The second section of the essay will provide a description of the Eighteen Stages ritual and its place in the larger context of the Shingon Training in Four Stages, whereas the third will give an analysis and interpretation of the rituals from the perspective of analytic psychology. The fourth section will focus on theoretical ramifications. In it I will seek to point out the limitations of a purely symbolic interpretation of ritual and suggest a mimetic theory of ritual as an alternative to existing theories that misinterpret the shido kegyō rituals by reading onto them inappropriate understandings of ritual dynamics.

THE SHINGON BUDDHIST RITUAL TRADITION

Shingon is the sect of Japanese Buddhism that is solely devoted to the practice of Tantric rituals. Shingon (Chinese: *ch'en yen*, literally "true word," deriving from the Sanskrit *mantra*) was founded in Japan by the monk Kūkai (posthumous title Kobo Daishi) in the early part of the ninth century. Kūkai had been initiated into the Tantric Buddhist[12] lineage in China, where he had traveled as a member of a Japanese imperial embassy. Although many Tantric Buddhist texts had been translated into Chinese from as early as the third century,[13] the Tantric lineage per se was transmitted from India to China in the early part of the eighth century, just a century before Kūkai's arrival in China.

The characteristic of Tantric Buddhism that makes it unique in relation to most of the rest of the Buddhist tradition lies in its emphasis on the possibility of realizing enlightenment in this very lifetime. The practices that facilitate this realization are based for the most part on rituals which reach back through China to India, and in some cases to the Central Asian homeland of the Indo-European peoples. In contemporary Japan, the training a Shingon priest undertakes to receive initiation as an *ajari* (Sanskrit: *acarya*); that is, a priest who can perform rituals on the basis of his own authority, is structured around four rituals that the priest learns to perform.[14] As such, these four rituals are fundamental to the tradition's ritual culture as a whole. The following description of the Shingon ritual tradition is based on my own experiences training as a Shingon priest during the summer of 1982, as well as my subsequent historical and textual studies of various Shingon rituals.

For the Shingon tradition the goal of practice is the realization of the practitioner's identity with the Dharmakāya Buddha Mahāvairocana. Tantra, in both its Hindu and Buddhist forms, begins from a basic assertion that human beings are fundamentally identical with the highest form of being. Śaivite Tantra identifies this highest form of being as Śiva,[15] whereas in Shingon the highest form of being is identified as the Dharmakāya Buddha Mahāvairocana. The ordinary person is fundamentally not different from the fully enlightened Buddha. However, because of mistaken ideas and feelings (Sanskrit: *kleśa*, Japanese: *bonnō*), people do not realize this originally enlightened character to be their own true nature.

The means of realizing[16] original enlightenment is Tantric ritual practice. At the core of Shingon ritual practice is *kaji* (Sanskrit: *adhiṣṭhāna*, though the Shingon usage seems to be at some variance from the meaning in Indian Buddhist usage), which is the threefold identification of the practitioner's body, speech, and mind with Mahāvairocana's body, speech, and mind. Through this ritual practice the practitioner is experiencing his or her own identity as being the fully enlightened Buddha Mahāvairocana. This ritual experience may be understood as a kind of remembering—a remembering that is not memory as making a past event mentally, or ritually, present. Rather, this is a remembering in the sense of reconstructing the practitioner's personal identity.[17] This view of ritual efficacy is based on the idea that each individual's own self-concept is itself a construction, subject to being dis-membered and re-membered.[18] Such a view of the self-concept is itself in keeping with Buddhist views of human existence.[19]

In the Shingon tradition ritual *practice* is the repetitive reexperiencing of a present reality, the true *identity* of the practitioner and the Buddha. This identity is not a past event that is made mentally present, but rather an ever-present reality which is made conscious through repetition of the ritual.

Body, speech, and mind are a traditional Buddhist way of talking about the existential whole of the human individual. The identification of the practitioner's body with the body of the Buddha is accomplished through the performance of *mudrā*. *Mudrā* are hand gestures that are performed throughout the ritual performance, but in the act of identification the practitioner assumes the same mudrā as that of Mahāvairocana. Identification of speech is accomplished through the recitation of mantra and *dhāraṇi*, that is, verbal formulae that embody some especially potent aspect of the Buddhist teachings.[20] Identification of mind is accomplished through yogic meditation. Identification is not a single movement on the part either of the practitioner or of the Buddha Mahāvairocana, but rather it is the result of a dual movement: that of the practitioner toward the Buddha Mahāvairocana and that of the Buddha Mahāvairocana toward the practitioner.[21] It is important to recall that Mahāvairocana Buddha is not external to the practitioner as some kind of supernatural being, but rather simply is the enlightened quality of the practitioner's own consciousness. The personification of the enlightened quality of the practitioner's own consciousness is not to be understood as literally indicating an external, separately existing being, much less some Platonic metaphysical absolute.

Shingon ritual practice, then, mediates the ordinary consciousness of the practitioner with the goal of practice—enlightened consciousness—through the practice of kaji, the triple identification of the practitioner with the Buddha Mahāvairocana. The Training in Four Stages develops this identification by engaging the practitioner in progressively more complicated rituals.

THE TRAINING IN FOUR STAGES

The Training in Four Stages takes its name from the fact that the practitioner learns to perform four rituals in the process of training for initiation as a Shingon Buddhist priest, that is, an ajari. The complete training sequence entails a series of preparatory practices that set the stage for the one hundred days of training. During the training period itself, the practitioner learns to perform the four rituals in order, to wit, the Eighteen Stages is the first of the four, and once practice of it is complete, the practitioner proceeds to the next, and so on.[22]

The Eighteen Stages is followed by the "*Vajra* Realm" ritual. The vajra is a symbol and ritual implement common to the entirety of the Tantric Buddhist tradition, giving that tradition one of its names: *Vajrayāna*, the vajra vehicle to awakening. The symbol is rooted in the thunderbolt implement of the high god, and is found throughout Indo-European religious culture. The thunderbolts of Zeus are directly related to the vajra of tantric Buddhism. As the thunderbolt, it is understood as pointing to the sudden illumination of awakening. At the same time it is also described as adamantine (or sometimes, diamond), that is, it cannot be destroyed or affected by anything else. The Vajra Realm is the world experienced under the condition of awakened wisdom, which is unmoving and immovable.

When wisdom is awakened, it becomes the basis of awakened action, that is, compassionate action, "the means by which the mind of enlightenment is perfected," according to Todaro.[23] Compassionate action is symbolized as the Womb-store Realm (Sanskrit: *garbhakoṣadhātu*), which forms the basis for the third ritual of the Training in Four Stages. The last of the four is the *Goma* Ritual devoted to Fudø. The goma (Sanskrit: *homa*) is a votive ritual that employs fire as the means by which the offering is made. In the case of the Training in Four Stages, it is devoted to the figure of Fudō Myōō. Fudō means Immovable, and Myōō means King of Wisdom.[24] The Eighteen Stages is the first of the four rituals the practitioner learns, and the others are expansions of its basic structure.

The Eighteen Stages takes its name from the eighteen mudrās and their accompanying mantras that formed the earliest version of this ritual. Over time mudrās and mantras have been added to the text of the ritual until the present form contains twenty-six.[25] The ritual is divided into five parts, referred to by Taisen Miyata as:

1. Purification of human nature
2. Construction of a cosmic center
3. Encounter with Vairocana Buddha
4. Identification
5. Dissociation[26]

Basically, the dramatic theme of the ritual is a feast. This dramatic theme (or semiosis) is the same as that of classic Indian Vedic ritual practices. The similarity results from the historical continuity between the Vedic rituals and Tantric Buddhist rituals in Japan. Through the performance of mudrās, mantras, visualizations, and other ritual acts, the practitioner enacts the following sequence of events.

The first ritual step is the preparation of the practitioner. If we develop an extended colloquial analogy, this corresponds to showering and changing clothes in preparation for the arrival of guests. Expressed more traditionally, the practitioner purifies his or her own actions of body, speech, and mind, these being considered to be the three kinds of actions that a human being can perform. The practitioner then "dons the armor of great compassion and by this act the army of Mara is put down."[27]

The second step, construction of a cosmic center, corresponds to cleaning and straightening the house so that one's guests will be comfortable. In the ritual this is enacted as first purifying the earth, which entails erecting four pillars at the four corners of the altar. The altar is then enclosed and purified, and a pavilion for the guest is ritually constructed.[28]

The third step, encounter, corresponds to sending an invitation and greeting one's guests upon their arrival. The practitioner sends a jewelled carriage to his or her guest, the Dharmakāya Buddha Mahāvairocana, who is invited to mount the carriage, which then returns to the altar. The ritual enclosure is then sealed against demonic influences. The guest is bathed in perfumed waters and led to a throne formed from a lotus. He "is entertained with music by means of ringing the bell; he is refreshed with powdered incense; flower garlands and burning incense are presented to him with which to adorn and perfume his body; food and drink, representing the best of field and stream, of mountains and seas, are offered to him to eat; lights are given to him to light his way; and hymns are recited in his praise."[29]

As with other Tantric rituals, identification—visualized, ritually enacted—between the practitioner and the "central deity" (Japanese *honzon*) is the main purpose of the Eighteen Stages ritual.[30] This forms the fourth step of the ritual and is the soteriologically most important event of the entire ritual sequence. Identification comprises three facets: identification of bodily actions, identification of speech actions, and identification of mental actions. In this way the practitioner visualizes and, therefore, experiences her or himself as identical with the absolute body of enlightened consciousness. The psychological impact of ritual identification is key to the efficacy of this ritual and will be discussed further.

Following the completion of identification, the final ritual stage, dissociation, is begun. A final set of mantras is recited and ritual offerings are made to the chief deity, Mahāvairocana Buddha. Merit generated by the practice of the rite is transferred from the practitioner to all sentient beings equally so that they may attain enlightenment more rapidly. The enclosure is opened, the deities take their leave and depart from the altar. The ritual ends with the practitioner reciting the mantra for protection, stepping down from his or her seat, making prostrations, and departing the hall of practice.

Ritual practice in the Shingon tradition is understood to be the means by which one moves from a condition of unrealized, inherent enlightenment to a condition of realizing one's inherently enlightened condition. In his *Ihon Sokushin Jobutsu Gi*,[31] Kūkai schematizes this movement from inherent enlightenment to realized enlightenment into three phases.[32] In the first of these phases, because a human being exists, he or she is inherently already a Buddha.[33] This phase is known as *rigu*, or "inherent principle." In the second phase, known as *kaji*, or "ritual identification,"[34] the practitioner engages in practice which allows him or her to experience his or her own enlightened consciousness within the ritual setting. The third phase, *kendoku*, or "attaining realization," is the goal of practice, that is, when the experience of enlightened consciousness becomes a permanent condition, rather than one that is delimited by ritual practice. Thus, through the repetitive re-experiencing of a present reality, the practitioner moves to make that reality an ever-present condition—he or she has successfully re-cognized/re-membered him or herself as an enlightened being, as a Buddha.[35]

The pattern of repetition found in the Shingon training is related to other kinds of pedagogical practices in Japan. Indeed, given the early date at which Shingon ritual practice entered Japanese culture, it is tempting to consider the possibility that it was the training procedures of Shingon that provided the model for the other forms in which this emphasis on repetitive, structured, detailed practice is used. Dorinne K. Kondo has described this Japanese pedagogy in relation to her own experience at *Rinri Gakuen*, the "Ethics School" that serves as the main training center for the "Ethics" movement which arose in postwar Japan. She says that as with

> other methods of learning and self-cultivation, one first learns through imitation. Stereotyped movements are repeated endlessly; for example, as a student of tea ceremony, one begins with seemingly simple tasks such as how to walk properly, how to fold a tea napkin, how to wipe the tea utensils. Unlike similar movements in everyday life, these are precisely defined, to be executed "just so." Later these learned actions are orchestrated into a ceremony that is the epitome of "natural," disciplined grace. The martial arts, also arts of "the way" (*dō*), practice their *kata*, patterned movements, until the movements are inscribed in muscle memory. In a sense, for these arts, content is secondary to repetition of form.[36]

As mentioned previously, the Shingon tradition itself has a soteriological explanation of the efficacy of the training rituals based on the idea of inherent enlightenment being gradually revealed and becoming the experiential reality of the practitioner. However, alternative explanations may be developed that would provide a different perspective on the transformative efficacy of the ritual practice.

A PSYCHOLOGICAL INTERPRETATION OF THE SHINGON RITUAL TRAINING

Analytic psychology can provide a metalanguage in which to discuss the efficacy of Shingon ritual that is more accessible to contemporary, psychologically oriented Westerners than the language of Shingon Buddhism itself. At the same time, by looking at the interactions between these two systems of thought, both of which describe the process of personal transformation, it is hoped that the psychodynamics of purposeful intra-psychic change may be better understood.

Analytic psychology takes as one of its basic premises the concept of the Self[37] as distinct from the ego. Jung explains his distinction between these two in "Transformation Symbolism in the Mass," his only extended study of ritual per se. There he describes the "Self" as the "unconscious substrate" upon which the "ego" as the personal sense of self-identity rests:

> The ego stands to the self as the moved to the mover, or as object to subject, because the determining factors which radiate out from the self surround the ego on all sides and are therefore supraordinate to it. The self, like the unconscious, is an *a priori* existent out of which the ego evolves. It is, so to speak, an unconscious prefiguration of the ego. It is not I who create myself, rather I happen to myself. This realization is of fundamental importance for the psychology of religious phenomena. . . .[38]

However, he continues, this "can be only half the psychological truth," since the ego experiences itself as free, rather than as entirely determined by the Self, which would be implied by the description just given. This situation leads to the tension between ego and Self—the conscious ego aspiring to self-determinancy, "hybris" in Jung's terms, and the unconscious Self as supreme, "supraordinate." Jung continues,

> This conflict between conscious and unconscious is at least brought nearer to solution through our becoming aware of it. Such an act of realization is presupposed in the act of self-sacrifice. The ego must make itself conscious of its claim, and the self must cause the ego to renounce it.[39]

This tension between the ego and the Self is not an unmoving, static one. In his *Ego and Archetype* Edward Edinger has discussed intrapsychic transformation as a cyclic process that begins with the ego completely contained with the Self, that is, completely unconscious. This process culminates within the establishment of an ego-Self axis linking the separated, conscious ego with the self. Edinger asserts that "psychological development is characterized by two processes occurring simultaneously, namely, progressive ego-Self separation and also increasing emergence of the ego-Self axis into consciousness."[40] The ego experiences this process as moving through phases of inflation and alienation, inflation resulting from the ego mistakenly believing that it is identical with the Self, and alienation being the desolate sense of separation resulting from the failures the ego encounters when it attempts to act as if it were identical with the Self. According to Edinger, this cyclic process repeats itself again and again in the early phases of psychological development, each cycle producing an increment of consciousness. Thus, gradually consciousness is built up:

> Once the ego has reached a certain level of development, it does not have to continue this repetitious cycle, at least not in the same way. The cycle is then replaced by a more or less conscious dialogue between ego and Self.[41]

This latter condition is referred to as individuation, which Edinger describes as itself being a process, or "urge":

> Speaking generally, the individuation urge promotes a state in which ego is related to Self without being identified with it. Out of this state there emerges a more or less continuous dialogue between the conscious ego and the unconscious, and also between outer and inner experience.[42]

This model of psychic development provides an understanding of the way in which the rituals of the Shingon training can produce intrapsychic change. The separation of the ego from the Self and the establishment of a communicating bond between the ego and the Self requires that there be some means by which the ego can conceptualize the Self. As Edinger points out, one of the functions of religious symbols is to provide the ego with images that are imbued with the numinous quality of the Self.[43] The figure of Mahāvairocana Buddha, presented simultaneously as the enlightened quality of consciousness itself and as the cosmic existence of the Buddha, is certainly an appropriate symbol for the Self.

Mahāvairocana means the Great Illuminator, which is translated into Japanese as *Dainichi*, or Great Sun. Symbolically, this combines the imagery of the illuminating quality of enlightened consciousness with the imagery of the sun as the source of life. Mahāvairocana is considered to be the Dharmakāya, or the absolute body of the Buddha. Originally a way of pointing to the universal validity of the Buddha Shakyamuni's teachings, the concept of the dharmakāya came to be understood as the universal awakened consciousness beyond all distinctions and descriptions.[44] Whereas many Buddhist thinkers consider the Dharmakāya to be passive, the Shingon tradition understands it to be active, and to be personified in the form of Mahāvairocana.[45]

As the practitioner visualizes Mahāvairocana, he or she is creating a concrete image of the Self as external to his or her own ego. The practitioner's ego is then confronting the Self in the image of Mahāvairocana. An example of such a concrete image may be abstracted from the Garbhakoṣadhātu Recitation, the third ritual of the training sequence:

Imagine that above the great circle of the earth is the syllable "vaṃ" which forms a great ocean. Within this ocean there is the syllable "ram" which forms the flames of great wisdom. Within these flames is the syllable "a" which forms an eight-petalled lotus blossom, the stalk of which is a vajra. Above the lotus there is the syllable "a" which forms the eight peaks of Mount Sumeru, surrounded by the seven mountains of gold and the circular mountain of iron, all full of the waters which bear within themselves the eight virtues.

On the highest peak of this mountain is the syllable "vaṃ" which forms the great wheel of action. Above this wheel is the syllable "huṃ" which forms the triple world (i.e., the realms of desire, form and formlessness).

Within this vajradhātu there is a four tiered maṇḍala altar. Within the altar is the syllable "aḥ" which forms a mountain peak. On it is a large, broad palace. Within this palace is a karma vajra, above which is the syllable "a." This forms a large, eight-petalled, white lotus throne. This throne emits countless rays of light, all surrounded by a hundred thousand lotuses. Above this there is the syllable "ah," which forms a lion throne of the fully awakened one. Above this is the syllable "a" which forms a great, jewelled, royal red lotus. Above him is the syllable "a" which forms a pure moon cakra.

Visualize that within this round, bright moon cakra there is the syllable "a" which forms the Dharmadhātu stūpa. This stūpa changes and becomes the Tathāgata Mahāvairocana. He is wearing a jewel crown of five Buddhas. He is sitting up straight, dressed in robes of fine silk and wears a necklace made of various jewels. His body emits an exquisite light which illumines the Dharmadhātu. Above the leaves of the lotus upon which he sits, in each of the eight directions are the eight syllables "raṃ," "vaṃ," "saṃ," "haḥ," "aṃ," "a," "vu," and "yu." These become the eight Buddhas and Bodhisattvas who attend Mahāvairocana, and they in turn are surrounded on all sides by the deities of the three tiered maṇḍala.[46]

This visualization process requires an intense psychological effort. At the same time that the wealth of details is being added, the entirety is to be maintained. Such an effort creates what can be referred to as an "imaginal space." As in liminal spaces, imaginal space is one in which the ordinary oppositional structures of everyday reality are made fluid. Psychologically, this can be very healthy, since it provides the possibility of restructuring psychic elements that in everyday reality are fixed.

Although structured visualizations of the kind described differ from spontaneous visions, it has been suggested that the content of structured visualizations has its origin in spontaneous visions.[47] According to August J. Cwik's summary of Jung's writings on active imagination, "The product of this work *must* be concretized in some form. That is, it can be written, drawn, sculpted, etc."[48] It would also be possible for such concretization to take the form of ritual, especially in a religious culture, such as that of Tantric Buddhism, in which ritual is effectively a creative art form. For such rituals to be psychologically effective, however, they need to provide the ego with access to the Self.

Religious traditions carry symbols of the Self that are one means by which the ego can access the Self. As Jung says in regard to Western culture, "*Christ exemplifies the archetype of the self.* He represents a totality of a divine or heavenly kind, a glorified man, a son of God *sine macula peccati*, unspotted by sin."[49] For the Shingon tradition, Mahāvairocana is the symbol of the Self, as that which transcends all oppositions by being the totality of existence—the Dharmakāya Buddha.

In the imaginal space of the ritual visualization, Mahāvairocana is not only made manifest, but is to be experienced as identical with the practitioner. From the perspective of analytical psychology, the archetype of the Self is formulated as Mahāvairocana, and the practitioner is establishing a connection with the Self. This connection occurs within the imaginal space of the ritual enclosure. The ritual space is enclosed by the practitioner after the arrival of the "Chief Deity," namely, Mahāvairocana. In the case of the paradigmatic "Eighteen Stages," this is done with two ritual actions. In the first, "Jikai Kongo Ketsu," the practitioner is to:

> (i)magine that the world, down to the limits of the Vajra Cakra, becomes an indestructible Vajra world, which cannot be shaken or moved by demons of great strength. If even a small amount of effort is expended, one will obtain a great result. Through the power of this empowerment all filthy and evil things with the earth will become pure and clean. This world will become large or small in accord with the mind of the devotee.[50]

Once the world is firmly established and purified in this fashion, the practitioner then creates the enclosure within which the ritual actions will proceed. This ritual action is known as the "Kongo Sho In," or Thunderbolt Wall Mudrā. The practitioner is to imagine that

> flames pour out from this mudrā and that they circle about your body to the right three times. This fits in well with the previous Earth Element, creating an impenetrable, indestructible castle, so that no demon, evil person, tiger, lion or noxious insect can approach the devotee.[51]

It is into this ritual enclosure, or imaginal space, that the Dharmakāya Buddha Mahāvairocana is to be invited. The practitioner identifies her or himself with this ensymbolment of the Self, an action that facilitates the development of the link between the ego and the Self. The disidentification of the practitioner from Mahāvairocana that follows serves to strengthen the needed sense of separateness of the ego and the Self.

From a developmental perspective, however, the establishment of a relation between the ego and the Self entails certain difficulties. As described by Edinger, the ego begins life so completely identified with the Self that it has no independent existence. This is problematic because, as Edinger says, "Although the ego begins in a state of inflation due to identification with the Self, this condition cannot persist."[52] Affronts to this inflated identification with the Self result in injury to the ego and "damage to the ego-Self axis."[53]

Edinger employs the term *alienation* to capture the experiential quality of this phase of development. The inflated ego—inflated by its mistaken belief that it is the same as the Self—cannot actualize the self-image created by the inflation. Failure to actualize this self-image leads to a sense of failure and separation from the Self, i.e., alienation. In a healthy developmental sequence alienation is followed by a re-establishment of a connection between the ego and Self. Re-identification of the ego with the Self, however, leads again to inflation, followed by alienation. This dialectic cycling between inflation and alienation requires adequate support from the parents or other care-givers if it is to be successfully negotiated. Improper or inadequate support can produce at least two kinds of disorders, in Edinger's view. In one of these, "If the child is not fully accepted after punishment for misbehavior . . . the child's ego can be caught in a sterile oscillation between inflation and alienation that builds up more and more frustration and despair."[54]

In the other, the parents are so permissive that "The whole experience of alienation, which brings consciousness with it, is omitted, and the child gets acceptance for his [sic] inflation."[55] Alienation is important to the developing ego, since it is alienation that makes the ego aware of being unique, and separate from the Self. Without having conscious awareness of this separation, the ego cannot be in communication with the Self. At the other extreme, where the ego experiences itself as totally alienated from the Self, there is the same absence of communication between the ego and the Self.

The Shingon ritual training is structured so as to avoid these dangers of the developmental process. Not only does the practitioner repeatedly identify him or herself with Mahāvairocana Buddha, but also as a regular part of the ritual, disidentifies him or herself and self-consciously returns to being a limited, ordinary person—but one who knows that he or she is fundamentally identical with Mahāvairocana. As Miyata describes it, "In this last phase of the ritual the effective mode is to dissociate man [sic] from the visualized cosmos and interiorize the cosmos in the human body."[56] The visualized cosmos that Miyata mentions is the entire realm of Mahāvairocana which the practitioner visualized, as just described. In other words, the practitioner takes the imaginal ritual space within which he or she experiences him or herself as identical with Mahāvairocana and enfolds it within his or her ego, engaging in this dialectic three times a day for the one hundred days of the training. Repeated over and over again, this seems to be intended to build up the healthy structure of a separate ego connected to the Self. The use of a specific program of identification and separation within the imaginal space of the ritual allows for the self-conscious replication of the dialectic process of psychological development described by Edinger.

THEORETICAL RAMIFICATIONS

The etic perspective on Shingon ritual provided by analytic psychology produces a valuable insight into the *process* of the Shido Kegyō rituals, which are a form of practice intended to stimulate intrapsychic change. The efficacy of the ritual practice can be understood in terms of the creation of an imaginal space within which the connection between the ego/practitioner and the Self/Mahāvairocana can be experienced as one of identity. The broader ritual process as a whole, that is, including disidentification/separation, replicates the dialectic process by which the dual relation of clear separation between the ego and the Self, together with the maintenance of a communicating link between the two, occurs in a normal, healthy developmental process from childhood to adulthood.

Three conclusions may be drawn from this study of the rituals of the Shingon Shido Kegyō training sequence. The first of these is that an understanding of ritual which is solely symbolic obscures the efficacy of the ritual process by understanding the ritual as pointing to something other than itself. The second is that the Shido Kegyō rituals are an individual form of religious practice. As a form of progressive practice, they cannot be accurately understood as either commemorative or anamnestic in function. The third conclusion is that a mimetic understanding of ritual practice can integrate both the symbolic and performative aspects of ritual, while at the same time preserving the import of the rituals as practice. More broadly, the importance of ritual studies for the study of religion is that it can provide entree to religious activities, as distinct from religious beliefs.

A solely symbolic understanding of ritual[57] is one which would only focus on interpreting the symbols employed in the ritual.[58] Thus, for example, in the goma (the votive ritual that is the fourth and final ritual of the Shido Kegyō sequence) attention would be paid to the meaning of the fire and the offerings made into it. Various perspectives could be employed in this interpretive process. One approach would be to explore the indigenous (emic) understanding of the fire. According to the Shingon tradition, the fire symbolizes the transformative power of wisdom and the offerings are one's own obscuring attachments (bonnō). The fire of wisdom transforms the obscuring attachments to energies that can be directed toward penetrating insight and compassionate action.

Other interpretive approaches are possible as well. A Freudian interpretation might see the fire as expressing sexuality that has been repressed. A comparative approach would look to the similarities and differences between the goma and other votive rites, particularly those in which the offering is made into fire. These and other possible interpretive perspectives provide insight into the meaning of the symbols employed in the course of a ritual. A study of ritual that focuses solely on the symbols of the ritual, however, remains superficial to the ritual process per se. The ritual is not simply the presentation and manipulation of a variety of symbols according to a set of rules. To limit understanding of the ritual in such a fashion presents ritual as simply standing for, that is, representing symbolically, something else. Probably originating with the Christian rhetoric concerning idolatry, this arm's-length understanding of ritual as *solely* symbolic of something else trivializes the efficacy of ritual itself and obscures the centrality of activity to ritual. To say that item A (a ritual) stands as a symbolic representation of item B (some "greater reality") means that item A is just exactly *not* item B. At the same time such a view implies that it is item B—the "greater reality"—that is truly effective, rather than item A, the ritual itself. In a similar vein, Frits Staal has argued that if the meaning of ritual is understood solely referentially, then rituals are meaningless.[59] From the Shingon perspective the rituals of the Shido Kegyō are in themselves effective, and I believe one could assume fairly safely that the emic perspective of many traditions is the same.

As a form of religious practice, the ritual practices of the Shido Kegyō training are understood by the tradition as working toward the practitioner's permanently experiencing the always-present reality of his or her enlightened condition. Two of the popular theories of ritual that explain the meaning of ritual in terms of memory are not adequate to the study of individual ritual practice such as the Shido Kegyō. These two ways of understanding rituals are the commemorative and anamnestic. The commemorative understanding explains rituals as a means of keeping some past event present in memory as part of the social context of meaning. The public calendar of official holidays, such as, the Fourth of July and Christmas, exemplifies this commemorative understanding of rituals. The political struggles surrounding the addition of a holiday to the official calendar, such as Martin Luther King, Jr., Day, though often highly vocal, are mute testimony to the implicit recognition of the efficacy of the commemorative function.

Whereas the commemorative understanding is not a technically formulated theory, the anamnestic understanding has been promoted as an explanatory theory. Probably the best known and most quoted promoter of the anamnestic theory is Mircea Eliade. One of the most influential expressions of Eliade's views is his *Sacred and Profane*. Speaking of the events recounted in myth Eliade says:

> It is easy to understand why the memory of that marvelous time haunted religious man, why he periodically sought to return to it. *In illo tempore* the gods had displayed their greatest powers. *The cosmogony is the supreme divine manifestation*, the paradigmatic act of strength, superabundance, and creativity. Religious man thirsts for the real. By every means at his disposal, he seeks to reside at the very source of primordial reality, when the world was *in statu nascendi* . . . through annual repetition of the cosmogony, time was regenerated, that is, it began again as sacred time, for it coincided with the *illud tempus* in which the world had first come into existence; (and) by participating ritually in the end of the world and its recreation, any man became contemporary with the *illud tempus*; hence he was born anew, he began life over again with his reserve of vital forces *intact*, as it was at the moment of his birth.[60]

Highlighting the difference between the commemorative and the anamnestic understandings, Eliade goes on to say that the "ritual reactualizing of the *illud tempus* in which the first epiphany of a reality occurred is the basis for all sacred calendars; the festival is not merely the commemoration of a mythical (and hence religious) event; it *reactualizes* the event."[61]

As with many theories in the field of religious studies, this one is true for some part of the material studied.[62] Although expressed as universally true, Eliade was specifically describing ancient Near Eastern (Babylonian and Hittite), Egyptian, and Persian New Year festivals. The generalization may also apply to Australo-Aboriginal practices, which Eliade examined at some length in another work—although the validity of his use of the source materials and his interpretations have recently been called into serious question.[63]

One of the sources that is most convincingly supportive of the anamnestic theory comes from Navajo healing rituals. Here the ritual is of a different kind—a life crisis ritual rather than part of the annual cycle of rituals.[64] Donald Sandner, a psychiatrist trained in analytic psychology, found Eliade's anamnestic theory useful in his own study of Navajo healing rituals:

> the presentation of the origin myth in song, prayer, and sand painting is not only for the purposes of remembrance [i.e., commemoration—RKP] and education, but to allow the patient to identify with those symbolic forces which once created the world [i.e., another ensymbolment of the Self—RKP], and by entering into them to re-create himself, in a state of health and wholeness . . . the return to origins is the first principle of symbolic healing.[65]

Despite the usefulness of the anamnestic understanding of ritual for interpreting a variety of rituals, this does not demonstrate its universal applicability. The rituals of the Shido Kegyō neither commemorate any founding event, nor do they reactualize any primal time.

Another theory concerning ritual that is often found in conjunction with the commemorative and anamnestic theories explains ritual as being universally linked to myth: the myth is used as the text for the ritual, the myth explains the meaning of the ritual or the ritual enacts the myth, or some other variant in which myth and ritual are invariably linked to one another.[66] This approach also proves inaccurate for the Shingon tradition. For example, the *Mahāvairocana Sutra*, central to the Shingon tradition, gives no mythic story that is reenacted in the performance of the last of the four training rituals, the goma. What it does provide is a charter myth, a story that validates the goma as a part of Buddhist practice. A charter myth functions very differently from a creation myth, the recounting of which forms the core of some ritual performances, such as, the Navajo healing rituals discussed by Sandner. In the case of Tantric Buddhism, however, the ritual practice of goma already existed in Indian religious culture. Perhaps an argument might be made for seeing the goma as a ritual that was originally a reenactment of some Vedic myth, for instance, the *puruṣa-sūkta*, the story of the creation of the world out of the body of the sacrificed original human. However, to assert that the contemporary Japanese goma is "really" a type of reenactment ritual based on the Vedic sources would be a case of reading onto the evidence a preconceived interpretation based on theory, rather than looking to the goma to find out what its meaning is.[67]

Not only is no myth, such as, the puruṣa-sūkta, recounted in the performance of the goma, but the purpose of the goma is different from a variety of Vedic rituals that might be supposed to be the "real" basis of the goma. The purpose of the goma in the training sequence is expressly understood by the tradition as the conversion of the practitioner's mistaken conceptions about him or herself and the world into clear insight into the transitory nature of all phenomena. This may be conceived as a kind of purification. The Vedic forms of purification employ rebirth symbolism, and hence could be understood as anamnestic. However, a purifying transformation through burning is different from a purifying renewal through rebirth. As employed in the goma, a purifying transformation by means of fire does not fit with the concept of reenactment or reactualization.

Having rejected the commonly accepted theories of ritual, an examination of the rituals of the Shido Kegyō offers a fresh conception of how rituals are effective in producing intrapsychic change. As described, in the course of the ritual the practitioner visualizes and ritually creates a realm wherein the Buddha may be manifest. This space is not understood, however, as symbolizing the "primal time," but rather a present reality. The ritual manifests a present reality, the practitioner's inherently enlightened nature, not a past one. Given that the goal of practice is to make that reality ever-present, rather than present only during the period of the ritual performance, the ritual might be called a preenactment, or preactualization, rather than a reenactment or reactualization.

This notion of preenactment may be seen as a kind of mimetic process in which one acts as if one already possessed a certain quality in order to allow that quality to emerge in oneself. This is a more traditional use of the term *mimesis* than the common contemporary usage of the term to identify an aesthetic theory of art imitating nature. The origins of the term are traced by Tatarkiewicz to the Dionysian cult in post-Homeric Greece. "Imitation did not signify reproducing external reality but expressing the inner one."[68]

Much the same understanding of mimesis was carried forward through Plato[69] and Aristotle into the early Christian understanding of the processes of "moral reform," that is, intrapsychic change. The early Christian understanding is described by Karl F. Morrison:

> as though he, were an athlete training for a race, the Christian internalized the model of Christ, enduring grief, persecution and death. . . . But this internalization was only possible because a change had already occurred. The Spirit had revealed to the soul things that its animal nature could not grasp. . . . It remained for the Church Fathers to discover how this call to alienation from the world could be made into a program . . . for personal renewal.[70]

Mimesis may be used as a cover term for any strategy of intrapsychic change that sees the possibility for that change as being dependent on an existing internal quality upon which that change is built. Indeed, mimesis provides an effective means of conceptualizing the similarities between some kinds of ritual and other kinds of strategies for intrapsychic change, that is, some approaches to acting, some kinds of psychotherapy, and some of the popular "self-help" techniques.

The ritual setting and implements of Shingon practice—the temple, altar, ritual implements, and so on—serve as the props for the imaginal process.[71] The function of such props is to stimulate the imagination and create what Kendall L. Walton calls "fictional truths," that is, propositions which are true by reference to a fictional set of beliefs and injunctions such as those in a game of make-believe:

> Make-believe—the use of (external) props in imaginative activities—is a truly remarkable invention . . . props insulate fictional worlds from what people do and think, conferring on them a kind of objective integrity worthy of the real world and making their exploration an adventure of discovery and surprise. Yet worlds of make-believe are much more malleable than reality is. We can arrange their contents as we like by manipulating props or even, if necessary, altering principles of generation.[72]

Further, Walton suggests that the fictional world which is constructed by someone else (representational artists in his discussion) can be more effective in producing beneficial experiences than those which we construct ourselves. We both benefit from the artist's expertise and gain access to his or her own special insights.[73] What Walton has referred to as a fictional world is the same as the imaginal space opened up in the Shingon rituals. To the extent that we allow ourselves to enter into the fictional world of the rituals, crafted over centuries by Tantric Buddhist practitioners in India, China, and Japan, we open ourselves to discovering something beyond our own powers of imagination, and to being changed by that discovery.

Beyond the issue of theories of ritual, there is a broader issue concerning the possible contribution of ritual studies to the study of religion. A strong stream within the Western religious tradition has long given priority to belief. This emphasis on belief has also deeply influenced the Western intellectual tradition and takes the form of viewing belief as primary and action as derivative. In other words, because one believes something, one acts accordingly. The fact that this idea seems so obviously true indicates how deeply this view has entered into the presumptions of Western intellectual discourse. However, it seems to me very important to recognize that rituals are about actions,[74] and that the study of rituals can give us access to a dimension of religion which is different from belief and which is not accessible through the examination of rituals in terms of the beliefs they may be interpreted to represent.

In my own fieldwork in Japan, it was not uncommon that when I asked people why they were doing something—such as a midsummer festival in which everyone in the neighborhood visited all the small local shrines to be found on the streets, in the alleys, and in people's backyards throughout the neighborhood, giving away rice cakes and drinking *sake*—I would get the reply. "Because we've always done it this way."[75] Why should I judge this to be an inadequate answer? Why should I seek the "true meaning" or assume that there must be someone else who does know the meaning? Indeed, Frits Staal found that

> There is only one answer which the best and most reliable among the ritualists themselves give consistently and with more than average frequency: we act according to the rules because this is our tradition (*paramparā*). The effective part of the answer seems to be: look and listen, these are our activities! To performing ritualists, rituals are like dance, of which Isadora Duncan said: "If I could tell you what it meant there would be no point in dancing it."[76]

An ancillary problem is that dissatisfaction with an answer like "We've always done it that way," may contribute to the covert introduction of value judgments.[77] For example, if one person says that a ritual is performed in order to achieve full enlightenment, and another says that it is for good luck—or because we've always done it that way—the former may come to be considered to be a "truer," "higher," or "more worthy" understanding of the beliefs behind the ritual. The obscured value judgment at work here is based on my values (including the values I hold as a Buddhist priest and practitioner) and the values of my society, rather than the values of my informants and their society.

Clearly, one of the values that I and my society hold is the importance of a textual basis for belief—another inheritance from post-Reformation, Western religious tradition with its bibliocentricity. It would not be at all surprising to find that the person who explains a ritual as contributing to full enlightenment is able to give a textual reference for this interpretation, whereas the person who says that it is for good luck cannot. Thus, giving belief primacy of place in the study of religion may contribute to focusing only on an elite, literate tradition, obscuring the nonliterate tradition that also forms a part of every religion.

There may indeed be some rituals that are specifically created to express some set of beliefs (or meanings, or values), just as allegories are constructed to convey some specific idea. However, I believe that the actual number of these is very small, if indeed any exist at all. The efficacy of ritual depends in large part upon familiarity, such as, that of childhood experience, which is not an experience of a set of independent symbols representing particular meanings. Although rituals may be *interpreted* as expressions of "more basic" beliefs/meanings/values, it is the hermeneutic presumption of the interpreter to see the beliefs/meanings/values as "more basic." The ritual practitioners themselves are probably more concerned, first of all, with getting the ritual "right," and second, with the intended outcome of the ritual, for example, "good luck," or a bountiful harvest, or the remission of sins, than they are with expressing their society's values.

Finally, there is the issue, central to this collection of essays, of the power of ritual to effect personal transformation. A change of beliefs alone does not necessarily lead to personal transformation. A person may change his or her beliefs about the dangers of smoking without being able to quit. Likewise, knowing the "meaning" of an action does not necessarily lead to being able to perform the action with any efficacy. A person may "know" that the "meaning" of a particular movement in karate is "upper block" without being able to perform an effective upper block. It is only through repeated practice of the action that one becomes able to produce an effective upper block. At the same time, repeated practice leads to the point at which there is no longer any thought preceding the action. Repetition of form leads to a kind of knowing quite different from being able to identify the "symbolic meaning" of the motion. In contrast to this performative ability, an intellectual knowing or understanding may well run counter to or even interfere with an effective performance. Consider the novice driver who needs to think about the sequence of actions required to brake a car without stalling it, thereby turning a normal stop into a dangerous situation. Similarly, an anthropologist may come to "know" that in some society a certain set of actions "means" the transition from adolescence to adulthood, yet were the anthropologist to attempt to perform the actions it is doubtful that they would be considered as having produced the same transition. Indeed, it would not be surprising to find that such actions on the part of the anthropologist would be considered a source of pollution requiring further ritual remedy.

The ability to effect personal transformation is to be found in an individual's participating in the activity of the ritual rather than in the exegesis of the symbols employed in the ritual. As David I. Kertzer has pointed out for social rituals, participation in a ritual may lead to changes in political identity "without requiring a common belief."[78] To the extent that religion is more than meanings and beliefs, to the extent that religion has the capacity to effect personal transformation, the study of ritual that focuses on activity may serve to broaden and deepen our understanding of religions as things which people *do*, rather than simply as things which people think.

SUMMARY

Edinger's description of the developmental process, founded on the concepts of analytic psychology, has provided a perspective on the rituals of the Shido Kegyō training that brings into focus the importance of seeing the ritual performance as an entirety. Beyond an understanding limited to the symbolic meanings of the elements of the ritual, analysis must also take into account the activity of ritual performance as well. For example, the fact that Mahāvairocana can be interpreted as a symbolic representation of the Self is a necessary but not sufficient part of understanding the efficacy of the Shido Kegyō practice. It is the interaction between the practitioner and Mahāvairocana, the process of identification and disidentification that, by replicating within the imaginal space of the ritual the developmental dialectic of identification and alienation, makes the ritual an effective means of intrapsychic change.

As a corollary to this focus on the ritual performance as a whole, there are three different interpretive perspectives for any symbolic component of a ritual. First, there is the structural meaning of that component within the whole of the ritual performance. Second, the tradition itself may provide interpretations of the symbolic component. Third, and only after the first two have been established, comparisons between traditions can be employed to further explore the possible meanings of the symbolic component. Clearly, this ordering places primacy on the proper understanding of the unique and specific, rather than on the creation of a universal typology of symbols. Due attention to the specific and unique is necessary to avoid misleading interpretations resulting from superficial comparisons.

In addition to being viewed as a whole process, it is also important to see the Shido Kegyō rituals as a form of religious practice. As part of an initiatory training, for example, these are rituals that the practitioner him or herself performs for his or her own psychospiritual development. Rituals performed as religious practice require a different approach than do other kinds of ritual. Given the way in which the rituals are understood to be soteriologically efficacious, interpreting these rituals as anamnestic or as commemorative is inappropriate.

As an individual religious practice,[79] the ritual performance of the Shido Kegyō may be better understood as creating an imaginal liminal space within which the practitioner is able to re-member, that is, to organize anew, his or her self-conception. This progressive restructuring of one's self-conception seems to imply that memory is a much more dynamic process than is (sometimes) thought. Instead of simply being a mechanical process by which information is stored, the current situation serves as the defining context of memories, giving either new meanings or maintaining old meanings of past experiences.

The quality of ritual that makes it possible for it to be employed as a means for creating an imaginal liminal space may be called its mimetic quality. This is not asserted to be a defining characteristic of all rituals, but rather as one of the qualities that some rituals share—a family resemblance. The notion of preenactment may be seen as a kind of mimetic process in which one acts as if one were already at the goal in order to move toward that goal. The efficacy of the Shido Kegyō practice is directed toward the realization of a present reality, and therefore, the commemorative and anamnestic understandings of ritual are inappropriate. In place of these understandings, a mimetic understanding of how some rituals function to effect intrapsychic change is more appropriate. The combination of analytic psychology and mimesis used here is not being promoted as the only proper way to understand rituals, but rather as heuristically useful, particularly for rituals like those of the Shido Kegyō training which are an individual religious practice.

NOTES

1. Perhaps the most influential of these is J. G. Frazer, whose *Golden Bough* continues to be reprinted, despite its theoretical and methodological failings. See Robert Ackerman, *J. G. Frazer: His Life and Work* (Cambridge: Cambridge University Press, 1987), p. 1.

2. Cf. Stanley Jeyaraja Tambiah, *Magic, Science, Religion, and the Scope of Rationality* (Cambridge: Cambridge University Press, 1990), especially Chapters 1 and 2.

3. This assumption continues to pervade the introductory textbooks of religious studies, where ritual is marginalized in relation to belief.

4. See particularly David I. Kertzer, *Ritual, Politics, and Power* (New Haven: Yale University Press, 1988) regarding the ongoing social and political importance of ritual in contemporary society. For a critique of Kertzer, see Martha Ellen Stortz, "Ritual Power, Ritual Authority: Configurations and Reconfigurations in the Era of Manifestations" in this volume.

5. An at least similar perspective underlies the works of Marvin Harris, e.g., his *Cows, Pigs, Wars and Witches: The Riddles of Culture* (New York: Random House, Vintage Books, 1974), and *Cultural Materialism: The Struggle for a Science of Culture* (New York: Random House, Vintage Books, 1980).

6. One of the most important contributions to an understanding of the social efficacy of ritual is the performative approach as developed by Stanley J. Tambiah in his essay "A Performative Approach to Ritual" (1979); reprinted as Chapter 4 of *Culture, Thought and Social Action: An Anthropological Perspective* (Cambridge: Harvard University Press, 1985). Not only does Tambiah's understanding of ritual as performative go beyond seeing the ritual as solely symbolic, it also goes beyond seeing ritual as simply a *performance*, i.e., a set of actions performed according to a rulebound sequence. Tambiah's *performative* understanding of ritual is to be distinguished from an understanding of ritual as a *performance*. Performance theory of ritual would tend to place ritual in a context appropriate to other such rule-bound sequences of actions; for example, dramatic performances, child's play, games, and the codification of contractual agreements. See, for example, Richard Schechner and Mady Schuman, eds., *Ritual, Play, and Performance: Readings in the Social Sciences/Theatre* (New York: The Seabury Press, 1976); and Richard Schechner and Willa Appel, eds., *By Means of Performance: Intercultural Studies of Theatre and Ritual* (Cambridge: Cambridge University Press, 1990). This distinction between rituals as performances similar to dramatic performances and rituals as themselves performing some effective action may be referred to as the difference between a performance theory and a performative theory.

Tambiah's performative theory is developed by reference to Austin's now well-known concept of a performative utterance. See Austin's *How to Do Things with Words*, 2nd ed, J. O. Urmson and Marina Sbisà, eds. (Cambridge: Harvard University Press, 1962). A performative utterance is one in which the expression is itself the perfor-

mance of the action. Examples are such expressions as "I apologize."
Here the expression does not report (or symbolically represent) some
other reality. It is not for example a report on the emotional state of the
person making the utterance, but rather is itself the act of apologizing.
In the same way, rituals are not simply symbolically representative of
something else, but rather are themselves the performance of the indicated social or intrapsychic transformation. Even in contemporary
society in the United States, the wedding ceremony, whether religious
or civil, is still considered by many to be a requisite for a couple to be
married. Although the state of marriage is presumably primarily a matter of the relation between the two people involved, if that state is not
marked ceremonially, then the two may not be considered to be "truly
married." To this extent, then, it is the performance of the ritual itself
that is efficacious.

Another way of talking about this concept of a performative theory of ritual is to see it as an attempt to develop a scientific and neutral
cover term. This cover term is one that would be universally applicable and which would reflect what is discussed within a specific religious context, e.g., Catholicism, under the category of sacrament. As a
cover term, however, the concept of ritual as performative is intended
to be free from the metaphysical and religious assumptions that constitute the particular religious context.

7. Again, the kind of change discussed here is to be distinguished
from changes in social status, e.g., the rites of passage studied by
Arnold van Gennep, *The Rites of Passage*, tr. Paula Wissig (Chicago:
University of Chicago Press, 1960) and Victor Turner, *The Ritual
Process* (Chicago: Aldine, 1969).

8. At the same time, analytic psychology does not preclude
pathology as an aspect of personal psychology.

9. This is a phenomenology of religion as defined by W. Brede
Kristensen: the "task [of the phenomenology of religion] is to classify
and group the numerous and widely divergent data in such a way that
an over-all view can be obtained of their religious content and the religious values they contain." *The Meaning of Religion: Lectures in the
Phenomenology of Religion*, tr. John B. Carman The Hague, The
Netherlands: Martinus Nijhoff, 1960), p. 1. Such an understanding of
the archetypes avoids the philosophic pitfalls of attributing a metaphysical status to them.

10. See Richard K. Payne, *The Tantric Ritual of Japan: Feeding
the Gods, The Japanese Fire Ritual* (Delhi, India: Aditya Prakashan,
1990), Chapter 7. The analytic approach taken there is largely based on
the work of Frits Staal; see especially *Rules Without Meaning: Ritual*,

Mantras and the Human Sciences, Toronto Studies in Religion, vol. 4. (New York: Peter Lang, 1989).

11. Reprint 1972 (Baltimore, MD: Penguin Books, 1973).

12. There are other terms that may be more appropriate for this tradition within Buddhism. Tantra has come to be conventionally accepted in modern Western scholarship, though (or perhaps because) the term refers to a body of texts that include the term *tantra* in their titles, rather than being a term which is used by adherents and practitioners to refer to themselves. "Vajrayāna" (i.e., the way of the lightning bolt) is used by many authors as a general term to identify the whole of the tradition as found throughout Buddhist Asia, while the term *mantrayāna* (i.e., the way of mantra) might be used for the East Asian forms. Whereas elsewhere I have chosen to use the term Vajrayāna, in this essay I continue to employ the term *tantra* because there seems to be no other appropriate term that enables one also to make comparative statements between Buddhist and Hindu forms of what may be a tradition that arose independently of either and which was then integrated into both.

13. Michel Strickmann, "The Goma in East Asia," in Frits Staal, ed., *Agni* (Berkeley, CA: Asian Humanities Press, 1983), 2, p.424.

14. The social function of the shido kegyō to train priests can be seen not only as part of a rite of passage, but also as part of a broader characteristic of ritual—the role of ritual as providing the individual with a kind of authority that cannot be acquired in any other way. See both John Hilary Martin, "Bringing the Power of the Past into the Present", and Martha Ellen Stortz, "Ritual Power, Ritual Authority" in this volume.

15. For example, in Śaiva siddhanta, Śiva is considered to have "sovereignty over the entire universe." Richard H. Davis, *Ritual in an Oscillating Universe: Worshiping Śiva in Medieval India* (Princeton, NJ: Princeton University Press, 1991), p. 9.

16. Literally: making original enlightenment real, i.e., manifest, not reified, i.e., concretizing the concept into some ontological absolute.

17. Concerning the malleability of one's own perceived self-identity, see Dorinne K. Kondo, *Crafting Selves: Power, Gender, and Discourses of Identity in a Japanese Workplace* (Chicago: The University of Chicago Press, 1990): "it is the contention of this book that selves which are coherent, seamless, bounded, and whole are indeed illusions" (p. 14).

18. It should be noted that this wordplay is not etymologically based. Despite the superficial similarity, *dismember* and *remember*

derive from different Latin roots. If memory serves, I was first exposed to the notion of re-membering as "putting back together" or reconstruction in the writings of one of the existentialists, perhaps Heidegger, Merleau-Ponty, or Sartre.

19. Particularly relevant would be the interpretation of self-identity as a *prajñāpi*, i.e., a socially constructed reality. For analogous ideas see Alfred Schutz, *The Problem of Social Reality* (Phenomenologica, no. 11. 3 vols. *Collected Papers.* [The Hague, The Netherlands: Martinus Nijhoff, 1971], vol. I) and Berger and Luckman, *The Social Construction of Reality* (Garden City, NY: Doubleday, 1967]. Such a view is also supported by recent psychological research: "Researchers who study memory and the brain are discovering the brain's capacity to construct and invent reality from the information it processes. . . . [M]emory is not a fixed thing, with its own special place or file drawer in the brain. It is a *process* that is constantly being reinvented. A 'memory' consists of fragments of the event, subsequent discussions and reading, other people's recollections and suggestions, and, perhaps most of all, present beliefs about the past." (Carol Tavris, "Beware the Incest-Survivor Machine," *The New York Times Book Review,* January 3, 1993).

20. For background information on mantra and *dhāraṇi,* see Harvey P. Alper, ed., *Understanding Mantras* (Albany: State University of New York Press, 1989), and Andre Padoux, *Vac: The Concept of the Word in Selected Hindu Tantras,* tr. Jacques Gontier (Albany, NY: State University of New York Press, 1990).

21. Minoru Kiyota, *Shingon Buddhism* (Los Angeles and Tokyo: Buddhist Books International, 1978), p. 70.

22. For a complete description of the complexity of the training sequence, see Payne, *Tantric Ritual of Japan,* pp. 70–2.

23. Dale Todaro, "Commentary on the *Garbhakosadhatu Recitation Manual,"* In Miyata Taisen, ed., *Handbook on the Four Stages of Prayoga: Chūin Branch of Shingon Tradition* (5 vols.) (Koyasan, Japan: Department of Koyasan Shingon Foreign Mission, 1988), 1, p.70.

24. For further information concerning the figure of Fudø, see Payne, Richard, "Standing Fast: Fudō Myōō in Japanese Literature," *Pacific World, The Journal of the Institute of Buddhist Studies,* n.s., no. 3 (1987), and "Firmly Rooted: On Fudō Myōō's Origins," *Pacific World, The Journal of the Institute of Buddhist Studies,* n.s., no. 4 (1988).

25. Miyata Taisen, *A Study of the Ritual Mudrās in the Shingon Tradition* (Sacramento, CA: Northern California Koyasan Temple, 1984), p. 7.

26. Ibid., pp. 9–11.

27. Shōun Toganoo, *Shingon: The Japanese Tantric Tradition* tr. Leo M. Pruden. (Original title: *Himitsu Jisō no Kenkyū*. 1935. Xerographic copy, n.d. (ca. 1980), p. 74. This action provides another link to classic Vedic rituals in which there are three fires, the southern fire (*dakṣiṇāgni*) being to protect the offerings intended for the gods (*deva*) from being stolen by the demons (*asuras*). See Payne, *Tantric Ritual of Japan*, p. 41.

28. The construction of a cosmic center corresponds to the ritual enclosure, *kraton*, discussed by Clare B. Fischer, "Power in the Palace: The Investiture of a Javanese Sultan," and the emphasis on place given by John Hilary Martin, "Bringing the Power of the Past into the Present" both in this volume. It is worth noting, however, that both the Javanese and the Aboriginal traditions are what Lewis Lancaster and Lionel Rothkrug (work in progress) would call "fixed," i.e., attached to a particular location. In other words, the kraton and the sacred sites of the Aboriginal tradition are unique. In contrast, the ritual enclosure of the Vajrayāna Buddhist rituals can be ritually produced in any location. This is what Lancaster and Rothkrug would refer to as "portable" in the sense that the location in which the ritual may be performed can be moved from one place to another. It is not fixed in a particular site, e.g., a temple or geographic location. ("Reproducible" has also been suggested as a third category.)

29. Shōun Toganoo, *Shingon*, p. 75.

30. I am currently at work on another essay, tentatively entitled "Enacted Feast," which will include a discussion of the "syntactic" impact of inserting this "semantic" unit.

31. See M. Kiyota, *Shingon*, p. 126.

32. This essay does not attempt to lay out the history of Shingon exegetical thought, but rather presents Kūkai's views as one of the most authoritative emic understandings—one that is still referred to by members of the tradition up to this day.

33. Tantric Buddhist thought is not separate from the other intellectual developments within Buddhism, e.g., *tathāgatagarbha*.

34. Kaji is sometimes translated as "empowerment," which has certain specific meaning in the context of initiating practice, or sometimes (misleadingly) translated as "grace." The concept of grace carries the specific meaning of an individual receiving God's grace solely as the result of God's action, rather than through any action of his or her

own. Clearly, such a concept is inappropriate to a tradition of practice, particularly one such as the Shingon, which views the process as a dual one requiring the initiation of the process to be on the practitioner's side.

35. The idea of ritual identification, although suggestive of trance possession states, does seem to have some significant differences. Usually, descriptions of trance emphasize the experience of the personal ego being displaced by the possessing spirit, with varying degrees of remembrance after the departure of the possessing spirit. See, for example, Gilbert Rouget, *Music and Trance: A Theory of the Relations Between Music and Possession*, tr. Brunhilde Biebuyck (Chicago: University of Chicago Press, 1985), pp. 17–28.) Though it is possible that the Buddhist rituals described here have their probably prehistoric origins in trance possession practices, the emic explanation does not seem to indicate any experience of displacement by a separate entity, but rather an increasing recognition of identity between the practitioner and Mahāvairocana.

36. Kondo, *Crafting Selves*, p. 106. Kondo's comment regarding the primacy of the repetition of form over content relates to the limitations of a solely symbolic understanding of ritual discussed further infra.

37. This "Self" as a psychological concept is obviously not to be confused with the metaphysical concept of *atman*, which is often translated as "self," and which—referring to a permanent, abiding, absolute, unchanging reality—is rejected by (virtually) all Buddhist thinkers.

38. C. G. Jung, "Transformation Symbolism of the Mass" in *Psychology and Religion: West and East*, tr. R. F. C. Hull. Bollingen Series 20, Collected Works of C. G. Jung, vol. 11; 2d ed. (Princeton, NJ: Princeton University Press, 1969), p. 259.

39. Ibid., p. 260.

40. Edward Edinger, *Ego and Archetype: Individuation and the Religious Function of the Psyche* (1972 Reprint. New York: Penguin Books, 1973), p. 6.

41. Ibid., p. 42.

42. Ibid., p. 96.

43. Ibid., p. 65.

44. Toganoo Shozui, "The Symbol System of Shingon Buddhism," pt. 2, p. 55.

45. The problematics of the ontology of Mahāvairocana produced a complex variety of philosophic positions over the course of Shingon's

history. For a brief discussion of this, see Taiko Yamasaki, *Shingon: Japanese Esoteric Buddhism* (Boston: Shambhala, 1988), p. 42.

46. Dale Todaro, tr., "Garbhakoṣadhātu Recitation Manual" in Miyata Taisen, ed., *Handbook on the Four Stages of Prayoga: Chūin Branch of Shingon Tradition* (5 vols.) Koyasan, Japan: Department of Koyasan Shingon Foreign Mission, 1988), 4, p. 23–25. Mod. auct.

47. Ron Davidson, personal communication. Note that structured visualizations also differ from active imagination.

48. August J. Cwik, "Active Imagination as Imaginal Play-Space," p. 103, in Nathan Schwartz-Salant and Murray Stein, eds., *Liminality and Transitional Phenomena*, (Wilmette, IL: Chiron Publications, 1991), pp. 99-114.

49. C. G. Jung, *Aion: Researches into the Phenomenology of the Self*, tr. R. F. C. Hull, Bollingen Series 20, Collected Works of C. G. Jung, vol. 9, 2; 2d ed.; (Princeton, NJ: Princeton University Press, 1968), p. 37. Emphasis in original.

50. Miyata Taisen, tr. "The Basic Recitation Manual of Eighteen Rites" (In Miyata Taisen, ed. *Handbook on the Four Stages of Prayoga*, 2,16–17.

51. Ibid., p. 17.

52. Edinger, p. 37.

53. Ibid.

54. Ibid., p. 42.

55. Ibid.

56. Miyata, *Ritual Mudrās*, p. 91.

57. A distinction may be made here between an implicit symbol system (the presence and importance of which I am not contesting here), and the explicit, exegetical interpretation of rituals in terms of a symbol system. It is the tendency to accept the latter as a theoretical and methodological given that I find questionable. On this distinction, Dan Sperber has said that "a complex symbolic system can work very well without being accompanied by any exegetic commentary." (*Rethinking Symbolism*, tr. Alice L. Morton [Cambridge: Cambridge University Press, 1975.]) p. 18.

58. See, for example, Victor W. Turner, "Symbols in African Ritual," and David W. Murray, "Ritual Communication: Some Considerations Regarding Meaning in Navajo Rituals," in Janet L. Golgin, David S. Kemnitzer, and David M. Schneider, eds., *Symbolic Anthropology: A Reader in the Study of Symbols and Meanings* (New York: Columbia University Press, 1977), pp. 183–94 and 195–220, respectively; and Monica Wilson, "Nyakyusa Ritual and Symbolism," and Victor W. Turner, "Themes in the Symbolism of Ndembu Hunting

Ritual," in John Middleton, ed., *Myth and Cosmos: Readings in Mythology and Symbolism* (Garden City, NY: The Natural History Press, Doubleday and Co., 1967), pp. 149–66 and 249–69, respectively. Turner's concept of an "operational meaning" ("Ndembu Hunting Ritual," p. 254)—by examining the use of a symbol in a ritual—begins to point beyond simply equating a symbol with a meaning. In contrast, Wilson ("Nyakyusa Ritual and Symolism," p. 161) goes so far as to ask, "What do the rituals really express? . . . What ideas and attitudes underlie them?" Both these authors assume that the irreducible ground of analysis is social values, i.e., that the meaning of rituals is contained in the symbols employed in the rituals and that the symbols are to be understood as expressions of social values. The choice of social values as the ground of analysis a) is arbitrary, b) ignores the role of ritual in forming social values, and c) reduces ritual to simply yet one more symbolic expression of social values, rather than recognizing the performative power of ritual to effect change.

59. Frits Staal, *Rules Without Meaning: Ritual, Mantras and the Human Sciences*, Toronto Studies in Religion, vol. 4 (New York: Peter Lang Publishing, 1989), pp. 131–40. See also Staal, "The Meaninglessness of Ritual," in *Numen: International Review for the History of Religions*, 1979.

60. Mircea Eliade, *Sacred and Profane: The Nature of Religion*, p. 80, emphases and gender-exclusive language in original.

61. Ibid., p. 81.

62. For a parallel situation regarding "monolithic" theories of myth, see G. S. Kirk, *The Nature of Greek Myths* (New York: Penguin Books, 1974), Introduction.

63. See Jonathan Z. Smith, *To Take Place* (Chicago: University of Chicago Press, 1987), pp. 1–13.

64. These categories are part of a very basic typology of rituals as life crisis, life cycle, and annual cycle (or calendric). As a typology of ritual, this is the only one that seems to me to be heuristically acceptable for cross-cultural comparisons. I understand that some of the Vedic ritual theorists employed these same categories, but I have as yet been unable to locate a source for this.

65. Donald Sandner, *Navaho Symbols of Healing* (New York: Harcourt Brace Jovanovich, Harvest/HBJ Book, 1979), p. 112.

66. This is, of course, the famous "myth and ritual" theory, already thoroughly discredited. See, especially, Joseph Fontenrose, *The Ritual Theory of Myth*, University of California Publications Folklore Studies, no. 18, 1966 (reprint), California Library Reprint Series

Edition (Berkeley, CA: University of California Press, 1971), and G. S. Kirk, *The Nature of Greek Myths*, Introduction.

67. Speaking more technically, this would be a *petitio principii* fallacy of the following form:

1. All rituals are reactualizations of mythic events.
2. the goma must be a reactualization of a mythic event.
3. Since the goma itself does not appear to be a reactualization, it must "really" be the Vedic predecessors that demonstrate the reactualizing function of the goma.
4. Therefore, all rituals are reactualizations of mythic events.

68. *Dictionary of the History of Ideas*, s.v. "Mimesis."

69. Plato's concern with the destructive potential of drama as discussed in the *Republic* evidences Plato's recognition of the efficacy of mimesis. See Leon Golden, *Aristotle on Tragic and Comic* Mimesis, American Classical Studies, no. 29 (Atlanta, GA: Scholars Press, 1992), Chapter 3 for an extended discussion of Plato's views. Also cf. Philippe Lacoue-Labarthe, "Typography," in *Typography: Mimesis, Philosophy, Politics*, ed. Christopher Fynsk (Cambridge: Harvard University Press, 1989).

70. Karl F. Morrison, *The Mimetic Tradition of Reform in the West*, Karl F. Morrison (Princeton: Princeton University Press, 1982) p. 3.

71. See Kendall L. Walton, *Mimesis as Make-Believe: On the Foundations of the Representational Arts* (Cambridge: Harvard University Press, 1990), p. 21ff. for his distinction between "prompters" of imagining, "objects" of imagining, and "props." Props in his usage serve the essential function of generating fictional truths. It is this usage that I am following here.

72. Ibid., p. 67.

73. Ibid. p. 68.

74. "Ritual . . . is primarily activity. It is an activity governed by explicit rules. The important thing is what you do, not what you think, believe or say." Staal, *Rules Without Meaning*, p. 116.

75. Such responses are far from uncommon; for example, see Dan Sperber, *Rethinking Symbolism*, p. 17.

76. Staal, *Rules Without Meaning*, p. 116.

77. Sometimes such value judgments are blatant, especially in some of the older ethnographic literature. For example, Monica Wilson says, "The aim of Nyakyusa ritual is not that union with God, constantly sought in Christian ritual, but a separation, for close association with the pagan gods spells madness and death, not fullness of life." ("Nyakyusa Ritual and Symbolism," p. 158). John Middleton,

ed., *Myth and Cosmos: Readings in Mythology and Symbolism* (Garden City, NY: The Natural History Press, 1967), p. 158 [originally published in *American Anthropologist* 5612 (1954):228–241].

78. David I. Kertzer, *Ritual, Politics, and Power* (New Haven, CT: Yale University Press, 1988), p. 72.

79. The fact of the Shingon ritual training being an individual practice also calls into question the widely accepted interpretation of rituals as a form of societal or cross-generational communication. Although similarities between ritual and language are quite evident, such similarities do not warrant the claim that *all* rituals are a form of communication, unless communication is radically redefined.

4

Ritual Power, Ritual Authority

Configurations and Reconfigurations in the Era of Manifestations

MARTHA ELLEN STORTZ

INTRODUCTION

That period of Shaker history known as "Mother Ann's Work" remembers ten years between 1837 and 1847, when remarkable "gifts" graced the scattered communities. Ecstatic utterances and movements had long been part of Shaker history. Their very name distinguished Shakers from a branch of the English Quakers from which they separated in Manchester, England in the early 1770s: these were "Shaking Quakers," Quakers possessed and entranced, Quakers whirling and speaking in tongues. Shaking Quakers, or, more simply, Shakers, faced persecution and civil censure in England and left to try their fortunes in the British colonies in America. The Shakers, clustered around their leader and founder Ann Lee, arrived in the British colonies in 1774— only two years before the War of Independence.

Early reports of Shaker worship in the United States speak of "dancing in extravagant postures," which attracted all the attention and even some of the censure that similar religious practices had elicited in England. But over the course of fifty years in the new republic, Shaker worship and ritualizations had routinized to the point of boredom. Giles Avery complained in 1835: "We have meeting at home among ourselves and it is so dull that one would scarcely know whether we were trying to serve God or something else."[1]

105

One should be careful what one wishes. The situation of stasis to which Avery alluded was quickly to change in an unprecedented out-pouring of "gifts" that absorbed the considerable energies of the society beginning in 1837 and continuing for the next ten years. The period, variously known as "Mother's Work," "Mother Ann's Work," or "The Era of Manifestations," so enlivened worship that the Central Ministry at New Lebanon, New York, closed worship to outsiders for a period of about seven years; it also threatened to remove whatever was "united" about the United Society and implicitly attacked the central position of the Central Ministry. In the heat and passion of ecstatic worship, authority passed imperceptibly but powerfully from the hands of the Central Ministry into the hands of "instruments," those open to receiving the gifts.

The question of authority in the ritualizations of Shaker worship is central to this essay. I have not discovered new documents on Shaker history, nor have I dug in archives to retrieve old ones. Instead, I depend on the work of those who have done both, notably Stephen J. Stein's masterful new book, *The Shaker Experience in America*, and Priscilla Brewer's nuanced history, *Shaker Communities, Shaker Lives*.[2] Rather, my focus is on the crisis of ritual authority that the period known as "Mother Ann's Work" posed for the society. Initially a time of sponta-neous utterances and movement, the emphasis in "Mother Ann's Work" shifted quickly to distinctive ritualizations authorized by the Central Ministry and required of all villages in the Society. Three are of particular interest: the Midnight Cry, the Sweeping Gift, and the Mountain Feast. Following a description of the period and its context, I will proceed to analyze this period of intense ritual experimentation, not as ritual proofs to a specific theory, but as ritual practices that simultaneously configure and reconfigure certain relations of power and authority in the United Society at that time. Further, these ritual-izations reflect certain tensions between the society and the world and within the society itself.

The purpose of this investigation is threefold. First, it seeks to advance an area of Shaker history that has received little attention: religious culture. This aspect of the United Society has too often been overlooked in the fascination for its material culture. The imbalance has not been lost on the few remaining Shaker believers. Before she died, Eldress Mildred Barker of Sabbathday Lake, Maine commented, "I almost expect to be remembered as a chair or a table."[3] But second, this study seeks to redress an area in ritual studies that has received lit-tle attention: the question of ritual power and ritual authority, and how they are supported.[4] Finally, the study challenges a traditional tendency in ritual theory to align ritual with the conserving forces of culture by showing how ritualizations can both reproduce and resist established relations of power, how ritualizations can both configure and reconfigure power.

INBREAKING OF THE ERA OF MANIFESTATIONS

In August 1837, in the upstate New York community of Watervliet, several young girls began exhibiting some unusual behavior, marked by trancing, seizures, and spiritual communications. The spiritual awakening started with children in the South Family, also known as the Gathering Family, the social unit into which people from the world were "gathered" in preparation for possible assimilation into the society. The children, largely girls, were reported to "be very much wrought upon . . . they have diverous gifts, shaking turning and singing and the like."[5] They spoke with "angels"; they journeyed to heavenly places.

Manifestations continued at Watervliet throughout the late summer and into the early autumn, increasing in intensity and drafting adolescents and eventually adults into service as "instruments." At that time worship services were open to the public, and spectators thronged to see such ecstatic activities. The range of these activities was quite a spectacle, and historian John Whitworth enumerates:

> . . . physical seizures and trances unaccompanied by verbal revelations or with attendant glossolalia; pronouncements directed to the whole society or sect, purportedly from the spirits of leaders of the sect or, via intermediary angels, from the deity himself; revelations of new rituals or songs for the group; 'gifts', in the ordinary sense of the word, for individual members, and messages to individuals and to the whole sect from the spirits of persons other than past leaders of the sect.[6]

News of the ecstatic behavior moved quickly throughout the United Society, but the response of one village in particular was important. The United Society was often accused of being "united" in name only, but in fact the structure of the society figured critically in the dissemination of information and governance of the whole. The society as a whole had four tightly organized tiers. The smallest unit of belonging was the "family," a unit consisting of up to a hundred men and women. Elders and Eldresses were the designated leaders of the family. A village comprised two or more families, and was presided over by two men and two women known as "the local ministry." Two or more villages in proximity to each other were known as a bishopric, the head of which was the local ministry of the largest village. Overseeing the whole constellation of bishoprics, villages, and families was the Central Ministry, located at New Lebanon in upstate New York, south of Watervliet. The Central Ministry consisted of a team of two men, elders, and two women, eldresses, who assumed leadership over the society as a whole.[7] The spiritual was also political.

The responses from New Lebanon were varied. From the dye house in the village, Eldress Elizabeth Lovegrove followed the progress of the Watervliet revival in her *Dye House Journal*:

> Nov. 26, 1837—We attend to the reading of some remarkable visions seen by some of the Young believers at Watervliet, which was very interesting.
> Jan. 5, 1838—We receive intelligence from Watervliet that the visions continue.
> Jan. 6, 1838—Great anxiety about the visions, but no way at present to get any information.[8]

If there was "great anxiety" in the New Lebanon dye house regarding such visions, one can only imagine the response from the elders and eldresses who composed the Central Ministry. From the administrative center of the United Society the response was more ambivalent. In early October of 1837, two months into the revival, one of the two elders from the Central Ministry at New Lebanon, Rufus Bishop, paid a visit to the Second Family at Watervliet. After observing the manifestations, he offered both interpretation and caution. As Stein reports:

> He judged that these evidences of "the condescending goodness of God" were intended to strengthen faith in "the work of God" and to highlight the "state of rewards & punishment beyond the grave." He warned the instruments against "letting their sense rise or taking the honor of those gifts to themselves," and he urged that they "keep their joining to their Elders & to the living body or they would suffer great loss."[9]

However, Stein notes that privately Elder Bishop had doubts, which he registered in the Central Ministry Journal:

> [O]n the whole I considered it a good powerful meeting; but to be honest about the matter I think there was rather too much of the wind, fire & earthquake to satisfy Believers who have had a long & fruitful travel."[10]

Whatever Elder Bishop's doubts, the official word from New Lebanon regarding the visions was both immediate and enthusiastic. Priscilla Brewer interprets the response as "overwhelmingly positive" and excerpts a report from the Central Ministry to the Shaker village at South Union, Indiana in 1838:

> Many have become Shakers indeed which in times past hardly deserved the name of a Shaker at all! But now they shake wherever they go; whether at work, or at Table!.... It is truly a wonderful day. ... Numbers who have been spiritually dead for many years, have been raised to life, and are now living souls in the house of God.[11]

John Whitworth comments: "These visitations spread to the adolescent and adult members of the society and, shortly afterwards, the Ministry of the sect pronounced them to be genuine expressions of the Presence of the Holy Spirit."[12] Whitworth's remark reveals a good deal more than the official enthusiasm of the Central Ministry. It reveals the need and desire of the Ministry to establish itself as the arbiter of true and false visions; it also suggests that authenticity was more easily connected to age. Children, particularly girl children, having visions might strain one's credulity; adolescents and adults were easier to regard as "genuine" visionaries.

As news of the manifestations spread, visitors from New Lebanon and from the "world" were not the only spectators to come and witness. Shakers from other villages made pilgrimage to Watervliet to view the mysteries themselves. The accounts these visitors sent back to their villages are valuable records of the trajectory of revival. They also carried the revival outside of Watervliet. The power of suggestion and the passion of the moment combined to release similar manifestations in other Shaker villages throughout the United Society from the eastern villages into the western frontier.

By the early spring of the following year Elder Philemon Stewart of the community at New Lebanon became an instrument. Moreover, the gifts bestowed upon Philemon Stewart originated not from mere angels nor from departed spirits, but were messages from none other than Mother Ann and Jesus Christ himself.[13] Stewart quickly became a "pre-eminent medium," as Whitworth dubs him, both in the eyes of his contemporaries and in the works of modern Shaker historians.[14] Stephen Stein links Stewart's spiritual gifts with political ascendancy:

> By the year's end Stewart had moved into the First Order and was listed as one of the principal instruments at the village. ...

Stewart soon was playing a pivotal role in the society's affairs as a chosen vessel, communicating God's will to the Believers. Ultimately he became the "most prominent" as well as the most controversial instrument in the society.[15]

Priscilla Brewer regards Stewart with some skepticism, focusing on the aura of controversy surrounding him:

His existence on the fringes of the Shaker power structure may well have made him uncomfortable, particularly as his brother, Amos, was ascending the hierarchy as an Elder. As an instrument, however, Philemon rapidly became a force to be reckoned with.[16]

Once again, the spiritual was political.

With more and more leaders becoming visionaries, the charismatic authority passed from children to adults. Accordingly, the nature of the "gifts" changed. Seizures were replaced with censures; physical frenzies gave way to admonitions and exhortations. Messages from the founding mothers and fathers of the society expressed horror at dirt, gossip, sloth, and sexual attraction, all anathema to the Shaker ethos.[17] A contemporary Shaker believer, Isaac Youngs, noted that between the spring of 1838 and the spring of 1840, the messages from the spirit world became "more dignified, more weighty—more tending to be repulsive to common human feelings, more bordering on restraint, and designed to enforce strict Church order." Youngs also observed a shift in both style and gender of the communications: "The first messages were all given thro' male instruments, tho' in a general sense the females were much more gifted in outward operations and gifts."[18] Whitworth comments on the high degree of control exercised by the Central Ministry over the reception, interpretation, and authenticity of spiritual gifts.

The most important instruments worked in close conjunction with the ministries and, as early as 1840, the Central Ministry insisted that all spiritual communications should be written down and examined by the society ministries before being announced to the assembled members. This right and duty of the ministries to censor spiritual communications was duly confirmed by revelation from Ann Lee, who disclosed that she had given her servants "spiritual spectacles" in order that they might be able to detect communications from evil spirits.[19]

Fronted with a charismatic authority that threatened to unseat its power, the Central Ministry reserved the right to assess the authenticity of visions and to discern whether the inspirations were demonic or divine.

The emphases on admonition and discernment were not to be wasted. In 1841 the Central Ministry announced that Holy Mother Wisdom herself would visit all the villages: in preparation for her appearance, all villages were to be put in órder and all hearts purified. Footwashing and fasting, confession and repentance became commonplace practices in all the villages, engaged all the more rigorously after villages began reporting in on their visits with this female manifestation of the Godhead. Stein describes a the visitation at New Lebanon in 1841:

> On the appointed day in April, Holy Mother Wisdom spoke through Miranda Barber, a chosen instrument, telling of the intention to "set a Mark on every person over 18 years of age, that when the destroying Angels should be sent forth they know who were vessels of mercy, & who were by their own works excluded from the protection of God." After bestowing "Gold Breastplate[s] set with pearls & precious stones of 35 colors" on the men and "Robes of needlework, covered with flowers of 18 Colors" on the women in the central ministry, as well as many "comforting words" on both, Wisdom worked her way through the ranks of the church. Every Believer repeated these words: "I am bound for the Kingdom of Heaven, O bless me with thy blessing! give me wisdom, strength & power O Holy Holy Mother!" The "divine parent" then spoke words of encouragement or admonition, set a mark on each member, and placed around each person's head a "Gold band" on which was written, "Touch not mine Anointed."[20]

The glitter of gold and the dazzle of precious stones ought not obscure what was actually going on here: the female manifestation of the Godhead first coronated members of the Central Ministry, then worked her way through the ranks of the faithful. One may well wonder who "chose" the chosen instrument. The appearance of Holy Mother Wisdom 1840-1841, then, served to reinforce the position of the Central Ministry and its representatives within the society at large at a time when that position was sorely tested.

In 1842 the Central Ministry announced several ritual gifts and prescribed them for every village in the Society: the Midnight Cry, the

Sweeping Gift, and the Mountain Festival. These required rites had come out of a secret session that Holy Mother Wisdom and Mother Ann had with the elders and eldresses of the New Lebanon community during her visitations there. The gifts, then, related directly to the female deity in the Godhead, both as preparation for her future visits and as a means of sustaining the standards of purity and repentance established in the wake of past visits.

The Midnight Cry

This ceremony was led by six men and six women who had given evidence of having received "gifts" and who were therefore "instruments." Bearing lamps, the mediums headed up a company that marched through the rooms of every building in the village, a journey that lasted nearly two weeks in some of the larger villages. At midnight on the third day, each family was aroused by solemn songs:

> Awake from your slumbers,
> for the Lord of Hosts is going through the land,
> He will sweep, he will clean his holy sanctuary.
> Search ye your Camps, yea! read and understand
> For the Lord of Hosts holds the Lamps in his hand.

The household then joined the ranks of the marchers. The next night all were aroused again and gathered for worship in the middle of the night.

The Sweeping Gift

A day was set aside for cleaning houses, shops, kitchens, and outbuildings—wherever "evil spirits" had hidden in dust and dirt. On the appointed day, a band of "instruments," led by elders, eldresses, and singers, marched throughout the community singing, chanting, and wielding spiritual brooms. The male instruments traversed the fields and barns, the hogpens and carpentry shops; the female instruments marched through the kitchens, schoolrooms, dairies, and infirmaries. All instruments wielded spiritual brooms and purified the space through which they passed. While they marched, traveling in their spiritual labor, the remaining sisters and brothers engaged in some temporal labor of their own: sweeping rooms with the real brooms that Shaker ingenuity had created, mopping floors, cleaning out pigpens, picking up bits of wood, glass, and paper, and burning rubbish. A village already "notorious for neatness, wore an aspect fifty per cent more tidy than usual."[21]

The Annual Mountain Feast

From the Central Ministry in the spring of 1842 came instructions for one of the most unusual ritualizations of this remarkable period: a mountaintop feast. A hill near the village was set aside, cleared, and set with a huge hexagonal stone, known as the "fountain."[22]

Preparation for the festival included fasting, confessions of sins, and prayer, as well as dress appropriate for the ceremony. The evening before the feast spiritual garments were distributed to the brothers from an imaginary chest. The brothers received coats of twelve different colors; a sky-blue, gold-buttoned jacket covered with fine needlework in characteristic floral patterns; white trousers spangled with stars; a white silk handkerchief bordered with gold; and a silver-colored fur hat. The sisters received gowns of twelve different colors; silver shoes; muslin caps; silver bonnets; and blue silk gloves. The community was clothed in heavenly garb, which symbolized the virtues of holiness, innocence, meekness, freedom, and peace.

The following day the believers gathered in the early morning and marched two abreast up toward the mountain. At various points during their ascent, they would stop, bow, clap, and shout at the village below them. When they arrived at the mountaintop clearing, they received spiritual spectacles through which they could view more clearly the events about to transpire.

The hill ceremonies commenced with a blessing of the instruments, those particularly gifted with visions and prophecies, whereupon the entire company commenced to dance. These were not the measured, formal steps that usually crossed a meetinghouse floor, but were rather a return to the ecstatic and involuntary whirling and shaking that had characterized the movement at its inception and had reappeared in the early weeks of "Mother Ann's Work." After the dancing, other spiritual gifts were bestowed, and this portion of the ceremony ended with a cleansing at the foot of the fountain.

Following this an altar was built, and each member processed to the altar, naming an offering she or he would make of the "most choice things" that each had to offer. The divine response to such offerings was the bestowal of more spiritual gifts: either spiritual guns for defending the believers against a hidden enemy or spiritual seed for sowing and watering in the world.

The culmination of the ceremony was a spiritual feast, similar to a Christian Eucharist. The believers piled onto tables the harvest of their fields—apples, pears, grapes, strawberries, milk and honey, bread and butter—and spiritual food like wild honey, locusts, and manna. The company sat down and feasted until midday.

After the feast a final gift was bestowed and celebrated. The prophet Daniel's love was received as a ball of yarn unwound through the company of believers. After this the group departed the holy mountain, marching back to their village and singing:

> I will march I will go
> In this pretty shining way
> In freedom's lovely valley
> On my organ I will play.

The annual mountaintop ceremony was celebrated faithfully for several years. Whatever its origins, whether from Mother Ann herself or from a ministry anxious about containing spiritual manifestations, the ceremony served to celebrate the outpouring of spiritual gifts, to restrict these gifts to a place apart from the workplaces and fields, and to restrict the ecstatic potential of Shaker worship to the space of a single day.

CONTROLLING AND CONTAINING THE MANIFESTATIONS

The Central Ministry prescribed these three ritualizations for all Shaker villages, claiming for them direct inspiration from Mother Ann and Holy Mother Wisdom. They could also be seen as attempts to control and contain the outpouring of spiritual gifts. Probably a truth of the purpose of these ritualizations lies somewhere in between the two alternative interpretations.

Whatever its worries in regard to its relationship within the society, the Central Ministry was also concerned about its interface with the world. In 1842 the Central Ministry decreed that meetings were to be closed to the public. In the same year Philemon Stewart had a series of visions that were published in 1843 and disseminated to the Boston consulates of hundreds of nations. Stewart's book, *A Holy, Sacred and Divine Roll and Book*, was a compilation of scriptural citations, theological reflection, and moral counsel, which rambled on for more than four hundred pages, filled two volumes, and exhorted believers to humility by threat of punishment. For it Stewart claimed direct inspiration: he wrote what was dictated to him by an angel, Al'sign te're Jah' by name.

The King of Sweden alone wrote to thank the Central Ministry for the gift of Stewart's book. There is evidence that among believers reception of the book and its author was less enthusiastic. Brewer records an anonymous journalist's entries:

> March 2, 1841—D. Boler leaves Elders. P. Stewart goes in.
> Nov. 26, 1842—P. Stewart leaves Eldership. (Joyful)
> April 20, 1843—P. Stewart G. Avery go Eastern Societies.
> Sept. 13, 1843—D. Boler to Canterbury after P. Stewart (wild).
> Jan. 30, 1844—P. Stewart Doctor (Trying to be one).
> Sept. 14, 1846—P. Stewart takes Grt. Garden.[23]

Disbelief did not attach to Stewart alone. A letter of January 1845 from the New Hampshire Ministry to the Central Ministry was marked "Confidential" and expressed exasperation:

> Unbelief in the present manifestation is too prevalent. Even their former Elder Brother James Pote seems to have very little if any faith in the present work—in the Sacred Roll or Book, or in preparing the Sacred Feast Ground; and there is no doubt that some of the young have gathered weakness from him, Paul Nowell, and perhaps others.[24]

Throughout the villages of the United Society there was evidence that the Era of Manifestations had come to a close. Worship had calmed to such an extent that in 1845 the Central Ministry decreed that meetings could once again be open to the public. Mountain festivals slowly ground to a halt, and fountain stones toppled and collected moss. A number of believers defected to the world, including some prominent instruments, which further undermined their credibility and created a sense that "Mother's Work" had come to an end.

BACKGROUND AND CONTEXT OF THE ERA OF MANIFESTATIONS

Background of the American Shaker Movement

The origins of the United Society are difficult to trace. On one hand, there is very little written. Documentary evidence about the origins of the sect in Manchester, England is sparse. The founding mother and fathers were probably lacking in any formal education; they left no records like Eldress Elizabeth Lovegrove's *Dye House Journal* of fifty years later. Such journals required literacy, security, and space. In its early years in England and in the United States, the society had none of these. Moreover, Shakers favored religious experience over holy words. What mattered in these early years was what the Spirit did in the moment, not what it had dictated in writing by inspired angels. The origins of the Shakers, or Shaking Quakers, as they were known in England, are shrouded in obscurity.

On the other hand, however, there is entirely too much written about the origins of the sect—but it was written by American Shaker historians and theologians almost thirty years after the tiny band of Shaking Quakers had settled in their first American community.[25] What is written then about the origins of the sect and the life of Ann Lee borders on hagiography. Interestingly, the earliest public testimonies of Shaker missionaries do not mention the figure whom later historians and theologians would lift up as the founding mother of the sect and elevate to a status that approached the divine.[26]

Ann Lee was probably born around 1736 in Manchester, England. Her father was a blacksmith, and as a child Ann began working in a factory preparing cotton for the looms and cutting velvet. She joined a small Quaker sect led by Jane and James Wardley. The group was much influenced by the French Prophets, or Camisards, a radical sect of Calvinists who had sought refuge in England after revocation of the Edict of Nantes in 1685. In exile the sect began preaching the imminence of the second coming of Christ and engaging in ecstatic worship with singing, shouting, dancing, visions, and prophecies. Worship appears to have been unstructured, beginning with the silence of a typical Quaker meeting, but continuing as the worshipers

> were seized with a mighty trembling, under which they would express the indignation of God against all sin. At other times they were affected, under the power of God, with a mighty shaking; and were occasionally exercised in singing, shouting, or walking the floor, under the influence of spiritual signs, shoving each other about—or swiftly passing and repassing each other, like clouds agitated by a mighty wind.[27]

The teachings of the "Shaking Quakers," as they came to be called, were as unstructured as their worship, but included a call to repentance, confession of sins, and conviction of the end of the world and the Second Coming of Christ.

Ann quickly assumed leadership in the group and came into conflict both with the Wardleys and with municipal authorities for disturbing the peace. These conflicts prompted Ann's departure, with eight of her followers, for the American colonies on a passage ship called the *Mariah*. The group landed in New York three months later and scattered to earn a livelihood. Within two years they had purchased a piece of land near Albany which they named Niskeyuna (later renamed Watervliet), reunited whomever of the original group remained, brought over family and provisions, and begun building farm buildings and houses. The Great Awakening and the New Lights revival movement had preceded the establishment of the colony at Watervliet and prepared the American colonists for the style of Shaker worship and the substance of their teachings. People came in droves to Watervliet, and public meetings were held regularly and with effect. Converts of all classes augmented the number of the "believers," and the wealthier among them added to the property and holdings of the community. New settlements sprang up in Connecticut, Massachusetts, New Hampshire, and New York; the frontier spirit carried Shaker communities into Kentucky, Ohio, Indiana. The communities thrived. Despite sporadic persecution, suspected Tory sympathies, and ongoing charges of family wrecking and kidnapping, Shaker villages grew in land, wealth, and prosperity.

The death of Ann Lee (or Mother Ann, as she came to be known) in 1784 and the expansion of the sect brought with it shifts in leadership style and theological presentation. By 1787 and under the able leadership and organizational genius of Joseph Meacham, the society entered a new phase.[28] His *Concise Statement of the Principles of the Only True Church* in 1790 was the first written exposition of the Shaker faith.[29] Richard McNemar published another exposition of the faith, *The Kentucky Revival*, in 1807, which was followed in 1808 by a more definitive, collaborative statement of Shaker belief and practice by western Shakers Benjamin S. Youngs, David Darrow, and John Meacham, *The Testimony of Christ's Second Appearing*. Eastern Shakers Seth Y. Wells and Calvin Green responded with a second edition of the *Testimony* in 1809, following with *A Summary View of the Millennial Church* in 1823. These documents all served a dual purpose: they routinized doctrine and practice within a movement that was now geographically diffuse, and they offered an apologetic of the Shaker faith to a public that accused them of everything from treason to kidnapping. Yet, whatever their stated purpose, the publication of these documents had an important consequence. With the emergence of a theological elite in the society who wrote and carried on the apologetic task of the institution, relationships of power between the sexes shifted subtly and irrevocably. Men took on the public task of writing, explaining, and defending the faith; women moved more and more into the private and domestic realm. Stephen Stein comments: "At this point women had little opportunity to participate in the male-dominated world of theology."[30] Thus, in the formative period the Shakers "evolved from an apocalyptic sect into a millennial church."[31] The sect depended on the leadership of a woman, Ann Lee, and boasted an equality of power relationships between the sexes; the church increasingly turned to leadership from its male theological elite.

Context of the Era of Manifestations

The Shakers arrived in America in 1774, initially scattered, but settled on the site at Watervliet by 1776. With Meacham's accession to leadership in 1787, however, the hub of the Shaker universe shifted from Watervliet west of the Hudson River to the town of New Lebanon east of the Hudson. The Era of Manifestations erupted in 1837 at Watervliet into a sect that had become an institution, the United Society of Believers. The intervening years, over sixty of them, brought changes into the group, changes that shaped their common life, their worship style, and their relationship to the world: geographic expansion, assimilation of converts, organizational style, routinization of charisma, rigidification of worship, lack of creative and competent leadership, increasing problems with youth, and economic crisis.

The United Society experienced solid expansion into the southern, northern, and particularly the western frontiers of the United States. This was as much due to missionary efforts on the part of the society, as to the surrounding religious sensibilities. Whitworth comments: ". . . Ann Lee constantly exhorted her followers to labour, and encouraged them with revelations which promised that soon thousands would flock to the sect and that the Shakers' testimony would 'overcome all nations.'"[32] But the Shakers were not the only religious groups with revelations and testimonies. The New Lights movement and the War of Independence contributed to a sense that the last days were at hand. People flocked to observe a group that practiced forms of ecstatic ritualizations and which tried to integrate work and worship.

The earliest converts to Shakerism, then, were often people from other revival movements. One of the most powerful revival preachers in New Lebanon, Joseph Meacham, made the short trip to Watervliet to observe Shaker life and was so impressed with its teachings, worship, and way of life that he converted to become one of the most powerful leaders in the second generation of Shakers in America. In 1805 Mother Lucy Wright, another convert appointed by Meacham to minister with him, made a decision to "open the gospel" to the West and authorized missionary expeditions in the Ohio Valley. Shaker villages were established at North Union, Whitewater, Union Village, and

Watervliet in Ohio, at West Union in Indiana, and at Pleasant Hill and South Union in Kentucky.

Geographic expansion was a mixed blessing for the United Society. Financing outposts on the frontier was a drain on the finances of the eastern villages. Financial drain contributed to a subterranean rivalry between eastern and western villages, that often threatened to break through to the surface. Attentive to the dynamics of this rivalry, Stephen Stein observes that the first impulse for Shaker theological apologetics came from the west. When western leaders Benjamin S. Youngs, John Meacham, and David Darrow produced their *Testimony* in 1808, eastern leaders Seth Y. Wells and Calvin Green issued a second edition of their own version of *Testimony* in 1809. Such rivalries were not uncommon.

Expansion—and the potential for faction that accompanied it— necessarily affected organization. Ann Lee's charisma had largely resided in the power of her person and the felicity of her speech—at least as it was recorded in the *Testimonies of the Life, Character, Revelations and Doctrines of Our Ever Blessed Mother Ann Lee* some 32 years after her death. Ann Lee's personal piety and example communicated powerfully to those around her. But what would happen when not all Shakers could interface with Mother Ann on a daily basis? What would happen after Mother Ann died? How then could her charisma keep a society together?[33] The situation that faced the Shakers after the death of Ann Lee was not unlike the situation facing early Christian leaders after the death of Jesus or the death of the disciples. Not surprisingly, their reactions were similar. The Shakers too would turn to written instead of oral testimony; they would organize and institutionalize their communities; they would centralize their structures.

With the spread of villages into the west, visits and face-to-face contact no longer served to keep the United Society united. "Letter writing became a bureaucratic science among the Shakers,"[34] as elders and eldresses of the various villages wrote to each other and wrote back and forth to the Central Ministry in New Lebanon. What marks the institutionalization of the society is the appearance of records, journals, diaries, and reports, which became the connective tissue of an expanse of Shaker communities.

After the death of Ann Lee in 1784, leadership passed easily into the hands of James Whittaker, who vigorously visited Shaker communities in New England, preferring contact to written communication. Whittaker was the last of the founding group who'd crossed the Atlantic on the ship *Mariah.* He was succeeded by the convert from

New Lebanon, Joseph Meacham, who institutionalized the society. Meacham initiated a plan for the succession of leaders in the Central Ministry: the male-female team would themselves choose their successors. In addition, Meacham stressed the importance of unity among the various villages and established New Lebanon as the hub of American Shakerism, articulated the importance of equality betwen male and female, presented instructions for the education of youth, and argued the importance of communal living. In the arena of worship, Meacham routinized the ecstatic character of Shaker worship. Stephen Stein observes: "The need for union and order led him to curb the spontaneous movement of the spirit in the meetings."[35] He regularized both the time and structure of worship. Under Meacham's direction "solemn songs" replaced ecstatic utterances and "laboring" or ritualized dances replaced trancing, whirling, and shaking. Collective expressions of worship supplanted individualized and Spirit-filled communications.

Perhaps it was the routinization of ecstatic movements that led to the "spiritual torpor" that had crept into Shaker worship in the early decades of the nineteenth century. Giles Avery registered his dissatisfaction. Writing from the hub of the Shaker cosmos in 1835, two years before the manifestations, he observed: "We have meeting at home among ourselves and it is so dull that one would scarcely know whether we were trying to serve God or something else."[36] Worship had fallen into a wooden routine.

Gone were creative leaders like Father Joseph Meacham and Mother Lucy Wright, who might have addressed such ritual monotony with fresh energy. Indeed, one historian remarks that "[t]he quality of leadership . . . had declined noticeably."[37] In the place of strong and able leaders, villages were filling up instead with a growing proportion of children and young people.

> Children and youths, often indentured or bound over by their parents or guardians, fled from the Believers with striking frequency. Family journals throughout the society record in astonishing detail the steady stream of youthful rebels who tried to escape the Shaker confines. Usually pursuit by the Believers followed their departure. Parents sometimes returned the runaways; others successfully eluded capture.[38]

The economic crisis of 1837 hit hard at the manufacturing economy of New York state and continued to erode the state's economy for several years.[39] Doubtless, the security and regulation of a Shaker village were attractive to families who could no longer support their own children.

Had the children been able to make choices for themselves, they might have chosen a less rigorous alternative to the Shaker ethos. Problems with youth fill Shaker journals and letters. Contemporary believer Isaac Youngs charged the youth with what he sensed was a growing spiritual decline in the society; it was direct consequence "of the ingathering of youth and children and those that had never known [Mother Ann] on earth, nor truly understood her gospel."[40] Letters like this and family journals explicitly expressed frustration with young people and implicitly revealed the dissatisfaction of the youth themselves. Disciplinary problems were rampant; runaways were all too common.

The United Society on the edge of the Era of Manifestations was highly complex, geographically extensive, and demographically diverse. If both gift and order were principles that governed the religious ethos of the society, as Stephen Stein suggests, this was a time when "gift" was clearly subordinate to order. It was a society that had grown from a sect into a highly structured organization characterized by patterns of domination and subordination so deeply etched into the common life as to be unquestionable. The Era of Manifestations was to unmask all these dynamics of power and both to configure and reconfigure, to reinforce and resist them.

ANALYSIS

RITUAL THEORY IN GENERAL

A cursory review of ritual theory reveals some interesting and common commitments about the dynamics of power in ritual. Peter L. Berger argues that the symbol systems embedded in ritual practice function as a "shield against terror."[41] David Kertzer elaborates on "terror" as fear of chaos and argues that it is through ritual actions that "we confront the experiential chaos that envelops us and create order."[42] In their attempt to liberate ritual from an almost exclusive association with magical and religious rites and examine its presence in secular ceremony, Barbara Myerhoff and Sally Falk Moore locate ritual in the ordering and structuring side of social life:

> Every ceremony is par excellence a dramatic statement against indeterminacy in some field of human affairs. Through order, formality, and repetition it seeks to state that the cosmos and social world, or some particular small part of them, are orderly and explicable and for the moment fixed. . . . Ritual is a declaration of form *against* indeterminacy."[43]

Victor Turner juxtaposes a structuring side of the social world with an antistructuring side, or communitas. He defines the pilgrimage on which ritual embarks as a journey from structure into communitas and back again:

> ... men are released from structure into communitas only to return to structure revitalized by their experience of communitas. What is certain is that no society can function adequately without this dialectic.[44]

Here is a universal, totalizing theory of ritual ("no society can function adequately without") with structure as its goal. Mary Collins expresses the same with lapidary simplicity: "ritual functions to master the chaotic and to disclose good order."[45]

The values in these explanatory universes are clear: unity, order, structure, purity, and indivisibility. Plurality, chaos, multivocality, and heterogeneity are either negative qualities or transitory, embraced for a time and then abandoned. Blatant is the assumption that ritual begins and ends in the landscape of structure, with a brief foray into chaos. But what if chaos, plurality, and polyphony could be entertained as values as well? What if ritual were seen both to present and to resolve chaos? What if ritual were to begin and end, not only in structure, but in indeterminacy as well? Perhaps ritualizations contain far more plurality, chaos, and even ambiguity than these thoughtful and above all orderly scholars can admit in their haste to participate in the rites of academic explanation.[46]

If these questions could be admitted into the discussion, then we might be able to acknowledge elements of resistance and subversion in ritualizations.[47] We might begin to understand that the explanation of ritual that emerges above masks the questions: *whose* idea of order? *whose* idea of structure? *whose* idea of unity? In his observation of and participation in rituals of healing in the Putumayo highlands of Colombia, anthropologist Michael Taussig argues against the orderly paradigms articulated above. Watching healing rituals among peasants whose lives begin and end in chaos, he suggests that the only hand of healing is "the left hand of anarchy"—certainly not *someone else's* idea of order.[48] Taussig challenges traditional theories of ritual and its universe of assumptions about ritual as ordering, conserving, or, at its most "wild," reordering. He invites an understanding of ritual that can also embrace chaos and resistance. He challenges ritual theorists to account for relations of power embedded in the social structures and the social beings in which various ritualizations are enacted and embodied.

Taussig's challenge has not gone unmet. In her impressive work on ritual, Catherine Bell suggests a broadly dialectical understanding of ritual: "Ritualization is a strategic play of power, of domination and resistance, within the arena of the social body."[49] Only such a broadly dialectical understanding of ritual and ritualizations will enable us to understand the ritual practices in the Shaker Era of Manifestations.

In part, what is going on is a confrontation between various kinds of power and authority, which are socially articulated by certain structural differences: adult-child, male-female, center-periphery, written-oral. We shall first examine the issues of power and authority, then investigate the ways in which these are articulated.[50]

Dominative power

The first kind of power is the power of domination or control, which assumes a relationship of superordination or subordination between two or more parties. Certainly, this is the power that evolved the United Society as it shifted from a persecuted sect into a millennial church, with a network of villages spread out from the institutional hub at New Lebanon. Third generation leader Joseph Meacham could see the need for the society to take on this kind of power more clearly than the founding mothers and fathers could. To that end, then, he organized the society, routinized its worship, and regulated its behavior.

This kind of power has usually been interpreted as oppressive, but it is also the power on which infants and young children depend, as they begin to grow into a new and uncharted world. For the Shakers, exercise of this kind of power was essential in both literal and metaphorical senses. Throughout its history the sect had taken in children and converts, people who were young both chronologically and religiously, given the values and practices of a Shaker ethos. Early on, the society had to attend to the education of its youth and the instruction of its converts. Again, part of Joseph Meacham's legacy was to focus particularly and in writing the issues of youth and converts.

Dominative power is the power exercised in institutions, which can at times constrain, but at other times organizes and orchestrates complex social arrangements. Given the diverse composition of a typical Shaker village, the unique Shaker choreography of work and worship proved equally foreign to everyone and thus was common ground for all. One family was in charge of new members and potential converts, much like the Gathering Family in Watervliet, in which the manifestations started. Other families managed temporal affairs and economic interface with the world. Still other families claimed pastoral ministry as their domain of expertise. In addition, chores involved everyone in an intricate division of labor that rotated believers from kitchen to dyehouse to garden or from tanning shop to the smithy to the fields according to their skills and interest.

This first form of power claims its authority externally, publicly, and institutionally. Leaders exercising the power of domination are often publicly appointed or elected, ruling with consent or, failing that, coercion of the governed. Governance was one of the first issues that Joseph Meacham tackled. He made New Lebanon the institutional center of the society, and he ensured an orderly succession of leaders for the Central Ministry, securing the public authority of that body for future generations.

This first form of power figures critically into the Era of Manifestations. Early on, the Central Ministry at New Lebanon was informed of the revelations at Watervliet; early on, Elder Rufus Bishop, one of four members of the Central Ministry team, visited Watervliet in person to witness firsthand what was going on. As noted, his official word was one of approval; privately, however, he had his doubts. The Central Ministry attempted to regulate the manifestations, urging elders and eldresses at various villages to ascertain whether or not the visions were authentic—and implicitly investing them with the authority to do so. The "pre-eminent mediums" were usually not the children who'd been the initial instruments. Rather, the spiritual elite was more often composed of elders and eldresses who could buttress their institutional power with a charismatic patina. The Central Ministry further decided when meetings were to be open or closed to the public, an ambiguous decision that may have been a plea for privacy, but may equally have been an attempt to starve the fire of spiritual gifts by denying it outside oxygen.

Finally, the Central Ministry prescribed ritualizations for all Shaker villages a few years into the Era of Manifestations. The supernatural origin of the various ritualizations is less an issue than their possible effect. In a stylized procession through every room of every building in a Shaker village, the Midnight Cry and the Sweeping Gift placed and kept under surveillance Shaker bodies and Shaker buildings. Dirt, slovenliness, and sloth—anathema in the Shaker ethos and a distinct problem in the period directly preceding the Era of Manifestations—were immediately apparent to the entire community, subject simultaneously to public view and communal censure. The Sweeping Gift was not at all subtle about its intentions: following on the heels of the instruments who swept with spiritual brooms were rank-and-file believers who were to continue the labor with real brooms and real brushes. The Mountain Feasts in effect moved the space for spiritual gifts outside the villages where there was work to be done and up to a place apart. The Feasts also restricted the time for ecstatic worship to one or two days per year, rather than allowing the spirit to blow where it would through every Shaker meeting. Finally, the Feasts opened ecstatic revelations to all believers, each of whom received spiritual gifts, wore spiritual spectacles, put on spiritual clothing, and ate spiritual food. By spreading these gifts out among all believers, the Feasts deemphasized the power of individual instruments. Thus, dominative power circulated in and throughout the Era of Manifestations, striving to check the visions and contain the mysteries.

Charismatic power

A second form of power is charismatic power, the power of a prophet, a popular leader, or an instrument.[51] This power often operates outside institutional structures and sanctions. It is the power that was edited out of the emerging institutions in the early Christian church, as evidenced in the various warnings against "false prophets" and "wandering teachers." It is the power of all those who "dream dreams" and "see visions" (Joel 2:28), necessitating close institutional surveillance in the form of spiritual directors, delegated to discern whence the mysteries come.

But lest this power be too quickly adopted as antidote to the coercive potential embedded in dominative power, it must be acknowledged that charismatic power too has the potential to enslave. Its unique form of oppression is *im*pression in the guise of devotees who turn their wills and their bodies over to hypnotic and mesmerizing fanatics.[52] Moreover, charismatic power is inherently unstable, often waning in those who possess it or disappearing after their deaths.[53]

Throughout the history of institutions dominative power has existed in an uneasy equilibrium with the personal magnetism of charismatic leaders. The political articulations of each form of power operate to subvert the other. This story is only repeated in the annals of Shaker history. The sect organized around Ann Lee, a charismatic figure—her person, her example, her visions of the spiritual world, and her sayings. For a poor and probably illiterate woman in religious and cultural institutions that were dominated by wealth, literacy, and men, all routes to institutional power were blocked. Lee exercised the only kind of power available to her: a power that depended neither on institutional authorization nor on external backing. She appealed to people who faced similar obstacles to institutional power. The charismatic power of Ann Lee and her other followers carried the Shaking Quakers across the Atlantic and into a settled existence along the Hudson at Watervliet.

With the death of the founders, however, came what sociologist Max Weber refers to as the routinization of charisma: the institutionalization of the society, the regulation of behavior, and the routinization of worship. Interestingly, the figure who almost singlehandedly accomplished this, Joseph Meacham, was possessed of a great deal of charismatic authority himself. But he also had an administrative genius that turned itself to the organization of the society through writing. The inbreaking of the Era of Manifestations was a second eruption of charismatic power into an institution that had routinized it.

The authority of charismatic power, unlike dominative power, is internal, generated by the personal magnetism of an instrument. The testimony and trancing of young girls at Watervliet alone established their authority. Later, the visions would pass on to those who had institutional authority as well: adults, elders, and eldresses in the village. Their combination of institutional authority and the privileges of age and gender would override the raw charismatic power of the earliest instruments. Interestingly, the figure named as the "pre-eminent medium" of the society was a man, Philemon Stewart, whose pre-eminence was further manifested in a publication, a written translation of kinesthetic, visual, and oral testimonies.[54]

Often the charismatic authority of an instrument was buttressed by the acknowledged source of the gifts. The trajectory of the Era of Manifestations reveals an escalation in the claimed sources of visions. The earliest mediums mentioned angels and departed spirits. Gradually, founding mothers and fathers appeared as sources: Father James Whittaker, Father Joseph Meacham, Mother Lucy Wright. Eventually, Mother Ann Lee would make her appearance. Ultimately, Holy Mother Wisdom entered the scene, a visitor to all the villages announced by the Central Ministry.[55] Indeed, a secret and closed meeting between Holy Mother Wisdom and the leaders of the Central Ministry at New Lebanon issued in prescribed ritualizations for all of Shakerdom: the Midnight Cry, the Sweeping Gift, and the Mountain Feasts.

Thus, charismatic power and its internal authority, backed supernatural sources, figured importantly in the Era of Manifestations, operating in direct tension with the dominative power of the Central Ministry. The tension expressed itself in the form of structural dichotomies that were unmasked in the Era of Manifestations. These dichotomies were both resisted and reproduced in the trajectory of the revival. These tensions run throughout the description and the analysis above. They are important to name, and they merit discussion: adult/child, male/female, center/periphery, and written/oral.

Adult/Child. As we have noted, Shaker journals and letters before and during the Era of Manifestations are replete with problems concerning children and youth. They were a problem for the society, and the frequency of runaways suggests that the society was a problem for the children.[56] The ecstatic ritualizations initiated by children at Watervliet exposed and resisted the domination of children by adults, elders, and eldresses in the society. For a brief time, children were revered for their visions and respected as chosen mediators of spiritual wisdom.[57] Quickly, however, the traditional patterns of domination ritually reasserted themselves. Elders and eldresses gained the right to adjudicate among authentic and inauthentic visions. Gradually, these leaders began to have visions themselves, and their visions were judged to be more credible than those of the youthful believers. As has been shown, the "pre-eminent mediums" were all adults. Ritual bodies shifted during the Era of Manifestations first to invert the dominance of adults over children, then to reestablish it.

Male/Female. A society that boasted equality between the sexes had increasingly alienated women from positions of power in its concern to present itself theologically and in writing to an outside world. The Era of Manifestations was in part a reassertion of a charismatic power that had initially resided in a female founding figure: Mother Ann Lee. Suddenly, girls and women were seized by the spirit and filled with gifts.[58] In time, however, men began to manifest spiritual gifts, and their charismatic power combined with a privilege of gender to elevate them in status as instruments. Finally, the revelations of a pre-eminent medium, Philemon Stewart, were published, a written and authoritative translation of the manifestations for public dissemination. Female ritual leaders in the Era of Manifestations initially challenged a male-dominated spiritual elite. Eventually, however, men too became ecstatic ritual leaders, and their visions restored men to their previous dominance.

Center/Periphery. The institutional hub of American Shakerism was the village of New Lebanon, where the Central Ministry resided. The center of Shaker operations moved there with the accession of Joseph Meacham to power, and there it remained into the twentieth century. But if New Lebanon was the brains and central nervous system of the

United Society, Watervliet was its heart. Here was where the exiled band of Shaking Quakers had settled and where Mother Ann Lee had lived and died. Significantly, the Era of Manifestations began, not at the institutional core of the Shaker cosmos, but at its spiritual heart. For a time, all believers watched with fascination and awe the events at Watervliet. In time, however, New Lebanon asserted its institutional authority, visiting Watervliet, authorizing the visions, and reporting on the revival to the rest of the Shaker world. Some four years into the revival, the Central Ministry announced a visit of Holy Mother Wisdom, but she visited first not Watervliet, but New Lebanon. The ritual center of the Era of Manifestations shifted to resist and then to reproduce relationships of power in the society.

Written/Oral.   Shakerism had initially evolved out of a tradition of ecstatic movement and spoken words. But as the society settled and expanded, as the era of the founding mothers and fathers faded into memory, writing became more and more important both internally and in the society's interactions with the world.[59] Writing captured the regulations and rules that an increasingly complex social organization needed, and writing offered explanation and rationale of the society's beliefs and behavior to an always curious and often suspicious public. The Era of Manifestations was a reassertion of the importance of ecstatic experience and oral testimony.[60] Gradually, however, the authoritative versions of the experiences and the testimonies were written down, and the dominance of the written ritual text reasserted itself over ritual practices.

CONCLUSION

The Shaker Era of Manifestations offers a fascinating study in various forms of ritual power and authority and kinds of ritualizations that attend each. At base is a clash between dominative power and charismatic power, each with its unique articulation in ritualizations. The initial ritualizations were a return to the formative period of Shaker history, a time when chaos was ritually courted in the form of ecstatic movements. These ritualizations, unruly, unpredictable, seemingly uncontainable, resisted the woodenness of Shaker worship at the time. But they also unmasked and inverted relationships of power within the society. Young women from the Gathering Family at Watervliet started having visions and seizures. Therein lie the inversions of age, gender, location, and genre at the base of these ecstatic ritualizations.

Almost as soon as these dynamics of power were revealed, they were redressed with counter-ritualizations prescribed by the Central Ministry for all Shaker villages. Rites like the Midnight Cry, the Sweeping Gift, and the Mountain Feast gradually routinized the spiritual manifestations and returned relationships between adults and children, men and women, the center at New Lebanon and outlying Shaker communities, and the tension between written and oral testimonies back to an established order. It was a period of "whirlwind, earthquake, and fire," as a contemporary Shaker observed.[61] But forever the question would remain: whose definitions of natural disaster were descriptively operative?

NOTES

1. Priscilla J. Brewer, *Shaker Communities, Shaker Lives* (Hanover, NH: University of New England Press, 1986), p. 115.

2. Stephen J. Stein, *The Shaker Experience in America* (New Haven: Yale University Press, 1992) and Priscilla J. Brewer, *Shaker Communities, Shaker Lives*. See also, Edward Deming Andrews, *The People Called Shakers* (Oxford: Oxford University Press, 1953); Henri Desroche, *The American Shakers: From Neo-Christianity to Presocialism* (Amherst, MA: University of Massachusetts Press, 1971); Edward Horgan, *The Shaker Holy Land: A Community Portrait* (Harvard, MA: Harvard Common Press, 1982); Flo Morse, *The Shakers and the World's People* (New York: Dodd, Mead & Co., 1980); Marjorie Procter-Smith, *Women in Shaker Community and Worship* (Lewiston, New York: The Edwin Mellen Press, 1985); Diane Sasson, *The Shaker Spiritual Narrative* (Knoxville, TN: University of Tennessee Press, 1983); John M. Whitworth, *God's Blueprints: A Sociological Study of Three Utopian Sects* (London: Routledge & Kegan Paul, 1975).

3. Quoted in Stein, p. xiii.

4. See Clare B. Fischer's article in this volume, "Power in the Palace," for very different ritualizations of power and authority. Benedict R. O'G. Anderson has articulated persuasively the differences between Western understandings of power, which this essay presupposes, and Javanese understandings of power, which Fischer's ethnography describes. See the essay "The Idea of Power in Javanese Culture" in Anderson's book *Language and Power: Exploring Political Cultures in Indonesia* (Ithaca, NY: Cornell University Press, 1990), p. 22ff.

5. Quoted in Stein, p. 168.

6. Whitworth, p. 51–52.

7. For more information on the organization of Shaker communities and their governance, see Stein, pp. 133–134, and Edward Deming Andrews and Faith Andrews, *Work and Worship: The Economic Order of the Shakers* (Greenwich, CT: New York Graphic Society, 1974), pp. 25–28.

8. Quoted in Brewer, p. 116.

9. Stein, p. 169.

10. Quoted in Stein, p. 169.

11. Quoted in Brewer, p. 116.

12. Whitworth, p. 50. His comment is telling: did the Central Ministry approve the visions shortly after their inception? or only shortly after the visions spread from the children to more credible adolescents and adults? Whether intentionally or not, Whitworth raises the question of the relative status of children, adolescents, and adults in the society.

13. The prominence of the founding mothers and fathers in these visions invites comparisons to the particular significance of ancestors in The Dreaming, described in John Hilary Martin's article in this volume, "Bringing the Power of the Past into the Present: Murrinh-patha Ritual."

14. See Whitworth's description of Stewart's visions, p. 51.

15. Stein, p. 174.

16. Brewer, p. 125.

17. Mother Lucy Wright, from the third generation of Shaker leaders, most often appeared with these sorts of scoldings. See Brewer, pp. 120–121.

18. Quoted in Brewer, pp. 126, 128.

19. Whitworth, p. 51.

20. Stein, p. 174–175.

21. Quoted in E. Andrews, p. 161.

22. The inscription on the "fountain" at Hancock reads:

> Written and placed here
> By the command of our Lord and Saviour Jesus Christ
> The Lord's Stone.
> Erected upon this Mt. Sinai, May 4th, 1843.
> The Word of the Lord
> Here is my Holy Fountain,
> Which I have placed here.
> For the healing of the Nations, who shall here seek my favor.

23. Quoted in Brewer, p. 126.

24. Ibid., p. 131.

25. Some of these early publications include: Joseph Meacham, *Concise Statement of the Principles of the Only True Church* (1790); Richard McNemar, *Kentucky Revival* (1807); Benjamin S. Youngs, *Testimony of Christ's Second Appearing* (1808); Rufus Bishop and Seth Y. Wells (eds.), *Testimonies of the Life, Character, Revelations and Doctrines of Our Ever Blessed Mother Ann Lee* (1816); John Dunlavy, *Manifesto* (1823), and Calvin Green and Seth Y. Wells, *Summary View of the Millennial Church* (1823). Note that the book *Testimonies* on the life and sayings of Ann Lee was published 32 years after Ann Lee died in 1784.

26. Stein reviews the creation of Shaker history and the spinning of a unique "myth of origins" in detail, pp. 66–87.

27. Quoted in Edward Deming Andrews' *The People Called Shakers: A Search for the Perfect Society*, p. 6.

28. Marjorie Procter-Smith suggests that at least part of the novelty involved in the transition from Lee to Meacham is that the sect was finally released from a liability: the suspicion attending the female leadership of Lee herself. "For a struggling young religious group, attempting to win converts away from larger, more established groups, having a woman as founder and leader must have been a liability. Attempts to downplay Lee's leadership . . ., absence of mention of Lee in the group's first publication, and the increasing prominence of the male 'Elders' on public occasions can be seen as attempts by the community to make itself more respectable and acceptable to the world's people." (Procter-Smith, pp. 24–25.)

29. Commenting on the *Concise Statement*, Stephen Stein writes: "Notably absent from the tract are any mention by name of Ann Lee or the Shakers and any explicit reference to the practice of celibacy or communal living. Meacham may have downplayed these elements in his public statement for strategic reasons. It is also possible that these concerns had not yet become definitive elements within the Shaker gospel." Stein, p. 47.

30. Stein, p. 76.

31. Ibid., p. 118.

32. Whitworth, p. 15.

33. For more on the nature of charismatic authority, see Max Weber, "The Sociology of Charismatic Authority," and "The Social Psychology of the World Religions," in H. H. Gerth and C. Wright Mills, eds., *From Max Weber: Essays in Sociology* (New York: Oxford University Press, 1958), esp. pp. 245–252, 297. For a critique and expansion of Weber's notion of charismatic authority, see Dorothy

Emmet, *Function, Purpose and Powers: Some Concepts in the Study of Individuals and Societies* (Philadelphia: Temple University Press, 1972), pp. 206–238. For a simplification of Weber's notion of charismatic authority and a cultural anthropological perspective to complement his sociological and psychological perspectives, see Benedict R. O'G. Anderson, *Language and Power: Exploring Political Cultures in Indonesia*, p. 74ff.

34. Stein, p. 125.

35. Ibid., p. 47.

36. Quoted in Brewer, p. 115.

37. Brewer, p. 115.

38. Stein, p. 162.

39. Whitworth addresses this economic crisis, but focuses on its religious aspects: nativism, anti-Catholicism, a general pessimism in reform, and a resurgence of millennial prophecies. See Whitworth, p. 51. He does not speculate about the effect the economic situation must have had on the demographics of a Shaker village.

40. Quoted in Brewer, p. 115.

41. Peter L. Berger, *The Sacred Canopy: Elements of a Sociological Theory of Religion* (New York: Doubleday, 1967), p. 22.

42. David I. Kertzer, *Ritual, Politics, and Power* (New Haven, CT: Yale University Press, 1988), p. 22.

43. Sally Falk Moore and Barbara G. Myerhoff, eds., *Secular Ritual* (Amsterdam: Van Gorcum, 1977), p. 17. Emphasis theirs.

44. Victor W. Turner, *The Ritual Process: Structure and Anti-Structure* (Chicago: Aldine Publishing Company, 1969), p. 129. Gender-exclusive language his.

45. Mary Collins, *Worship: Renewal to Practice* (Washington, DC: The Pastoral Press, 1987), p. 171.

46. James E. Gibson distinguishes "tame" and "wild" theories of ritual, drawing on Nietzsche's opposition of the Apollonian and the Dionysian in his article "Celebration and Transgression: Nietzsche on Ritual," *Journal of Ritual Studies* 5:2 (Summer 1991), pp. 1–13. In a different vein, Michael Aune, in his article in this volume, "The Subject of Ritual," challenges the assumption of traditional ritual theories that rituals are about "resolving contradictions, disguising conflicts, or changing people and things." Whereas the point of my essay is to show ritualizations that *state* contradictions and unmask conflict, Aune is concerned with "changing people and things." Countering what he considers to be a romantic claim that ritual transforms people and things, Aune argues for a more modest effect that enables people to reconfigure and reinterpret their world more constructively.

47. Kertzer's judgment that ritual has a "creative potential" but a decidedly "conservative bias" has less to do with actual practices of rituals than with the fact that Kertzer, in observing them always expects to find order and, if not consensus, then at least solidarity (Kertzer, p. 12).

48. Taussig writes that "the yage nights pose awkwardness of fit, breaking-up and scrambling, the allegorical rather than the symbolist mode, the predominance of the left hand of anarchy—as in Artaud's notion of theater of cruelty with its poetic language of the senses, language that breaks open the conventions of language and the signifying function of signs through its chaotic mingling of danger and humor, 'liberating signs,' Artaud said, in a disorder that brings us ever closer to chaos." Michael Taussig, *Shamanism, Colonialism, and the Wild Man: A Study in Terror and Healing* (Chicago: The University of Chicago Press, 1987), p. 442.

49. Catherine Bell, *Ritual Theory, Ritual Practice* (New York: Oxford University Press, 1992), p. 204. See also pp. 83–88 and her article "The Ritual Body and the Dynamics of Ritual Power," *Journal of Ritual Studies* 4:2 (Summer 1990), pp. 310–311. Bell has been criticized for her lack of attention to actual ritualizations. In fact, she is doing an ethnography of the academy, examining the ritualizations of scholarly explanation, its presuppositions and its silences. As an anthropology of the academy, the book is both provocative and insightful.

50. For further development of these various kinds of power and authority—dominative power, charismatic power, and a third form of power not here named (coactive power, see my *PastorPower* (Nashville, TN: Abingdon Press, 1993), and "'By the laying on of hands and by prayer': An Analysis of Power in the Rite of Ordination," *Consensus* 20:1 (1994), pp. 9–28. The typology is derived from Starhawk, *Truth or Dare: Encounters with Power, Authority, and Mystery* (San Francisco: Harper & Row, 1987), pp. 9ff. Yet Starhawk follows the lead of many feminists, dismissing dominative power as always coercive and embracing uncritically charismatic and coactive power as liberatory. She ignores the potential positive uses of dominative power, as well as the ambient dangers lurking in charismatic and coactive power. Discussion with Clare Fischer, however, suggests to me that these various kinds of power and authority are distinctively Western—and may not be applicable across cultural boundaries. See her article in this volume, "Power in the Palace." Again, Benedict Anderson distinguishes between Western and Javanese understandings of power in his essay "The Idea of Power in Javanese Culture," *Language and Power*, p. 19ff.

51. See Benedict Anderson's qualification of charismatic power, as he shifts from Weber's sociological and psychological focus on charisma to his perspective informed by cultural anthropology: ". . . it is less a real quality of the leader than a quality attributed to him by his followers." "The Idea of Power in Javanese Culture," p. 74. Gender-exclusive language Anderson's.

52. See Dorothy Emmet's discussion of hypnotic charismatic leadership, pp. 233–238.

53. On this point, see Max Weber, "The Sociology of Charismatic Authority," in H. H. Gerth and C. Wright Mills, eds., pp. 248–250. See also Anderson's challenge to the instability Weber perceived in this form of power. In Javanese society, Anderson finds charismatic power "not a temporary phenomenon of crisis, but the permanent, routine, organizing principle of the state." *Language, Power*, p. 76. "The Idea of Power,"

54. This is John Whitworth's designation, p. 51.

55. Again, compare this to the ritualizations surrounding ancestors in John Hilary Martin's essay in this volume.

56. Joseph Driskill's article in this volume, "The Significance of Ritual in the Case of Joanne," raises some fascinating questions in view of this documented tension between adults and children in the society. Were these ritualizations registering such tensions? To what kinds of situations did these ritualizations react?

57. Again, the predominance in these early visions of the founding mothers and fathers constituted a remembering that threatened to be a re-membering of the community: a return to ecstatic worship, an acknowledgment of the gifts and powers of women and youth, a revaluation of orality and spontaneity. Perhaps these early visions had the potential to preenact a new kind of community—which is precisely why they were stifled. On memory as re-membering and the mimetic qualities of ritual, see Richard Payne's article in this volume, "Realizing Inherent Enlightenment: Ritual and Self-Transformation in Shingon Buddhism."

58. For a fascinating study on trancing and possession among women whose status is changing, see Aihwa Ong's *Spirits of Resistance and Capitalist Discipline: Factory Women in Malaysia* (Albany, NY: State University of New York Press, 1987).

59. The significance of score and story line are critical, as John Hilary Martin has noted in his article in this volume, "Bringing the Power of the Past into the Present: Murrinh-patha Ritual." At issue here is whether the score and story lines were scripted or not, whether they were written down, transmitted orally, or utterly spontaneous.

60. Volney Gay, in his article in this volume, "Ritual and Psychotherapy," compares ritual and personal uses of altered states of consciousness (ASC). Two elements that both uses share are prominent here: the space ASC creates to express wishes and recount facts—in this situation, tensions—that are officially denied; and the resistance ASC presents to official powers who would wish to deny such tensions.

61. Cited in Brewer, p. 115.

Part II

Liturgical Explorations

Introductory Essay

MICHAEL B. AUNE

The two following essays are explorations of particular rituals or ritualized activities in several Christian traditions. They are situated within a disciplinary configuration known as "liturgical studies." Originating as a modern discipline in the mid-nineteenth century among Jewish and Christian scholars, its primary object of study has been the texts or literary remains of the activity called "worship." Texts are investigated, critical editions of those texts are published, and interpretations of these materials are offered that claim to uncover their import and power for the communities who used them.

Although the study of texts has continued to be significant, the discipline, in recent years, has also moved beyond them in order to understand more fully the wider historical and cultural contexts in which liturgical practices take place. This move "beyond the text" to the people who use it has brought liturgical studies into the

> borderlands between theology and some of its neighboring human disciplines, such as the sociology of knowledge, the philosophy of language, the anthropology of ritual, the psychology of belief, and the theory of action.[1]

The expanding or revamping of liturgical scholarship has been rooted in the realization that what it has been studying is not what people are doing in church or synagogue. Our focus on texts and their messages has neglected the human activity of worship. What needs to be uncovered and explored, however, is lived liturgical practice, what Lawrence A. Hoffman calls "the liturgical field."[2] This is "the holistic network of interrelationships that bind together discrete things, acts, people, and events into the activity we call worship—or better still, ritual."[3]

The authors of the essays in this section, Aune and Slough, have moved "beyond the text" in several ways. In doing so, we have encountered a whole new set of issues about the ways liturgies and ritual events work. The move to the communities who live beyond the texts—a community of Norwegian immigrants living on the Dakota prairie over a century ago and participants in hymn-singing events— brings into focus the meanings and ritualized patterns that make the worshipers' or participants' worlds uniquely their own.[4] We find expressions of unfolding self-identity in ritual and effects of ritualization on those taking part—especially their experience and how it is created within a specific religious context.

As we explored ritual practices in specific communities, we found that the initial organizing theme of our project—"ritual as mediator of memory and meaning"—was both hindrance and help. We came to share an uneasiness with what one writer has called "meaning madness" or the "meanings-under-every-rock" approach and analysis associated with certain kinds of ritual study, including liturgical study.[5] We sensed that something salient would be missing if we did not try to understand the experience of ritual participants—its power and significance.

For example, Rebecca Slough found that "memory and meaning-making" were not always satisfying ways to orient and to interpret ritual experience. Although participants in hymn-singing events reported that such an experience was "significant" and even "meaningful," they were certainly not engaged in deciphering social-religious messages inscribed in hymn texts. Rather, what was significant about these events was that in the experience of singing, participants "knew" or "came to know" something—what unity in a community was like, what a sense of transcendence might be. These noetic aspects of hymn-singing events, according to Slough, seemed to be a more suitable way for both singers and leaders of these events to speak of and to interpret what was occurring.

Michael B. Aune found the themes of memory and meaning to be a bit more workable, provided they were given a more subjective, affective nuance. In particular, in struggling with how to understand what constitutes effective ritual from a participant's viewpoint, Aune discovered that its power and significance involved much more than interpretations of theological claims, labels, and intentions. Rather, as an instance of what he termed "ideology and experience in action," he found that the human subject of religious ritual—at least in the tradition he was exploring—sought a practical reinterpretation of the world that could provide a sense of what was involved in being a particular kind of person. Interest in the subjective experience of ritual participation surfaced issues of "meaning-creation." But the meanings that were created were not those of doctrines and ideas so much as they were values, feelings, perceptions, and relationships. In short, a subject of ritual is about the task of "making sense," of deploying, so to speak, a lived, practical consciousness.

These "liturgical explorations"—some implicitly, others more explicitly—provide a point of entry into the area "lived experience" ("meaning" or "a way of knowing") that has been shaped and reshaped by what can be called an "ideology" or "collective memory." Both refer to those historically conditioned procedures and categories by which a person organizes experience and constructs meanings. And "meanings," as some cultural theorists would assert, have less to do with encoded messages that "stand for something" that is somewhere else and more to do with

> the activity of composing and being composed by the connections among things. To have meaning in one's life is to recognize pattern in the disparate elements of existence, to seek order, significance, and wholeness. Meaning is anchored in trust and is the ground of hope. Without it, human beings cannot survive. In its most comprehensive dimensions, this meaning-making activity is the activity of faith, carried out in a dialectic between fear and trust, hope and hopelessness, alienation and belonging. . . .

> We are personally engaged in this meaning-making, symbolizing, faith activity, *yet ultimately we cannot do it alone; it is a profoundly relational activity.*[6]

Traditionally, however, liturgical and ritual scholarship has been weak, vague, or nonexistent when it comes to these experiential, noetic, and affective dimensions of participation in this manner of acting and speaking. In fact, scholars have often declared these dimensions as simply off limits because they are both ineffable and inaccessible.[7] Add to this our own convictions and concepts of experience as individualistic, subjective, personal, and esoteric, and we continue to have that "enormous barrier to an understanding of the subject [of ritual]."[8]

Yet the chastening events of this twentieth century have challenged, questioned, and criticized many of our cherished assumptions about the unity and autonomy of the individual and the ideals of self-expression and subjectivity. In the wake of such severe criticism, however, contemporary thought and research have sought to develop new ways of thinking and, in doing so, have clarified, elaborated, if not reconceptualized, just what it is we mean by "experience" or "subjectivity."[9]

Along with the difficulties, challenges, and criticisms noted above, there has been also an increasing weariness and dissatisfaction in both the humanities and social sciences with fragmented, unreal, and detached analyses of social, personal, and cultural realities that are removed considerably from those whose "realities" they are. As a result, scholarly efforts have begun to come to terms with how it is that human beings perceive their world and the events of their lives in ways that make some sense to them.

Another way to state this kind of sensibility is that it seeks to understand the affective, felt quality of human existence. It embodies—or better, persons embody and interweave—feeling and thought so tightly as to make them indistinguishable. Those of us who seek to understand just what it is that people experience when they engage in ritual or in worship should realize, then, that their (and our) own sensibility is shaped by intellectual, social, psychological, and aesthetic structures and dynamics.

What these two essays contribute to the larger contemporary discussion of the nature and force of ritual is most likely different when compared to former ways of thinking about this way of acting and speaking. Whereas ritual, by certain definitions, is and may be (in certain phenomenological sense) "a nonordinary sort of activity,"[10] nevertheless certain understandings are facilitated through participation in it and bear a problematic relationship to the ordinariness of everyday life.

The way in which mystifying and romanticizing approaches to ritual, past and present, address this problematic relationship is to claim for ritual the capacity and the necessity "to transform the inconsequential banality of ordinary life."[11] We found in our explorations, however, that it was precisely the affirmation of ordinary life that was at issue.

At times, we discovered an altering of imagination and insight, belief and emotion "at a single stroke," as Susanne Langer once emphasized.[12] Or there was a rearranging or confirming of visions of life for individuals or groups in which ritual participants felt "incorporated, empowered, activated, euphoric"[13] and better situated in "quality space," that sensation of wholeness, belonging, identity, and relationship that characterizes meaningful cultural experience.[14]

Our thinking about and interpreting how it is that rituals do certain noetic and affective things necessitated an important shift away from an assumption that the fundamental task of ritual is to "resolve" basic conflicts or contradictions that have emerged in personal/social life such as those which exist between religious belief and the real world.[15] We sensed that if rituals actually "worked" in this fashion, that is, as solving or resolving contradictions and conflicts between religious belief and the real world, those who participated in them would handle their problems with great aplomb or be healed of whatever it is that ails and afflicts them.[16] Thus, we found Catherine Bell's recent proposal of proceeding with a radically different assumption about what the central dynamic of ritual is to be very useful for our explorations.[17] That is, we assumed instead that rituals do not address nor purport to resolve "fundamental contradictions" or "conflicts" at all, because they are rather practical activities in which people participate in order to deal practically—both noetically and affectively—with their specific circumstances.

Although "resolution" of these circumstances may be implied in a ritual, we had a sense that it was more nearly accurate to say that this way of acting and speaking provides a way to know the world and to act on and in such a world. And the manner in which one comes to know this is through an emotional experience of insight and connectedness to others and to the world. Both essayists found these noetic and affective dynamics to afford a certain sense of identity and to enable ritual participants to have some sense of reality by virtue of which they can live in communication and relationship with others.[18]

It is significant, if not provocative, we think, that our respective essays connect with some current culture writing and theorizing as well as some contemporary philosophical discussions of identity and selfhood. Stephen A. Tyler has written recently, for example, that a postmodern ethnography

> does not move toward abstraction, away from life, but back to experience. It aims not to foster the growth of knowledge but to restructure experience, not to understand objective reality, for that is already established by common sense, nor to explain how we understand, for that is impossible, but to reassimilate, to reintegrate the self in society and to restructure the conduct of everyday life.[19]

Although rituals, liturgical expressions, and congregational hymn-singing events may not always do or perform what is ideologically or theologically claimed for them, nevertheless they still do things for those who participate. But it is time to have the two essayists speak for themselves.

NOTES

1. Geoffrey Wainwright, "A Language in Which We Speak to God," *Worship* 57 (1983), p. 309; cited in Lawrence A. Hoffman, *Beyond the Text: A Holistic Approach to Liturgy* (Bloomington, IN: Indiana University Press, 1987), p. 2. The title of Hoffman's book sums up well the sort of interest and style of inquiry than animate much contemporary liturgical study.

2. *Beyond the Text*, p. 173.

3. Ibid.

4. Ibid., p. 182.

5. Ivan Strenski, "What's Rite? Evolution, Exchange and the Big Picture," *Religion* 21 (1991), p. 221.

6. Sharon Daloz Parks, "Communication, Ritual as," *The New Dictionary of Sacramental Worship*, ed. Peter E. Fink, S.J. (Collegeville, MN: The Liturgical Press, 1991), p. 236. My emphasis.

7. E.g., Barbara Myerhoff noted how this was the case in certain anthroppligical studies of ritual. See "The Transformation of Consciousness in Ritual Performances: Some Thoughts and Questions," *By Means of Performance: Intercultural Studies of Theatre and Ritual*, ed. Richard Schechner and Willa Appel (Cambridge: Cambridge University Press, 1990), p. 245.

8. Barbara Myerhoff, Linda Camino, and Edith Turner, "Rites of Passage: An Overview," *Encyclopedia of Religion*, ed Mircea Eliade et al., vol. 12 (New York: Macmillan and Co., 1987), p. 383.

9. E.g., *Reconstructing Individualism: Autonomy, Individuality, and the Self in Western Thought*, ed. Thimas C. Heller, Morton Sosna, and David E. Wellbery with Arnold I. Davidson, Ann Swidler, and Ian Watt (Stanford, CA: Stanford University Press, 1986); Charles Taylor, *Sources of the Self: The Making of the Modern Identity* (Cambridge: Harvard University Press, 1989). The emphasis is placed on human sociability, relatedness, and interaction with others, with a culture, with a tradition.

10. Michelle Z. Rosaldo, *Knowledge and Passion: Ilongot Notions of Self and Social Life*,Cambridge Studies in Cultural Systems (Cambridge: Cambridge University Press, 1980), p. 61.

11. Evan Zuesse, "Ritual," *Encyclopedia of Religion*, ed. Mircea Eliade, vol. 12 (New York: Macmillan, 1987), p. 405.

12. *Philosophy in a New Key* (Cambridge: Harvard University Press, 1942); cited in Barbara Myerhoff, "The Transformation of Consciousness in Ritual Performances: Some Thoughts and Questions," p. 246.

13. James W. Fernandez, *Persuasions and Performances: The Play of Tropes in Culture* (Bloomington, IN: Indiana University Press, 1986), p. 23.

14. Ibid., pp. 39–43.

15. See Catherine Bell, *Ritual Theory, Ritual Practice* (Oxford: Oxford University Press. 1992), pp. 35–37.

16. See F. Allan Hanson, "The Semiotics of Ritual," *Semiotica* 33, 1/2 (1981), pp. 169–178.

17. *Ritual Theory, Ritual Practice*, pp. 35–37, 69–117.

18. Ibid.

19. *The Unspeakable: Discourse, Dialogue, and Rhetoric in the Postmodern World.* [The Rhetoric of the Human Sciences] (Madison, WI: University of Wisconsin Press, 1987), pp. 211–212.

5

The Subject of Ritual

Ideology and Experience in Action

MICHAEL B. AUNE

INTRODUCTION

An Experience of Religious Ritual

Sunday dawned and the immigrant families living on the prairie of eastern South Dakota gathered for worship in the sod hut of Per and Beret Hansa. Beret's immigrant trunk, draped with a white cloth, was their altar. A paten, a chalice, and two candlesticks rested upon it. A long, low bench, made up of several small benches, ran along in front of the improvised altar. All kinds of prairie wild flowers, either in bouquets of various sizes hanging under the ceiling or in glasses and bowls, adorned the sod hut. In this setting, the small community participated that day in the simplest of worship services: they heard the Scriptures read and preached, and ate and drank together in the Lord's Supper, and then went home.

In his sermon, the minister stated or claimed what was expected to happen that day: "Love itself, eternal and boundless, is present here. [God] is ready and willing to lighten your burdens, just as a mother cares for her nursing child. . . . Come and receive freely of the abundance of grace. Come and behold the glory of the Lord."[1]

Interpretations of what did happen diverged wildly. The minister was very gloomy about what had taken place. As he drove off in his cart, he thought, "Never before have I failed so miserably in any ser-

147

vice!"[2] The participants, however, reacted differently. One of them noted a few days later that he

> probably lacked a proper conception of the wonders the minister preached about; yet this he knew for certain, that nothing so glorious as that Communion service in Per Hansa's sod house had he ever before experienced and the happiness of that hour was still glowing with steady warmth in [his] heart.[3]

For yet another participant, her experience seemed to exemplify what anthropologist James W. Fernandez calls "the quality of cultural experience," where one is so situated as to have a sensation of wholeness and empowerment.[4] Her "heart [was] made strong by its nurturing connection with voices of the past that join the present in essential continuity."[5]

These scenes from Ole Rölvaag's classic novel, *Giants in the Earth*, offer something important to an understanding of the nature and power of religious ritual. One might ask, "How so?" There is little of the texture and detail normally associated with an ethnographic account of a ritual event. Nor is there any mention of text, rubric, and gesture. There is only a brief description of the setting, the participants, the major actions, and the impact of what occurred for those who were present.

Yet what was said, seen, and done exhibited many of the "qualities" that scholars often find in ritual.[6] In fact, Rölvaag's description is "dense" with them, as Ronald L. Grimes' outline makes clear[7]:

- performed, embodied, enacted, gestural (not merely thought or said)
- formalized, stylized
- repetitive, rhythmic
- collective, institutionalized, consensual (not personal or private)
- patterned, standardized, ordered
- traditional
- valued highly, deeply felt, sentiment-laden, meaningful, serious
- symbolic, referential
- religious
- functional

How I Became A Ritual Critic

As I have reflected on these scenes from *Giants in the Earth* over the years, as well as on my own location in this ethnic and religious tradition—Norwegian and Lutheran—that is enacted in ritual, I have been more concerned with this activity's intellectual markedness—its theological understandings of God, Christ, faith, church, grace, revelation, and the like—rather than with its emotional power. In my thinking and writing about ritual, I have sought to remain neutral, impartial, and objective. Emotion and subjectivity tended to unhinge me as an observer of, participant in, and interpreter of rites. I had been taught to regard such matters as vices to be avoided.

Yet I kept coming back to Rölvaag's description of a rite that eluded all intellectual markedness, interpretive categories, and standard ritual theories which generally assumed that this activity is about resolving contradictions, disguising conflicts, or changing people and things.[8] I had to acknowledge such matters, if only at first in hedged prose. I had to see, finally, that this description possessed a deep personal significance. With that insight, I began to realize that I wanted to say something that expressed my passionate interest and prior knowledge and experience.[9] In the words of political theorist Michael Walzer, I was approaching the role or stance of "a connected critic."[10] Or, as Ronald Grimes might have it, I was moving toward the posture of "a connected ritual critic."[11] But I did not quite know, as yet, how to be one.

Eventually, I realized that the divided voices in Rölvaag's account were each mine. The minister approached the Communion service by trying to analyze its effect in terms of the theological and intellectual truths he thought were to be clearly communicated and found it a failure. Participants approached the same service attentively and were powerfully moved. I was both of these people simultaneously: ashamed to be moved, yet terribly bored and somewhat suspicious of head trips. Was I finally becoming "a ritual critic"?

According to Ronald L. Grimes, a ritual critic is one who interprets a rite or a ritual system with a view to implicating its practice.[12] A ritual critic, so defined, can be both an involved participant and one who can also exercise distance and perspective. The criticism which she or he offers can be theoretical and interpretive as well as applied. In our current context, this critic may seek to change ritual experience, both what is experienced and how experience occurs. In turn, these changes might lead to a differently understood—if not constituted— self.[13]

From another point of view, namely that of liturgical studies, what I have wanted to present is "a poetics of religious ritual."[14] Such an undertaking involves an investigation of how prayers and/or texts produce or create "meaning" in a participant. I would continue to be interested in how this "meaning" is intellectually or theologically marked. But my attention was also now fastened on "meaning" as emotionally felt—an understanding of a particular way of being-in-the-world, "the self-interpretation of a subject."[15]

This Essay

These initial considerations provide both backdrop and point of entry for this essay in which I want to explore religious ritual's capacity to define and construct a human subject in relation to its world. Or, to use the splendidly simple expression of Howard Eilberg-Schwartz, I want to better understand how this activity we label "religious ritual" can be an interpretation of "what it means to be a particular kind of person."[16] To undertake such a task of exploration and understanding, I propose a return to the scenes from *Giants in the Earth* with which I began in order to ask what constituted effective ritual from a participant's viewpoint: this is the topic of Part I. In Part II I want to inquire whether a useful way to better understand such effectiveness is via an approach to ritual as a matter of "ideology and experience in action."[17]

Such an approach was first suggested to me in this almost throwaway line of liturgical historian Robert F. Taft. Although he did not pursue or define what he meant by "ideology," he did indicate that he was incorporating some of Victor Turner's ideas about ritual. Turner viewed ideology as a culture's normative meaning that becomes emotionally significant in ritual performance.[18]

More recently, rejuvenated and broadened concepts of "ideology" have been articulated by cultural historians and literary theorists.[19] These concepts move beyond Marxist notions of dispensable and oppressive fictions to include "modes of feeling, valuing, perceiving, and believing" that persons receive from their culture and employ to make their world intelligible.[20] As such, ideology's basic characteristic is to construct human subjects or subjectivities,[21] and this strikes me as potentially useful for the interpretation of how a ritual is significant or effective from a participant's viewpoint.

But the study and interpretation of ritual is often associated with "belief" because of the assumption that the primary task of this way of acting and speaking "is to express beliefs in symbolic ways for the purposes of their continual reaffirmation and inculcation."[22] This traditional association of "belief" and ritual has been sharply challenged in recent years. And as we will see, symbols and symbolic action do not always communicate clear and shared understandings, for the pastor in the ritual described by Rölvaag thought he had failed miserably. Yet from the viewpoint of the participants, what was said, seen, and done had "worked" in some constructive, even redemptive way.[23] Their experience involved more than interpreting theological claims, labels, and intentions. Recall that one of the participants noted his lack of "a proper conception" of what the minister had preached about.[24] As Ronald L. Grimes has observed, the operative vocabulary that ritual participants employ in their assessment of what takes place is "nontechnical" and "nontheological."[25] Moreover, whatever it is that this activity does or "means" for and to them is not simply composed of the thoughts or ideas they have had while doing it.[26] Other dynamics and factors were at work. The task is now to see what they might be.

I. AN EXPERIENCE OF RELIGIOUS RITUAL ONCE AGAIN

Introductory Comments

Ole Edvart Rölvaag's *Giants in the Earth* is the story of a Norwegian immigrant family who settled on the South Dakota prairie during the last quarter of the nineteenth century. This novel is considered one of the two or three best fictional accounts of immigrant experience, and its author has been regarded as a consummate artist who portrayed the courage, strength, vision, and painful psychology of the immigrant in America. Rölvaag was also the kind of writer who sought to appropriate and interpret what was being construed during his time as "the crisis of modern American culture."[27] He was well aware, as are contemporary cross-cultural and bilingual writers, of the necessity of retaining cultural integrity and an organic sense of unity over against a surrounding dominant cultural system with its ideology of the autonomous individual.[28] As some critics have observed, Rölvaag's firsthand knowledge of the immigrant experience presented him with an acute sense of the anguished search for a new selfhood in America.

Critics have also noted Rölvaag's strategic placement of the Communion scene in the novel. These immigrants experienced the strain of living in a desolate land bereft of the psychological, cultural, and religious sources that had previously given their existence some measure of coherence and meaningfulness. The life which they had left behind was an interweaving of cultural, political, and religious threads. A prominent theme in this novel, therefore, is a remembering of what this life had meant to them.

The focus of such remembering for Beret, the novel's central character, is her immigrant trunk, a great chest strapped with iron bands and marked with the faintly visible letters *Anno* 16--. As the novel unfolds, the trunk becomes increasingly a symbol of the country that had been left behind. It "is the only tangible link with the life and culture of the old country. . . ."[29] For her, the trunk functioned as a practical kind of strategy, an artifact, by which she could connect past and present. In so doing, Beret was attempting to construct a self and a version of experience with which she could live.[30] When those attempts failed, she fantasized that the trunk was her coffin. In fact, the lowest point of the novel is undoubtedly when Beret actually lies in the trunk, lid closed, and holding her son and daughter. When Per flung the lid open, what he saw "made his blood run cold."[31]

But the trunk not only symbolized the presence of the old country. Later in the novel, the immigrant trunk also served as the altar for the communion service that occurred in the sod hut of Per and Beret Hansa, thereby functioning as a "medium" of something at stake for the worshipers—perhaps a sacred presence. It seemed to bring things together in relation to one another—traditional ties of culture with the need for what can be termed "relevance"—that which was at stake in living.[32]

The pastor who officiated at this service spoke of the promise of the love of God for God's children, a promise not constrained by the threatening boundaries of either space or time but extended to each of the worshipers personally and to their community as a whole. A looking back had occurred in order to move forward, to alter their relationship to the present and to the future: "Just imagine! He [the pastor] had made them sing exactly the same hymns here in this sod house as the people sang in the churches in Norway. . . ."[33]

Einar Haugen, a scholar, writer, and educator in the field of Scandinavian languages and literature, notes, "It has been said, and it may be true, that at this point the story should have ended."[34] The tension between Beret and Per has been resolved. The psychological deterioration of the community has been reversed. From the viewpoint of a certain ritual theorizing, especially the kind that rests on the "lovely idea" that this way of acting and speaking resolves fundamental contradictions between religious/cultural values and actual experience, Rölvaag's account would be an incredible instance that this is indeed how it works.

A Personal Report

The first time I read Rölvaag's account of this simple and austere worship service I was a student at St. Olaf College, his alma mater and where he also taught for a quarter-century. As I recall, it did not make much of an impact on me other than I thought it was somewhat "quaint," and from the viewpoint of my liturgical sensitivities and sensibilities at the time, rather "low church." When I read the account again some years later, I was the pastor of a small rural parish of three congregations located on the prairie of western North Dakota. This time it made more of an impression on me because of the strong similarity to what my parishioners would sometimes tell me had happened to them. Not only had my position and location changed dramatically, but also my angle of vision and life experience. But I was unable to appreciate fully what it was like in that small sod house on that particular Sunday over a century earlier and to hear that "Love itself, eternal and boundless, is present here." However, was this not the same claim—indeed the same promise—being proclaimed in the texts, actions, songs, movements of those people whose pastor I was?

Years later I found myself being drawn back to Rölvaag's account for several reasons. I had completed a doctoral program in liturgical studies, had written materials for the introduction of ritual forms now being used in many American Lutheran congregations, and was teaching in a theological seminary where I had an official intellectual responsibility to train women and men to lead and to cultivate an actually occurring system of religious ritual. My emphasis was on having them learn and perform the texts, structures, actions, and gestures of this particular ritual system. I wanted them to become experts in its intellectual and theological markings.

But as I found myself increasingly in the position of being a participant in ritual as a member of a congregation rather than as a leader or presider, I began to realize that my own understanding of worship as a particular ritual event had yet to account for the worshiper. My own stance as teacher, scholar, and now worship-*er* needed to include "the people, their meanings, their assumed constructs, and the ritualized patterns that make the world uniquely their own."[35] But how would I do this?

"Beyond the Text"

I needed to move "beyond the text," as Lawrence A. Hoffman has insisted in his recent study so entitled. I needed to augment my historical and theological studies with the methodologies and perspectives of a variety of disciplines in the humanities and social sciences. Liturgical theology has since been opened to the cross-cultural resources provided by anthropology and religious studies. As this occurred in my own teaching and research, I was confronted by topics such as the person, the self, and the emotions that were difficult to probe using the methods and tools of traditional scholarship .

But these were precisely the topics that had been lurking at the edges of my thinking about the significance and power of religious ritual. How would I address them? Expanded concepts of language and text proved to be useful for awhile. I learned that identities are embedded in texts, represented in discourse, encoded in an amalgam of orality, gesture, and written content. I also learned that the generation of meaning and individual meaning that was "intelligible and fraught with sense"[37] could not be understood apart from the social relations of a specific community and its practices that form the self in relation to the world.

These expanded concepts of language and text, however, could not help me answer the question I had been asking: "How does religious ritual offer an interpretation to a participant of what it means to be a particular kind of person?"—where "interpretation" refers to a moment in the process of understanding by which one "makes sense of" or comes to know something.[38]

I returned to the account in *Giants in the Earth* with an increased awareness of Rölvaag's own interest in issues of the self and how the self is defined when far from home, order, history, and ritual. My interest, like his, stood in marked opposition to a Romantic celebration of the expanding and ultimately non-historical, autonomous self. Thus, Rölvaag made the central point in *Giants in the Earth*

> the cost incurred when independence, attenuated beyond traditional ties of culture, turns out to be only the autonomous self. In Beret he creates a character who not only recognizes the false claims of self-sufficiency but knows that true strength and wholeness eventuate within relationships, not apart from them. From relationships within one's native culture as well as from those beyond it comes strength greater than the autonomous self, even when empowered with imagination, is able to generate.[39]

Rölvaag was so aware of the need to have "a sense of belonging to what gives life wholeness and consecration."[40] Thus, his placement of the Communion scene in the novel is significant because it provided a particularly focused, even strategic, way for the immigrants to regain their bearings by living once more with reference to time, place, and other persons. It is clear that this ritual performed a strategic task of giving the immigrants once again a particular sense of identity and social reality.[41] In fact, what was said and done reversed the psychological deterioration of the whole community and was considered by them to be the zenith of their lives. But Rölvaag was too orthodox and too Lutheran to be so naive as to think that religious ritual was transformative. All one has to do is to read the rest of the novel to realize that the immigrants had not been transformed into different people. Their situation had not been dramatically altered or resolved. No "transformation of the inconsequential banality of ordinary life"[42] had taken place. The romantic notion of ritual as a central, transformative process was not at work here. Yet something did occur. Some kind of modest empowerment had taken place that enabled them to reinterpret and construe the world and their place in it in a more constructive, even "redemptive" manner.[43] "How so?" is the question to which I now turn.

II. PARTICIPATION IN RELIGIOUS RITUAL: IDEOLOGY AND EXPERIENCE IN ACTION

The Subject of Ritual

How religious ritual might work as a powerful ideological arena for the construction of human subjects and subjectivities is a question that presents a major problem for theologically and anthropologically trained theorists. They assume that this way of acting and speaking is necessarily group-oriented and hence collective and social. Because of this assumption, ritual cannot reveal important insights about the self, much less construct one.

Given the importance of the theme of subjectivity (or "selfhood" as some prefer) in Western thought generally and the recurring ideas of "self" and "experience" to explain the nature of ritual more recently in popular as well as psychotherapeutic literature,[44] the lack of more critical scholarly attention is indeed surprising. There seem to be at least two major reasons for this state of affairs. One is definitional; the other is cultural. First, as I have just noted, the usual scholarly view is that ritual is a group-oriented, social, and collective phenomenon and hence has little or nothing to do with the self.[45] Second, the burgeoning literature on individualism and self-culture continues to castigate our narcissistic, individualistic, and therapeutic seeking of self-realization and self-fulfillment. It is extremely difficult, therefore, to conceive of the self in a more productive way that would assist a consideration of the subject of ritual, even though we know better or know again that this subject is a cultural construction.[46]

Ritual theorists often prefer, however, the individual/collective dichotomy, thus privileging this way of acting and speaking on the collective side. "But the self itself is a cultural construction," states Ronald L. Grimes. He concludes that since "[t]here is no such thing as an unsocialized individual . . . ," the individual/collective dichotomy must be rejected,

> because taking seriously either term in the self/society pair always leads to the other term: bodies are enculturated and cultures are embodied. For this reason it is necessary to reject much that is assumed about ritual and the individual.[47]

Moreover, religious ritual, according to certain traditions of performance and interpretation, allows participants to see, feel, and understand their social reality and subjective identity. In Judaism, for example,

> [t]he self is known and knowable through its relationships to others. The distinction between private and public is not one of conflict, but of complementarity. Balance is the quintessential experience of the Jew. He [sic] is, when observant of Jewish law, in harmony with himself [sic] and the community, the community and God, himself [sic] and God. The repetition of liturgy and the experience of worship, the outer and the inner, are possible and appropriate. The discipline of prayer recognizes and facilitates the integration of the individual and the community, and his [sic] participation in the community is experienced personally and individually in the prayer ritual.[48]

Other traditions speak of a heart being moved,[49] raising a mind to God,[50] reconnecting a self to a web of communication by which the fabric of human life is composed and recomposed,[51] thereby bringing about a kinship with other human beings, a different self-perception or identity altogether.[52]

Yet not enough scholarly work has been done on how this way of acting and speaking can define the human subject in relation to its world. A significant mark or prevailing theme in those attempts to understand how ritual acting and speaking can define the human subject ritual is to romanticize what takes place. The resulting emphasis is on how humanization takes place as symbols are shared and community is affirmed.[53] Individualism and subjectivity have been deftly avoided.

As I have read these withering attacks on "selfism" and the ideology of individualism that ritual is somehow able to overcome,[54] I am tempted to conclude that subjectivity is a recent phenomenon, unknown to earlier, simpler times. But just as literary critics and cultural historians have been reminding us "that subjectivity is a human characteristic that has always been part of our history, albeit in different configurations and with different powers and values,"[55] so too should students of ritual realize that this way of acting and speaking necessarily involves a participant who is a "subject."

The problem of the "subject" is basic to any humanistic or social scientific inquiry that seeks to better understand the dynamic nature of culture (and ritual is certainly a cultural matter!). But to speak of the "subject" or "subjectivity" is *not* the same as "subjectivism." The latter refers to sense perceptions and impressions, feelings of the here-and-now, and consciousness of incomparable individualism. The former, however, refers to how a person or an individual is where things happen or to whom things happen, and *not* that one who makes things happen.[56] That is, a *subject* is not a source and master of meaning or signification but emerges through the discourses and practices of a culture—"the 'I' is not something given but comes to exist . . . as that which is addressed by and relates to others."[57]

These ways of viewing the *subjective* and *subjectivity* are critically important for the study of individual participation in ritual. Instead of approaching this activity as a relatively enclosed dramatic frame having to do primarily with a group or a community, the focus is now on how to understand what is said, seen, and done as formative of a distinctive experience of personhood or self-definition.

At first glance, terms such as *subject, subjective, subjectivity, person(hood), self(hood)* appear to be synonymous or, as some have observed, "possibly coterminous."[58] They refer to an individual, an aware human being. Yet these terms, for others, are very controversial and require closer definition and more rigorous distinction in their usage. For example, some theorists regard "the individual" as simply an illusion of whole and coherent personal organization. "The subject" refers to a conglomeration of positions—for example, cultural, economic, political, religious—into which a person is called by the practices, discourses, and the world that he or she inhabits.[59] To be a "subject," therefore, is to be both "subject-of" and "subject-to." In my instance, for example, I have been assigned "a subject position" according to gender, race, ethnicity, family, and region. More specifically, I am a male, white, Norwegian-American, son, and Californian. Each of these subject positions is a part of me. I inhabit them, but I do not determine them. That is, my own subjectivity is an ascribed "position" within various discourses and practices. I am "constituted" or "constructed" by them—what used to be called "culture." More recently, the constitution of a concrete individual, a subject, is regarded as a function of "ideology" in its rejuvenated and broadened sense.[60]

Ideology and Religious Ritual

But why do I employ a concept such as "ideology" in order to engage so fundamental a question of how religious ritual can be said to work? Why not use "belief" or "theology"? As noted earlier, theological claims and labels do not play much of a salient role in how participants seek to make sense of ritual. In fact, when they are asked about what happens or what this activity means, rarely do they revert to theological terms or abstract doctrines. Rather, they voice their responses in terms of feelings, values, perceptions, and relationships—"the stuff which makes us uniquely what we are, constitutive of our very identities. . . ."[61] And such "stuff," as Terry Eagleton has written, is "ideological" in the rejuvenated and broadened sense of our lived relations to the world that are a crucial part of what it is to be ourselves.[62] Such relations are "subjectively active"—"they *move* us. . . ."[63] This subjectivity, moreover, "focuses on the 'who I am' or, as important, the 'who we are' of culture, on individual and collective identities."[64]

There has been a line of thought in the study of ritual that sought to account for inner workings of this activity by distinguishing between its sensory and ideological poles. According to Victor Turner, the sensory pole was composed of physiological phenomena such as desire, willing, and feeling.[65] Ritual's ideological pole was constituted by a culture's normative meanings and values. These might include moral matters such as kindness, reciprocity, generosity, respect, and obedience to political authority. When ritual is performed, according to Turner, what happens is an interchange between these sensory and ideological poles by which ideological social norms are transformed into emotionally felt individual desires. Hence, the effect of the performance is at once cognitive *and* affective.

This theoretical depiction of ritual's inner dynamics would be helpful, except for one major difficulty.[66] It invokes dichotomous categories—most particularly, thought vs. action, society vs. individual, objectivity vs. subjectivity, cognition vs. affect. A dominant assumption in such theorizing is that these dichotomies are useful. So what ritual is seen as doing is reintegrating, even fusing these divisions of human experience, thereby making more readily apparent what this activity means. In fact, ritual needs to work this way, especially if the central dynamic or need of cultural and social life is "resolution" or "problem solving."

It should not be surprising, however, that a problem-solving approach or fusion theory of ritual does not quite ring true. If this way of acting and speaking indeed performed such an integrative task so as to solve the fundamental contradictions between religious and social values and actual experience, would there not be some results? Would not one be able to discern a reshaping of consciousness, a creating of meaning, and a restructuring of perception in how ritual participants think and feel?

Ritual theorists and liturgical theologians would like to answer "yes" to these questions, because we want to think that this is indeed what happens. But as Lawrence A. Hoffman has noted recently,

> It would be nice if Christians leaving their Christmas mass walk out on a world where the reality of the Christian promise makes them over into hopeful charitable Christians; where even the most mean-spirited Scrooge among them sees the light, as we say. But as often as not, it is any one of the other meanings that carry the day, the public understandings that everyone except the experts recognize as the rite's message, or the private meanings that individuals hold, perhaps only inchoately but certainly nonetheless—Ms. Fahy's walking away from the icon of Mary with the happy feeling that she has been among believers, for instance. Forget the theology of the occasion; she came to be with people like herself, and leaves with the feeling that the cynical folk, including her own bishop who told her to stay away, the people, that is, who populate the world of officialdom, are not the ones who matter.[67]

Because what ritual does for the participant is quite different from what the experts say, one's critical and interpretive task should be to get at what this is.[68] To do so, what might be helpful is to pick up once again the notion of "ideology." I noted earlier that with its rejuvenation and broadening, modes of feeling, valuing, perceiving, and believing are now included. Whereas these modes are certainly "subjective," they are *not* private. Unlike earlier Marxist approaches to "ideology" that were so rationalistic, a broadened concept allows us to attend to our affective and unconscious relations to the world. Because "ideology" attempts "to analyze the ways in which the individual is addressed, involved, or constituted,"[69] we are presented with a vantage point from which to reevaluate what is meant by both "subjectivity" and "experience"—and, hence, to develop a better understanding of a subjective experience of ritual participation.

Participation in Religious Ritual as Subjective Experience

The report of an experience of ritual and its interpretation with which I began this essay might easily convey the impression that participants in this activity seek or expect a sort of experiential high, a psychological state inducing health, solidarity, and change. Recall that one of the participants in the Communion service in Per Hansa's sod hut had concluded that he had never before experienced anything "so glorious . . . and the happiness of that hour was still glowing with steady warmth in [his] heart." Is this an instance of that "soggy subjectivism"[70] so castigated by various cultural critics?

It is the case that "ritual participation quite often moves people to tears, and sometimes to conversion, joy, or cure . . . ,"[71] thereby serving as a vehicle of affective change and deep emotion. There is also a more familiar psychological and pragmatic sense of why one participates in this activity in the first place—such as "to induce, indulge, explore, and often to reflect upon the things one feels," as well as to organize and actualize feelings and understandings about oneself and the world in which one lives.[72]

But, to regard these matters as "soggy subjectivism" is extremely problematic, if not wrong altogether, because of the failure to see that rituals do provide an occasion to reflect upon the things one feels. Such feeling, as some scholars remind us, is *not* simply elemental or idiosyncratic. Rather, it "tell[s] us how the world is, in a very vivid way. . . ."[73] Some theologians observe as well that so-called "subjective language" is not only a description of one's interior experience but also an expression of feelings in order to achieve a greater sense of one's own identity.[74] The whole person is involved and such involvement implies something about the relation of the person-as-a-whole to his or her environment. Feeling, understood in this manner, involves information about the relations of a person to his or her socially constituted world. It is feeling "that has become meaningful by being interpreted."[75]

Such a process of meaning-creation, moreover, is "intersubjective." It is "what happens in the field of self and other,"[76] that is, "experience."[77] And the defining character of experience is *overbearing practical relevance*, where relevance is "that which is at stake in living—that is, for survival, for coherence, for transcendence. . . ."[78] We can see an experience of religious ritual as providing a connecting link between persons and things—and, as a result of such a connection, sometimes "transforming," but more likely reinterpreting the relationship between context and person. In contemporary scholarly parlance, these matters have to do with subjectivity and ideology—where "ideology," as we saw earlier, "includes both everyday notions and 'experience' and elaborate intellectual doctrines, both the 'consciousness' of social actors and the institutionalized thought-systems and discourses of a given society."[79]

A suitably reformulated conception of "ideology" and "experience" can provide a coherent and plausible approach to a range of theoretical and methodological issues that are concerned with better understanding human action and interaction as well as the workings of symbolic forms and their roles in social life.[80] Thus, I find "ideology" to be a particularly useful and apt way to conceptualize the very process of meaning-creation.

Some scholars prefer "ideation" instead of "ideology."[81] Both terms are inclusive and are concerned with those historically conditioned procedures and categories by which one organizes and interprets experience and constructs meanings.[82] "Experience" is constituted by "this indissoluble mixture of feeling and ideation. . . ."[83] In this process of meaning-creation, "ideology is not simply a function or entity but the creation of people feeling, thinking, persuading, and struggling for meaning."[84]

> Indeed, [the] function [of ideology] . . . seems less to make sense of (naturalize) sociopolitical orderings than to make sense of feeling, to construct meaning out of the raw materials of needs, desires, expectations (both frustrated and fulfilled), fears, and anxieties. . . . [This] focus . . . stresses the mediating role of the psyche in all cultural production.[85]

In pursuing this line of inquiry—that ritual can be approached as an instance of "ideology and experience in action," an important point to remember is that when a person is engaged in the process of meaning-creation, he or she is not simply and dutifully appropriating or internalizing an already imposed "coherent set of ideas, statements, or attitudes."[86] Rather, what he or she seems to be doing is seeking, even grappling with, a "Real" in order to enter it and thereby live his or her life in a world that makes sense in varying degrees.[87]

Whether rituals make any sense to those who participate in them is a controversial question at the present time, especially since the publication of Frits Staal's essay, "The Meaninglessness of Ritual," over a decade ago.[88] Staal argued that rituals are meaningless because they do not refer to or communicate anything. Critics have pointed out subsequently, however, that referential theories of meaning have been regarded as inadequate for some time,[89] even though many scholars of ritual, especially liturgical theologians, continue to be overly preoccupied with "meaning-as-semantics" or as cognitive content.[90]

More recently, developments in both the humanities and the social sciences have alerted us to how "meaning" is not something that floats "out there" and that people occasionally snatch it.[91] Nor does "it" somehow exist privately within our heads. Rather, "meaning" is constructed through a relational process between persons.[92] Since it is difficult to conceive of or even have "shared meaning," or "common meaning," then it is necessary to struggle to create and locate togetherness or relationship, something "meaningful."[93] Moreover, as we have been learning, how we think of meaning depends on what we think meanings *do*.

Roy D'Andrade's observation on this matter is helpful:

Meanings in general, and cultural meaning systems in particular, do at least four different things. Meanings represent the world, create cultural entities, direct one to do certain things, and evoke certain feelings. These four functions of meaning— the *representational*, the *constructive*, the *directive* and the *evocative*—are differentially elaborated in particular cultural meaning systems, but are always present to some degree in any system.[94]

Moreover, D'Andrade reminds us that this differentiation is not always sharply made, especially in what things mean to the persons involved. Rather, these meanings "are simultaneously constructive, representative, evocative, and directive."[95]

A similar approach to meaning, this time presented in terms of ritual, is Wade Wheelock's notion of how the language of this activity is to be understood as "situating" rather than as "informing."[96] As a result, the "message" that is presented "is less an idea to be taught and more a reality to be repeatedly experienced."[97] Examples of looking at "meaning" in and of ritual activity in this fashion include the Vedic sacrifice that rehearses and celebrates the great mythic deeds of creation which gave humanity an ordered world or the Christian Mass as an expression of a fundamental value or important lesson/example of the divine concern for humanity and human response to the divine.[98]

More specifically, for a liturgical theologian "meaning" seems to involve primarily matters of "content" or "semantics." The said, seen, and done of Christian worship contain or express trinitarian and Christological, pneumatological and anthropological, ecclesiological and eschatological components of Christian faith. The task of those who are participating is somehow to discern these various components and find them to be personally significant and involving because they have been successfully "mediated" by a rite.

Liturgical scholars have a particular stake, then, in the expectation and/or conviction that rites "mean" something in a semiotic or referential sense. That is to say, rites [at least Christian rites] are regarded as telling us something about God, Christ, church, sacraments, and living a life of faith or as referring to these realities in some way. The task of a worshiper or participant is to "believe in" such realities.

It is evident, however, that worshipers/participants do not always find these basic symbols to be clear. Nor do they always interpret them in the same way. Thus, it is difficult to say that rituals have to do with the communication of *shared* ideas, values, and assumptions that are fundamental to a society.

Recall again the account with which I began this essay. The pastor thought that the ritual over which he had presided had not gone well, had not "succeeded," if you will: "In this heart he blamed himself bitterly; not only had he spoiled the Communion sermon. . . . 'Never before,' he thought, 'have I failed so miserably in any service!'"[99] Yet the worshipers experienced it as reversing the psychological deterioration of their community as well as providing them with a deeply felt experience of identity and understanding of what each person was, in the full sense of the past that had made them what they were, the present in which they sought to live what they were, and the future they hoped to be.[100] To speak of one pole of their experience as "ideology," then, calls attention not to monolithic worldview, social solidarity, or a coherent and agreed-upon set of ideas. Rather, what we seem to have is "a lived and practical consciousness," especially of relationships and a sense of belonging by which subjects are formed, re-formed, and enabled to live in an apparently meaningful world.[101]

Another way to state this understanding of "ideology" is that it signifies and provides the very terms in which one seeks to understand the affective, felt quality of human existence. It embodies, or better, a person or persons embody and interweave feeling and thought so tightly as to make them indistinguishable. According to cultural theorist Raymond Williams,

> We are talking about characteristic elements of impulse, restraint, and tone; specifically affective elements of consciousness and relationships: *not feeling against thought, but thought as felt and feeling as thought: practical consciousness of a present kind, in a living and inter-relating continuity.*[102]

Such "practical consciousness," however, is historically conditioned and culturally shaped and is a key element of the dialectic relationship between the subjective and the social. Yet theoretical and ethnographic accounts of ritual have tended not to give much attention to the impact of this way of acting and speaking on the individual, unless there is healing, exorcism, trance, or the like that are involved. More generally, scholarly considerations have tended to be preoccupied with how ritual either evokes and gives access to the sacred or reveals a particular social meaning for specific groups of people. Overlooked in both of these approaches, as a result, is a rather obvious feature, one which is underscored in theological/doctrinal claims and insider reports that I noted earlier about moving a heart,[103] raising a mind to God,[104] reconnecting a self to a web of communication by which the fabric of human life is composed and recomposed,[105] engaging with a personal and/or ultimate Other, or bringing about a kinship with other human beings, creating a different self-perception or identity altogether.[106] Yet it is this larger web of "ideology," as I have been calling it, which provides both backdrop and practical strategies that allow participants in religious ritual to experience, if not to know in some fashion, just how and why this way of acting and speaking makes possible beliefs, values, and personal identity.

CONCLUSION

Ronald L. Grimes has written, "One's sense of ritual is conveyed by the image one has of it, but it is actually generated by the experience one has of it."[107] Throughout this essay, I have been aware of how my own sense of ritual has changed. I recounted some of that history, not to be trendily reflexive, but because it was not entirely personal at all. For my thinking, teaching, and writing are embedded in a more general scholarly tendency that has characterized explanations and understandings of Western cultural practices and, to some extent, theological investigations of religious ritual. Hence, I have been participating in a shift away from a scholarship that analyzes what this activity should be to the use of critical methods and insights which can better illustrate what constitutes effectiveness for those involved. "The" meaning of a rite or a liturgy, asserts Grimes, "is a fiction, because meaning is always meaning-to-somebody."[108] Similarly, Catherine Bell has argued that ritual theory and interpretation need to focus on the strategies that participants employ in the act of ritualizing in order to understand better and more fully what comprises effectiveness for them.[109]

To do this kind of analysis I needed a reconceptualization of the experience of subjectivity, one that would allow me a broad range of definition and usage. Thus, subjectivity is an "I" with its own viewpoint; it is an other to Others, which also affects a sense of subjectivity; it involves being a subject of knowledge and discourse; it entails having a body that is separate from others and yet closely dependent on an environment; it is one whose viewpoint is partial and particular.[110] A common theme in this way of thinking about the human subject is that it is an ongoing construction because it "is dependent upon intersubjectivity, or the intersubjective nature of language and culture."[111] And, I would add, "ritual" as well!

What I had only intuited—namely, that I have my emotions, beliefs, abilities, values, perceptions, and so on because I am situated in a social, cultural, religious web of interpretation that helps me to make sense of my experience and my behavior—I now better understand. As a result, my sense of ritual and its capacity to say and to offer an interpretation of what it means to be a particular kind of person is because this saying and doing focuses on "who I am" and "who we are"—on an individual and a collective identity.

From a theological viewpoint, such a sense of ritual might not add up to much. It is rather modest. I have said little about marvelous, visible transformations of head and heart. The contradictions between religious and cultural values and lived experience are not miraculously resolved. Consciousness is not reshaped; new meaning has not always been created; perceptions have not been restructured.

For some ritual traditions, the notion that this way of acting and speaking is a central, transformative social process is both romantic and unworkable. It does not ring true. Yet experts and participants often place enormous pressure on rituals to be communally enthusiastic and personally meaningful. They are preoccupied with certain qualities such as "warmth," "togetherness," "feeling good," "getting some good out of it."

The critical question that is not addressed very often is, what is the power of ritual in a society such as ours?[112] If it does not provide a model of the world or a model for action in that world, then what does this way of acting and speaking *do*? Catherine Bell has suggested that we need to find a new language to speak about ritual expectation and participation.

In this essay I have sought to make a contribution toward this end. The scenes from *Giants in the Earth* struck me [and still do] as useful for an attempt to say something about how the goals of ritual go beyond the present moment with its embodiment of interpretive schemes—what I chose to term "ideology" because such schemes are the very stuff that make us human, that constitute our identities. Our values, feelings, beliefs, and perceptions are formed by and dependent on others. Hence, saying "I" is also a matter of saying "we."[113]

Although these connections are lauded by an ever-increasing number of literary and cultural critics—and rightfully so—they are not all that new or even startling. Ole Edvart Rölvaag knew the importance and, yes, the necessity of "a heart made strong by its nurturing connection with voices of the past that join the present in essential continuity."[114] This "heart made strong" was Rölvaag's "hard-won theory of personhood," expressed in his fiction and in the ritual that he depicted in *Giants in the Earth*. There, he answered the question of what it means to be a particular kind of person—one who receives and one who gives, one who "feels conjoined in this world and faithful to another."[115] The human subject who is so defined and constructed, so addressed and hailed in religious ritual, comes away with a strategic and partial reinterpretation of the world. She is empowered to experience that world in a constructive, even redemptive manner. He is enabled to say, "I understand (or I understand once again) what my life is about."

NOTES

1. O. E. Rölvaag, *Giants in the Earth: A Saga of the Prairie*, trans. Lincoln Colcord and the author (New York: Harper & Row, n.d.), p. 395. [Originally published in 1927].

2. Ibid., p. 396.

3. Ibid., p. 398.

4. *Persuasions and Performances: The Play of Tropes in Culture* (Bloomington, IN: Indiana University Press, 1986), pp. 11–25.

5. Harold P. Simonson, *Prairies Within: The Tragic Trilogy of Ole Rölvaag* (Seattle, WA: University of Washington Press, 1987), p. 8.

6. See Ronald L. Grimes, *Ritual Criticism: Case Studies in Its Practice, Essays on Its Theory* (Columbia, SC: University of South Carolina Press, 1990), p. 13ff.

7. Ibid., p. 14. Rather than attempting to discern and then to define what ritual "really is," some scholars now realize that this is not an entity to be discovered but rather a particular "how" of human activity to be explored. One looks for certain "qualities" characteristic of this activity. "When these qualities begin to multiply," notes Ronald L. Grimes, "when an activity becomes dense with them, it becomes increasingly proper to speak of it as ritualized, if not a rite as such" [*Ritual Criticism*, p. 14]. Similarly, Catherine Bell speaks of ritual or "ritualization" as a certain kind of "practical, strategic activity" that constructs and modestly empowers "a social person's" sense of reality and identity [*Ritual Theory, Ritual Practice* (Oxford: Oxford University Press, 1992), pp. 67-93]. Rebecca J. Slough (this volume) also finds useful Grimes' list of ritual qualities and Bell's notion of "ritualization" in her exploration of hymn-singing events as ritual behavior.

8. E.g., James L. Watson, "The Structure of Chinese Funerary Rites: Elementary Forms, Ritual Sequence, and the Primacy of Performance," *Death Ritual in Late Imperial and Modern China* , ed. James L. Watson and Evelyn S. Rawski (Berkeley, CA: University of California Press, 1988), p. 4ff. See Catherine Bell's criticism of this notion of ritual "as a type of myth legitimating the whole apparatus of ritual studies" [*Ritual Theory, Ritual Practice*, p. 37].

9. Here I want to acknowledge those colleagues (from whom I asked no mercy) who read various drafts of this essay: Martha Ellen Stortz, Donna L. Seamone, Gail W. Cromack, and Donna Stevenson.

10. *Interpretation and Social Criticism* (Cambridge: Harvard University Press, 1987), p. 39; cited in Renato Rosaldo, *Culture and Truth: The Remaking of Social Analysis* (Boston: Beacon Press, 1989), p. 194.

11. *Ritual Criticism*, pp. 18–27.

12. Ibid., p. 16.

13. Ibid., p. 26.

14. Michael A. Signer, "The Poetics of Liturgy," *The Changing Face of Jewish and Christian Worship in North America*, ed. Paul F. Bradshaw and Lawrence A. Hoffman (Notre Dame, IN: University of Notre Dame Press, 1991), pp. 184–198.

15. Ibid., pp. 193, 195.

16. Paper presented to the Ritual Studies Group, American Academy of Religion Annual Meeting (San Francisco, CA, November 22, 1992).

17. Robert F. Taft, S.J., *Beyond East and West: Problems in Liturgical Understanding* (Washington, DC: The Pastoral Press, 1984), p. 127.

18. *Dramas, Fields, and Metaphors* (Ithaca, NY: Cornell University Press, 1974), p. 55.

19. "Ideology" is a notoriously complicated and contested concept. Often it means "false and distorted consciousness" or is employed to deny human agency, even to conjure persons right out of existence. My preference in this essay is to use "ideology" in a looser sense so that I have a way to consider how meaning is produced and individual identity is created within a social-cultural context. Whereas some readers might expect that usage of a concept such as "ideology" would also involve a discussion of liberation theology, this is *not* a concern in this essay. I only want to have a way to talk about how we as individuals come to understand the world in which we live—and a loose notion of "ideology" helps me to do that.

20. Terry Eagleton, *Literary Theory: An Introduction* (Minneapolis, MN: University of Minnesota Press, 1983), p. 15.

21. Kenneth Thompson, *Beliefs and Ideology* (Chicester, Sussex: Ellis Horwood Limited, 1986), pp. 15–16.

22. Bell, *Ritual Theory, Ritual Practice*, p. 182.

23. See Catherine Bell, "The Authority of Ritual Experts," *Studia Liturgica* p. 23 (1993), 117.

24. See n. 3.

25. *Ritual Criticism*, p. 47.

26. Ibid., p. 43.

27. William Boelhower, "Ethnic Trilogies: A Genealogical and Generational Poetics," *The Invention of Ethnicity*, ed. Werner Sollors (New York: Oxford University Press, 1989), p. 158.

28. See Ramón Saldívar, *Chicano Narrative: The Dialectics of Difference* (Madison, WI: The University of Wisconsin Press, 1990).

29. John Helgeland, "Beret's Problem: An Essay on Immigrant Pioneer Religion," *Lutheran Quarterly* 28 (February 1976), p. 50.

30. See the recent discussion by Gayle Greene, "Feminist Fiction and the Uses of Memory," *Signs: Journal of Women in Culture and Society* 16/2 (1991), pp. 290–321; also Alan Radley, "Artefacts, Memory and a Sense of the Past," *Collective Remembering*, ed. D. Middleton and D. Edwards (London: SAGE Publications, 1990), pp. 46–59.

31. Rölvaag, *Giants in the Earth*, p. 338.

32. Arthur Kleinman and Joan Kleinman, "Suffering and Its Professional Transformation: Toward an Ethnography of Interpersonal

Experience," *Culture, Medicine, and Psychiatry* 15 (1991), pp. 277; 294–295.

33. Rölvaag, *Giants in the Earth*, p. 401.

34. Einar Haugen, *Ole Edvart Rölvaag* (Boston: Twayne Publishers, 1983), p. 89.

35. Lawrence A. Hoffman, *Beyond the Text: A Holistic Approach to Liturgy* (Bloomington, IN: Indiana University Press, 1987), p. 182.

36. See George E. Marcus and Michael M. J. Fischer, *Anthropology as Cultural Critique: An Experimental Moment in the Human Sciences* (Chicago: University of Chicago Press, 1986), p. 45ff.

37. This superb phrase, drawn from Michelle Rosaldo's book, *Knowledge and Passion* (Cambridge: Cambridge University Press, 1980, p. 28), expresses well, as I seek to show throughout this essay, that tight interweaving of knowing, feeling, and thinking—or, perhaps better, their coalescence into some kind of unity of experience that is compelling and powerful.

38. Grimes, *Ritual Criticism*, p. 16. See also Sandra M. Schneiders, *The Revelatory Text: Interpreting the New Testament as Sacred Scripture* (San Francisco: Harper San Francisco, 1991), pp. 17–18.

39. Simonson, pp. 20–21.

40. Ibid., p. 20.

41. Catherine Bell, "The Ritual Body and the Dynamics of Ritual Power," *Journal of Ritual Studies* 4/2 (Summer 1990), p. 299.

42. Evan Zuesse, "Ritual," *Encyclopedia of Religion*, vol. 12, ed. Mircea Eliade (New York: Macmillan, 1987), p. 405.

43. Bell, "The Authority of Ritual Experts," p. 117.

44. Grimes, *Ritual Criticism*, p. 109ff.

45. Ibid., p. 110.

46. Ronald L. Grimes, "Reinventing Ritual," *Soundings* 75/1 (Spring 1992), pp. 26–28.

47. Ibid.

48. Riv-Ellen Prell[-Foldes], "The reinvention of reflexivity in Jewish Prayer: The Self and Community in Modernity," *Semiotica* 30/1–2 (1980), p. 81.

49. "Apology of the Augsburg Confession," 13, 5, *The Book of Concord*, ed. and trans. Theodore G. Tappert (Philadelphia: Fortress Press, 1959), pp. 211–212.

50. "*Sacrosanctum Concilium*: The Constitution on the Sacred Liturgy 33," *The Documents of Vatican II*, ed. Walter Abbott (New York: Guild, America, Association, 1966), p. 149.

51. Sharon Parks, "Communication, Ritual as," *The New Dictionary of Sacramental Worship*, ed. Peter E. Fink, S.J. (Collegeville, MN: The Liturgical Press, 1991), p. 236.

52. See Fred Clothey, *Rhythm and Intent : Ritual Studies from South India* (Madras, India: Blackie and Son Publishers Pvt Ltd, 1983), pp. 1–7.

53. Bell, "The Authority of Ritual Experts," p. 112. She cites Robert Bellah et al., *Habits of the Heart* as an example of such a view.

54. E.g., Robert Bellah et al., *Habits of the Heart: Individualism and Commitment in American Life* (Berkeley, CA: University of California Press, 1985).

55. Lee Patterson, *Chaucer and the Subject of History* (Madison, WI: The University of Wisconsin Press, 1991), p. 12.

56. Jeremy Hawthorn, *A Concise Glossary of Contemporary Literary Theory* (London and New York: Edward Arnold, 1992), p. 180.

57. Jonathan Culler, *Structuralist Poetics: Structuralism, Linguistics and the Study of Literature* (Ithaca, NY: Cornell University Press, 1981), p. 28.

58. E.g., Brenda Marshall, *Teaching the Postmodern: Fiction and Theory* (New York: Routledge, 1992), p. 81ff.

59. Paul Smith, *Discerning the Subject* (Minneapolis, MN: University of Minnesota Press, 1988), p. xxxv. A way not to get bogged down in these terminological differences is to use, as Smith suggests, the term *subject/individual* "to designate the human entity to whom qualities of being a "subject" or an "individual" are commonly assigned" (p. xxxv). Another possibility is simply to stay with the terms "subject" and "subjectivity," but with the awareness of their broad range of senses [e.g., Regenia Gagnier, *Subjectivities: A History of Self-Representation in Britain, 1832–1920* (Oxford: Oxford University Press, 1991), pp. 8–9].

60. See Julian Henriques, et al., *Changing the Subject: Psychology, Social Regulation, and Subjectivity* (London: Methuen, 1984), pp. 2–3.

61. Terry Eagleton, *Ideology: An Introduction* (London: Verso, 1991), p. 20.

62. Ibid., pp. 18–20.

63. Richard Johnson, "What Is Cultural Studies Anyway?" *Social Text* no. 16, 6/1 (1987), p. 44.

64. Ibid.

65. *Dramas, Fields, and Metaphors*, p. 55.

66. Here I follow Catherine Bell's critique of this tendency to view ritual in terms of dichotomies. See her *Ritual Theory, Ritual Practice*, pp. 13–66.

67. "How Ritual Means: Ritual Circumcision in Rabbinic Culture and Today," *Studia Liturgica* 23 (1993), p. 82.

68. Ibid., 83. Hoffman cites Ronald Grimes' identification of one of the goals of ritual criticism as "precisely the deconstruction of official statements." See Grimes, *Ritual Criticism*, pp. 34 and 36.

69. Bell, *Ritual Theory, Ritual Practice*, p. 233, n. 109.

70. This expression is Terry Eagleton's. See his *Ideology*, p. 17. He contrasts "soggy subjectivism" with "steel-hard objectivism," that "realm of indubitable physical facts" as opposed to "a sphere of precariously floating values."

71. M. Rosaldo, *Knowledge and Passion*, p. 25.

72. Ibid.

73. Roy G. D'Andrade, "The Cultural Part of Cognition," *Cognitive Science* 5 (1981), p. 191; cited in Robert I. Levy, "Emotion, Knowing, and Culture," *Culture Theory: Essays on Mind, Self, and Emotion*, ed. R. A. Shweder and R. A. LeVine (Cambridge: Cambridge University Press, 1984), p. 218.

74. J. A. Appleyard, S.J., "The Languages We Use: Talking About Religious Experience," *Studies in the Spirituality of Jesuits* 19/2 (March 1987), p. 11.

75. Debora Kuller Shuger, *Habits of Thought in the English Renaissance: Religion, Politics, and the Dominant High Culture* (Berkeley, CA: University of California Press, 1990), p. 254.

76. See Jessica Benjamin, *The Bonds of Love: Psychoanalysis, Feminism, and the Problem of Domination* (New York: Pantheon Books, 1988), p. 20.

77. Kleinman and Kleinman, pp. 275–301.

78. Ibid., pp. 277; 294–295.

79. Göran Therborn, *The Ideology of Power and the Power of Ideology* (London: Verso, 1980), p. 2.

80. John B. Thompson, *Ideology and Modern Culture* (Stanford, CA: Stanford University Press, 1990), pp. 4, 7.

81. E.g., Shuger, *Habits of Thought in the English Renaissance*, p. 254. Yet early in her book, Shuger uses "ideology," not "ideation."

82. Ibid., pp. 8–9; 254–255.

83. Ibid., p. 254.

84. Ibid., p. 255.

85. Ibid., pp. 254–255.

86. Bell, *Ritual Theory, Ritual Practice*, p. 191.

87. "Real" is literary critic Ramón Saldívar's term for collective and historical processes into which a "subject," a particular being-in-the-world, is placed that allows him or her to see, to feel, and to understand his or her social reality [*Chicano Narrative: The Dialectics of Difference*, pp. 7 and 211]. When combined with Göran Therborn's understanding of ideology as "that aspect of the human condition under which human beings live their lives as conscious actors in a world that makes sense to them in varying degrees," we can begin to see how ritual is a component of that larger web of everyday notions, "experience," elaborate intellectual doctrines and the institutionalized thought-systems and practices of a given society [*The Ideology of Power and the Power of Ideology*, pp. 2–4]. By viewing ritual in this way, we can focus on the ways it operates in the formation and transformation of human subjectivity. It seems to work as "a lived and practical consciousness."

88. *Numen* 26/1 (1979), pp. 2–22.

89 Hans Penner, "Language, Ritual, and Meaning," *Numen* 32/1 (July 1985), pp. 1–16.

90. E.g., Gilbert Lewis, *Day of Shining Red: An Essay on Understanding Ritual*, [Cambridge Studies in Social Anthropology, No. 27] (Cambridge: Cambridge University Press, 1980), pp. 1–38; 112–120; Ronald L. Grimes, *Beginnings in Ritual Studies* (Washington, DC: University Press of America, 1982), pp. 1–69; Mary Collins, *Contemplative Participation* (Collegeville, MN: The Liturgical Press, 1990), p. 28.

91. See the discussion of the Fifty-Seventh Colloquy, March 13, 1988, Center for Hermeneutical Studies in Hellenistic and Modern Culture, David S. Steward and Rebecca Slough, "Teaching and Learning Practice: A Relational Hermeneutic for Professional Schooling," ed. James Duke (Berkeley, CA: Graduate Theological Union and University of California-Berkeley, 1989), p. 81ff.

92. See Roy G. D'Andrade, "Cultural Meaning Systems," *Culture Theory: Essays on Mind, Self, and Emotion*, ed. Richard A. Shweder and Robert A. LeVine (Cambridge: Cambridge University Press, 1984), pp. 88–119.

93. Peter G. Stromberg, *Symbols of Community: The Cultural System of a Swedish Church* (Tucson, AZ: The University of Arizona Press, 1986), pp. 78, 116.

94. "Cultural Meaning Systems," p. 96.

95. Ibid., p. 116.

96. "The Problem of Ritual Language: From Information to Situation," *The Journal of the American Academy of Religion* 50/1 (March 1982), pp. 58–71.

97. Ibid., p. 66.

98. Ibid., p. 65.

99. Rölvaag, *Giants in the Earth*, p. 396.

100. See Taft, *Beyond East and West*, p. 127.

101. Harold Simonson has observed how these relationships are a greater source of strength and empowerment than the autonomous self. See *Prairies Within: The Tragic Trilogy of Ole Rölvaag*, pp. 20–21.

102. *Marxism and Literature* (Oxford: Oxford University Press, 1977), p. 132. My emphasis.

103. "Apology of the Augsburg Confession," 13, 5, pp. 211–212.

104. "*Sacrosanctum Concilium*: The Constitution on the Sacred Liturgy 33," p. 149.

105. Parks, "Communication, Ritual as," p. 236.

106. See Clothey, *Rhythm and Intent*, pp. 1–7.

107. "Victor Turner's Definition, Theory, and Sense of Ritual," *Victor Turner and the Construction of Cultural Criticism: Between Literature and Anthropology*, ed. Kathleen M. Ashley (Bloomington, IN: Indiana University Press, 1990), p. 144.

108. Grimes, *Ritual Criticism*, p. 42.

109. "Ritual, Change, and Changing Rituals," *Worship* 63/1 (January 1989), pp. 31–41.

110. See Gagnier, *Subjectivities: A History of Self-Representation in Britain, 1832–1920*, pp. 8–9.

111. Ibid., p. 11. Teresa de Lauretis' discussion of "subjectivity" and "experience" has also been useful. See her *Alice Doesn't: Feminism, Semiotics, Cinema* (Bloomington, IN: Indiana University Press, 1984), pp. 158–186.

112. What follows has been very much shaped by Catherine Bell's conversation with GTU Area VII students and faculty ("Worship, Proclamation, and the Arts") held at Pacific Lutheran Theological Seminary, Berkeley, CA, on May 6, 1992 and her essay, "The Authority of Ritual Experts," *Studia Liturgica* 23 (1993), p. 117.

113. See Gayle Greene, "Looking at History," *Changing Subjects: The Making of Feminist Literary Criticism*, ed. Gayle Greene and Coppelia Kahn (London: Routledge, 1993), p. 21.

114. Simonson, *Prairies Within*, p. 8.

115. Ibid., p. 71.

6

"Let Every Tongue, by Art Refined, Mingle Its Softest Notes With Mine"[1]

An Exploration of Hymn-Singing Events and Dimensions of Knowing

REBECCA J. SLOUGH

Congregational hymn singing is one of the hallmarks of the Protestant Reformation. Martin Luther encouraged the development of congregational hymnody as a means for worshipers to engage actively in worship. Popular secular tunes acquired religious texts, and chorale tunes were composed for hymns that expressed new biblical and theological insights. Reformers in Geneva set biblical texts to tunes for congregational singing; English reformers introduced congregational psalm singing with the composition of a limited number of psalm tunes. As a result, congregational song became a significant feature of Protestant life.

Along the way to the twentieth century, hymn singing outside of set liturgical patterns became a pleasure in its own right. Eighteenth and nineteenth century religious revivals set congregational singing as a social event within the religious consciousness and sensibilities of Protestants in North America. Choral societies developed, and collections of tunes with religious texts were published. Music teachers and leaders held singing schools throughout the nineteenth century, providing the means for teaching music and literacy skills and for enhancing community life in both urban and rural areas. In the 1940s and '50s all-night hymn sings were popular among evangelical Christian groups. Descendants of Welsh immigrants still gather frequently, particularly around St. David's Day (March 6) or at the end of a competitive music festival, for a *Cymanfa Ganu* (singing gathering) to sing their traditional tunes and texts. Mennonite, Brethren, and Baptist churches often plan hymn sings with neighboring congregations. "Sacred Harp" singing conventions are held throughout the south in the summertime, and many local groups of Sacred Harp fasola singers keep that tradition alive during the rest of the year. Black gospel concerts feature one or more gospel groups with the audience clapping, singing, or dancing along. The agenda of the yearly Hymn Society of the United States and Canada meetings is dominated by hymn festivals. Since the Reformation, Christians have found singing together to be an important congregational and ecumenical activity.

My interest in hymn-singing events stems from my musical and liturgical training, my religious formation in Mennonite and Brethren congregations, my job as managing editor of *Hymnal: A Worship Book* (1992),[2] and my experience as a pastor. In all those spheres, I have known my own and others' joy, frustration, exuberance, and anger through singing in congregations and large public gatherings. The work I and a host of others did on the hymnal exposed me to the ferocious ardor and anger that congregational singing can unleash. The sources of these passionate responses were often barely articulate in our committees or by the people in the congregations we were to represent. Issues around the nature and gender of God, preserving the "tradition" (however tradition is understood), preferences for certain musical styles, power, leadership authority, and denominational identity fueled much debate. Frequently, impasses in our discussions could be overcome only by singing together (usually by singing a particular hymn that had sparked the controversy); at other times impasses were so great that only silence and distance from one another could dissolve them or focus the issue of debate more clearly. Singing was fundamental in our formation and understanding of ourselves as Christians, and yet we were often inarticulate in our expression of this self-understanding.

I have led and sung in many hymn-singing events in the last twenty years, with as few as ten people and as many as a thousand. The pattern of "hymn sing" with which I am most familiar allows the identified leader(s) to select several hymns to open or close the event, with most of the time given over for the singers to make requests. I have sung hymns and songs from books, from overhead projector slides, and from memory using organs, pianos, wind instruments, guitars, percussion, or a capella. Some events were completely planned by the leaders

with no congregational requests allowed; others were entirely spontaneous requests. Given the variety of planning strategies, in this essay I
am considering hymn singing events broadly as those gatherings of
people whose intent is to sing hymns and religious songs together for
any duration of time (minutes, hours, days) outside of the regular pattern of worship services and seasonal cycles.[3]

Although a good deal of descriptive work has been done on these
experiences of singing,[4] there has been little discussion of the ritual
function(s) of these events, and even less interest in the noetic aspects
of this ritual activity. Hymn-singing events present a unique perspective from which to look at dimensions of knowing through action.
After establishing hymn singing events as a form of ritual using Ronald
Grimes' list of ritual characteristics,[5] I briefly discuss the nature of
meaning and knowing. Theodore Jennings' essay "On Ritual
Knowledge"[6] provides a starting point for examining the interfaces
between ritual, knowing, and hymn singing events. Some of Catherine
Bell's insights from *Ritual Theory, Ritual Practice*[7] are woven into
Jennings' argument to nuance his claims. I have used Michael
Polanyi's[8] and Douglas Hall's[9] work on the nature of knowing, which
have implications on the cognitive, intersubjective, and spiritual
planes. These two epistemologies provide some means for "getting at"
dimensions of knowing in ways that are compatible with the commitments of the ritual theorists presented. Since this essay primarily is a
means for clearing the ground for more methodical and intense work
to begin, I close with several proposals that could orient this task.

Terminology poses an immediate problem, since Grimes,
Jennings, and Bell each use "ritual" in a different sense. In this essay
"ritual" will describe action that exhibits the characteristics of ritual
that Grimes outlines. "Ritual" also will be understood as practice that
is in some way set apart from the flow of normal daily activity, what
Bell means by "ritualization," which implies that such behavior is
planned or strategic in some way.[10] In Jennings' work "ritual" resembles Grimes' notion of "rite" and some aspects of Bell's notion of "ritualization." Thus, for the sake of simplicity, "ritual" will be used
throughout this essay, with the full acknowledgment that some
semantic shifts have been finessed.

SINGING EVENTS AS RITUAL ACTION

Various ritual theories do not easily account for hymn singing events
as ritual. The "meaning" of these events is not necessarily found in the
mediation of limit situations, nor in creating rites of passage with dan-

gerous periods of liminality,[11] nor necessarily in reconfirming specific social values or institutions, nor in explicitly dealing with the dichotomies of human experience, nor presenting a social-religious message to decipher. At least, these are not on the forefront of singers' minds in explaining why the event "works" (or doesn't work). There is no clear intentional goal to achieve, except to sing, and no guaranteed benefit to gain. There is no truth that promises to be revealed. From a skeptical point of view, these events are meaningless. Gathering to sing may provide a singer the opportunity to relive a good past experience,[12] but the power of these events (if there is any) to affect the singers' hearts, minds, and spirits in any way is experienced solely in the present. These events are performances of the moment tied to specific times, places, and people and the conditions of their lives.[13]

Grimes' work on the qualities of ritual removes a number of obstacles presented by other theorists in considering the ritual character of singing events. Hymn sings are a type of action that exhibits pattern and structure, but they do not enact or reenact a specific event or rite, frequently a defining feature of ritual, especially religious ritual.[14] Grimes claims that where these qualities are present in people's action, there is evidence of ritual.[15]

1. *Performed, embodied, enacted, gestural*
   Hymn singing events differ from concerts in that the participants create sound and perform the hymns themselves; soloists or small groups may be used to sing selected parts of a hymn or may entertain the participants during a period designed to rest their voices. There is no identified audience. The primary instrument of the ritual action is the human body: voice, breath, lungs, heart, mouth, ears, and hands.

2. *Formalized, elevated, stylized, differentiated*
   Singing events are not part of mundane experience; their special quality derives from the requirements of appointed times, appropriate acoustical spaces, musical leadership, a group of relative size, and long periods of singing without other verbal discourse. They often are anticipated for several weeks or months, though they can occur spontaneously. Music, in this case sung text, is the central feature of the action; few other daily activities rely on music so exclusively.

3. *Repetitive, redundant, rhythmic*

   Groups that value hymn singing events schedule them periodically into their shared community life. Some singing events are seasonally controlled. *Harmonia Sacra* hymn sings at Weavers Mennonite Church, Harrisonburg, Virginia, are on New Year's Day; Sacred Harp singing conventions are held frequently in the summer. Sunday evenings are traditional times for hymn singing in many congregations. Special seasons and holidays are frequently deemed to be appropriate times for singing events.

4. *Collective, institutionalized, consensual*

   Hymn sings are always collective events. The structure of the event is agreed upon by all involved insofar as they expect to sing religious hymns or songs and little, if anything, else during the time of the event. These events are institutionalized to the extent that leaders recognized for having musical competence guide the action. Some type of training to lead is presumed. Choices of leadership surface the issues of power and authority most specifically in the ritual action.

5. *Traditional, archaic, primordial*

   Hymn singing traditions have not developed nor changed among singing groups in a uniform pattern. Sociological and cultural factors affected the rate and the strength of singing traditions within various groups. Each has its traditional ways of singing and preserves that character as much as possible. In this way hymn singing embodies something of the past in the present that may feel archaic, yet is important to the experience of being Welsh, Russian Mennonite, or a Sacred Harp singer. These traditional ways of singing create a sense of social identity through speech and tone. The tension between replicating the tradition and experimental creativity, however these notions are understood by the singers and leaders, are played out continually in these events.[16]

6. *Valued highly or ultimately, deeply felt, sentiment-laden, meaningful, serious*

   Although there may be a good deal of joyfulness, laughter, and playfulness during a hymn sing, the activity is treated with respect and seriousness. The purposes of hymn sings may be nostalgic (for example, singing through the *Sacred Harp* of 1844), sentimental (such as singing the old hymns that are no longer popular), or recreational (singing for its own sake). Whereas broader social values might be identified by the group, the values of individual participants may not be shared widely. Conflicts in values, styles, and pieties are a constant threat to the ritual action. Portions of a singing group preferring certain styles of music/text may oppose the preferences of other portions of the group. When angry or offended, people will not sing.

7. *Condensed, multilayered*

Numerous layers of knowledge are required to participate fully in a hymn-sing event. Minimally, a participant would need to be able to "follow along" in a musical mode, either by knowing the basic elements of music, by reading music, or by being able to imitate others musically. Skills for reading text are essential in many hymn sing settings. Fuller enjoyment of a singing event would require increasing knowledge of the hymn's history, the musical periods in which the tunes were composed, variations of the tune, different musical styles, different performance possibilities, theological allusions in the text, literary devices and poetic structures, various metaphors, something of the religious or social experience of the author that gave rise to the text, and the musical idiom of the tune.[17] The musical medium carries embedded cultural markers that create and reinforce identity and knowledge.

8. *Symbolic, referential (not merely technological or means end oriented)*

The simplicity of many hymn singing events is striking. The primary technological tool is the printed book. In some events musical instruments, such as piano, organ, electronic keyboard, or electric guitar, are technological additions. Depending on the size of the group singing, microphones may be required for the leaders. What participants gain from the experience cannot be predicted in advance of the event. It has little, if any, teleological significance. Often, it leads only to the possibility of participating in other hymn-singing events or the rejection of such events as social forms.

9. *Dramatic, ludic [play-like]*

For people with adequate musical and social knowledge hymn-singing events are fundamentally recreational and creative. Dramatic and playful qualities are often built into the movement and rhythm of the tunes and texts. Individual music leaders can effectively highlight these qualities through their interpretations and experimentation with hymns. Variations in tempo, voicing, rhythm, selection of stanzas, styles of directing, and the like, can give the impression that "you will never sing this hymn this way again." When skillful directors attempt reinterpretations or experiments on familiar hymns, the effects can be a heightened awareness of the hymns' text or the musical qualities of the tune. When leadership is not skillful, the experience may be disappointing or downright bad.

10. *Mystical, transcendent, religious, cosmic*

Hymn-singing events can expand the singers' sense of self and increase their awareness that "the sum is more than its parts."[18] There is far more going on than meets the eye or ear. This experience has something to do with how the physical properties of sound create space and a sense of being; how various voices create different qualities of sound; how the singers share some basic beliefs, values, and/or commitments (religious or otherwise); or how camaraderie is experienced through knowledge and practice of similar skills, facts, operations, and processes.

11. *Adaptive, functional*

No two hymn-singing events are conducted in precisely the same manner; choices of what to sing and how to sing are dictated by the time and place of the event, the group gathered to sing, the skills and interests of the leaders, and the frequency of such events. New hymns/songs may be introduced; different styles of leadership must be accommodated; adjustments are made in the acoustical space. Astute leaders are aware of various political agendas found in the group and may attempt to sing a wide range of hymn styles to keep everyone happy or to find "place" or a "voice" in the event.

12. *Conscious, deliberate*
     Since hymn singing events do not happen in the routine
     course of everyday life and are not a prescribed part of
     the liturgical cycle, finding one's way into such an activ-
     ity requires conscious choice and deliberate action.
     However, how the event is experienced and interpreted
     may stir unconscious thought and feeling, since music
     by its nature can carry singers to knowledge beyond the
     ability of words to capture.

As Grimes notes, using these characteristics to identify ritual
behavior has advantages over definitions of ritual because 1) they
account for a fuller range of ritual activity and experience, and 2) they
do not imply that the presence of only certain characteristics qualify as
ritual.[19] This approach permits hymn singing events to count as ritual
action even if all its individual parts do not confirm a particular ritual
theory nor are understood to be rites of a particular tradition.[20]

These characteristics can also serve to illustrate tensions or "failures" within the ritual event. Conflicts that arise from a leader's mis-
use of power and authority threaten the integrity of the ritual. Singers
may experience a sense of alienation or separation from the other
singers for any number of reasons ranging from musical inexperience,
religious doubts, difficulties in relationships with other singers, to dis-
like for the type of music sung or inadequate social knowledge of the
group that is singing. The failures of this ritual in a particular instance
do not undermine its character nor its power as ritual. In fact, dissatisfaction or "failure" may demonstrate the necessity of a specific ritual
activity and highlight the inadequacy of the conventional or traditional action that has been assumed. In the last two decades singing
hymns has been difficult for many people at different times. Many
images and metaphors found in the hymn texts have been experienced
as exclusive (particularly in terms of gender and race), oppressive, mili-
taristic, or meaningless. Other people have found the traditional hymn
a tired-out style that did not release the energy and joy of faith.
Whereas some people have needed to stop singing for a period of time,
few have stopped entirely. New hymn texts and musical styles are
being created that expand the singing repertoire, which has led to an
adaptation of the ritual form in many regions of North America.

Identifying hymn singing events as ritual behavior refocuses
attention on the "doing" aspects of the singers' actions and sets these
events on par with drama, music, dance, and sporting events. Although

these ritual actions are culturally and socially significant, they are not meant to accomplish anything in a teleological sense.

RITUAL AND MEANING

The theme investigated by the ritual study group (religious ritual: the mediator of memory and meaning) posed a problem for my study of singing events. Reflecting on my own participation in hymn-singing events as a singer and as a leader, I did not find "meaning" an entirely satisfying term around which to orient my experience of this ritual.

Since the Enlightenment, the quest for meaning, especially referential meaning, has dominated Western thought.[21] Aided by the increase of scientific investigations, logical positivism, and a philosophical tradition that has tended to separate the mind from experience, philosophers, scientists, and theologians, as well as the average person on the street, sought "the meaning" as an objective reality that could be apprehended by an objective observer. The interpretive processes that give rise to meaning have tended to collapse significant details of particular contexts or performances into broad generalizations; "meaning" could become increasingly divorced from the experience of people living in those settings.

Part of the difficulty in discerning the meaning of hymn-singing events lies with the problems presented in determining the meaning of music in general. Diane Raffman, a philosopher of music and cognition, says, "Music may be intended, but it isn't intentional; it isn't *about* anything. Except in certain contrived circumstances, . . . music does not refer or bear truth.[22]" Explicating "the meaning" of experiences, artifacts, or sounds that are not intentional, referential, or truth-bearing is difficult, if not impossible. Certain words or actions may take on symbolic or metaphoric qualities that can orient many divergent associations, relationships, and actions that give rise to meaning. Over time the "meaning(s)" of complex events might be constructed or reconstructed at social and personal levels. The problem is, of course, that associations, relationships, and actions are never static; meaning is always changing.

My interest in hymn singing events as ritual centers more on the processes of meaning-making through action. Before I can make meaning out of an action I have to know the action as being something significant to me as a person in relationship with other people, artifacts, and things in the natural world. I must know that something exists before I can determine what it means. I have assumed in this essay that

processes of knowing precede the processes of meaning-making in ritual action.

RITUAL AND KNOWING

Interest in processes of knowing through action has increased in recent
years, perhaps replacing the pursuit of "meaning" as the primary focus
of some disciplines.[23] Clearly, "meaning" has not been abandoned as a
significant factor in human experience, nor as a requirement for
human interaction. However, the shift attempts to account for the
active knower in the process of gaining knowledge and to challenge the
assumptions of objectivity and positivism that have undergirded societies of the West.

"Knowing," the present participle of "to know," has to do with
perceiving, understanding, recognizing, and being aware; knowing is
attentive action. It can be associated with intimacy or the perception
of hidden or secret qualities, as in the biblical sense of "to know" with
its overtly sexual connotations. The shape of knowledge acquired
through the action is governed by the social context in which the
potential knower is acting. Knowing leads to types of knowledge that
are characterized by competence, a sense of personal connectedness,
creativity, and transcendence.[24] Fundamentally, knowing leads to
knowledge of the self (its character, competencies, and weaknesses), of
others, and the relationship between the experience of the self and the
experience of others.[25]

Knowing is a process of learning, but also is a state of readiness to
receive and to explore the different stimuli that are apprehended in a
particular moment in a particular setting. In the case of this essay, a
knowing singer is situated in a specific place (a hymn singing event)
with specific kinds of experience (for instance, religious and/or musical training) to bring to bear in singing knowingly (that is, being aware
of the particular constraints and opportunities to make music with
others) in that event. The knowledge gained through experience is the
"stuff" from which meaning is made at personal and social levels.[26]

Investigating the noetic aspects of ritual using the specific example of hymn singing offers opportunities to explore the interfaces
between the self and the group, or the self in relationship to the group
more directly. This approach honors the reality of social/cultural
knowledge that is taught and assumed to guide social interaction; it
also honors the noetic processes within a particular individual that
create a sense of self in relationship that gives rise to action in some
form.

RITUAL AS A PROCESS OF KNOWING

Theodore Jennings' "On Ritual Knowledge" is one of the few articles in English that explores the noetic functions of ritual. His work provides a way into the dimensions of knowledge found at the level of the ritual action itself. He proposes three significant moments in understanding how knowing occurs: 1) "ritual action is a way of gaining knowledge . . . [and] may serve as a mode of inquiry and discovery"; 2) ritual serves to transmit knowledge; and 3) "ritual performance is a display of the ritual and of the participants in the ritual. . . ."[27]

Of Moment 1 Jennings assumes that ritual activity changes over time. Studies in liturgical history and the history of religions show that aspects of rites and general ritual behavior have always been improvised, elaborated, contracted, and eliminated.

> . . . we may nevertheless maintain that it is the openness to novelty inscribed in ritual liminality and the exploratory quest for the appropriate action which constitute the possibility of a history of ritual action even within a relatively stable ritual tradition.[28]

In spite of the appearance of fixed ritual forms, each performance of a rite or ceremony is unique. Shifts in linguistic meanings, differences in leadership style, changes in cultural and societal symbols, changes in gender roles and task assignments, and varying demographics within a community are representative examples of cultural and social changes that must be continually negotiated in ritual action.

Catherine Bell claims that ritual[29] is "a strategic social activity," whose purpose is socialization.[30] The actions that define or give shape to particular ritual practices highlight certain social values or networks of relationship and sublimate others.[31] Thus, ritual participants gain knowledge of themselves in the presence of various types of relationships, and through a collective action explore how to act in the ritual context. Ritual practices change over time because social power structures are continually shifting within a community.

One example of the effects of social change among Mennonites is seen in the increasing number of women invited to lead hymn sings. Since the 1970s women trained in music (and frequently having some seminary training as well) have planned and participated in leading large gatherings of singers. Their presence in the event as leaders has "put a different face" on musical authority and explicitly demonstrated a new awareness of gender equality.

Examining how ritual is explored and discovered pushes Jennings to a second significant assumption: ritual knowledge is gained through the ritual participant's body in action.

> We might speak here of the "incarnate" character of ritual knowledge or say that it is gained through "embodiment." This would be somewhat misleading, however. It is not so much that the mind "embodies" itself in ritual action, but rather that the body "minds" itself or attends through itself in ritual action. When engaged in ritual action . . . I do not first think through the appropriate action and then "perform it." Rather it is more like this: My hand "discovers" the fitting gesture . . . which I may then "cerebrally" *re*-cognize as appropriate or right. I may then attempt to give an account of this appropriateness. These are different epistemological steps of which only the first (attending and discovering through the body) is constitutive of ritual knowledge.[32]

This is a particularly useful point for considering the processes of knowing through singing. First, singing itself is a bodily action that cannot be achieved simply by thinking about it; singing must be done. If the singer does not "mind" his or her body, the sound created will be off key, unrhythmic, breathless or breathy, harsh, too loud or too soft, and so on. He or she learns when to clap, when to move, when to stand or sit, when to be silent, when to laugh, when (or whether) to shout and dance in the event. Singing makes the singer aware of and attentive to his or her body and to ways of being expressive vocally and rhythmically with it.[33] By attending to the bodily dimensions of hymn singing, singers discover how to sing, where sound is located in the body, which musical styles demand different body responses, the nature of rhythm, the feel of silence, different vocal interactions, the nature of breathing, and the like.

However, this bodily knowledge also demonstrates musical incompetence and may manifest a fear of failure. Singers who do not know how to get their bodies to feel music so that they can produce pleasing sounds know what it is to feel separated from themselves. To be tone deaf, to have little rhythmic sense, or not to know the repertoire of hymns that is familiar to others can lead to a sense of alienation. This sense of separation can be heightened when singing with a group, because incompetence is hard to hide. Many people find singing in groups terrifying for good reason. Singers must be initiated into this ritual form over a period of time so that their bodies learn how to work and what to do.

The goal of singing with a group is not to focus attention on one's body, but through such bodily awareness to join with others in making organized and pleasing sounds and coordinated movement. Singing creates a body of relationships. When singing fails, there is no body; singers are out of tune, out of rhythm, out of relationship. Sometimes this "out of body" situation is transitory and the singing body is quickly restored; at other times the situation is indicative of deeper difficulties. By attending to his or her body, a singer learns to fit his or her sound appropriately with the body of sounds created by others.

Of Moment 2, Jennings claims that the ritual participant gains knowledge of the ritual pattern and the types of actions that achieve successful movement through it. Singers experience the shape of the event—whether it is thoroughly planned by a leader, often appearing more formal, or more spontaneous and free form. This type of knowing happens in at least two ways. First, new singers are initiated into the action of the event itself with the help of other experienced singers, or by paying attention to directions given by the leaders. Second, experienced singers who know the pattern experience the different musical and textual styles, experience different leadership styles, and possibly a new body mindedness (for example, when to exert energy, how to save it, and such), which can improve their vocal production and singing pleasure.

Singers acting within the context of a singing event over time become, in Bell's sense, a "ritualized body."[34] Their responses may be unreflected or intentional, but they know how to act in a fitting way with the other singers in the context. The pattern of action shapes the way they "know" in the ritual environment and how they understand themselves and their actions within that setting.

Concerning Moment 3, Jennings notes, "To participate in ritual is to know how the 'world' acts, how it 'comes to be.' "[35] Ritual action is circular. It reveals how the world acts and how ritual participants should act in that world. Since ritual shows how this "world comes to be," it also shows how participants create that world. Ritual shapes the participants by showing them appropriate and fitting actions. These actions stimulate a wide range of attitudes, emotions, and ideas that, in turn, guide participants' present and future choices in ritual action.

Bell attributes the circularity of ritual action to the confines of specific ritual environments and the patterns of social interaction existing in those contexts:

> A focus on the acts themselves illuminates a critical circularity to the body's interaction with the environment: generating

it, it is molded by it in turn. By virtue of this circularity, space and time are redefined through the physical movements of bodies projecting organizing schemes on the space-time environment on the one hand while reabsorbing these schemes as the nature of reality on the other. In this process, such schemes become socially instinctive automatisms of the body and implicit strategies for shifting the power of relationships among symbols.[36]

Ritual action is a creative process. Participants bring to the ritual environment social experiences and knowledge outside of that world which are brought to bear upon their actions in the ritual context. This dynamic continually gives rise to the needs for discovery and exploration.

"The world" created by singing is primarily a world of sound. Singing creates a ritual space with acoustic, not visible, boundaries. This world is structured by musical possibilities and constraints, and supported secondarily by verbal or visual characteristics. Movement is probably this world's most dominant feature, because music itself is primarily movement.[37] Therefore, the world created by singing events is transitory and somewhat ephemeral. Though the sound is created by human bodies and mechanical instruments, it is disembodied immediately after its creation, freed to loft upward and to dissipate.

"This world" is not ultimately dominated by hierarchical social relationships; usually singers in this context stand on socially level ground. Leadership of the event may be passed around to various competent leaders, decisions that can enter into the realm of politics. Authority to lead is granted to those who have been initiated into the musical tradition of the group or have shown musical competence appropriate for the group. Power to decide how hymns may be interpreted normally resides with the leader, but his or her power to lead is controlled by the groups' willingness to be led through the hymn. Opening the opportunity for singers to request their favorite hymns erodes the leaders' power base considerably; not all leaders are competent to lead the hymns singers randomly request.

Since singers committed to a religious tradition are the usual participants in hymn singing events, the acoustic world created is believed to have a sacred character. Singing religious texts to appropriate music opens to a type of "real presence," and for many singers, this kind of singing is sacramental.[38]

Coming to know the singing group, its ethos, style, commitments, and values, is another kind of ritual knowledge. Knowing the group comes only through action in it. Breathing together, creating sound, resting in silence, listening to each other may reveal more about the group's dynamics than descriptions of visually observable aspects of the event. Kenneth Nafziger is a music professor at Eastern Mennonite College who frequently leads congregational and convention hymn-singing events throughout North America. During the course of a weekend, he says, he can tell a lot about the state of a particular congregation or group by the way in which its members sing together. His clues come from how the singers listen to each other as they sing; how eager they are (or are not) to learn new hymns; how pleased they are with themselves when they have learned a musically difficult tune; how quiet they are after creating a particularly wonderful sound; or how energized they feel for a day or two after having a "good sing."

"The world(s)" created through hymn singing events are always different because the particular group of people singing together is always different. When conflict, alienation, or apathy are evident in the group, these realities will manifest themselves in the ritual world. This does not imply a failure of the ritual action to make "a perfect world"; rather, the ritual action demonstrates and perhaps even highlights the conflicts and unresolved issues within the group.

Jennings' essay highlights three spheres in which the noetic functions of ritual are experienced: knowing through the body; knowing the ritual action itself; knowing the social world of the community through a common action. Bell's view that ritual is a social strategy that creates a ritualized social body and realigns relationships helps to focus Jennings' work by showing more clearly the purpose of ritual action.

Michael Polanyi's investigation into personal knowledge complements Jennings' and Bell's points. His explorations take this discussion more directly into the realm of knowing processes in the individual, which neither Jennings or Bell address.

RITUAL AND PERSONAL KNOWING

Polanyi pursued his investigation of personal knowing in the context of the scientific community working under the belief that all investigations could be objective, unaffected by the personal experience of the observer observing. His concerns are reflected in these themes that circle throughout his writings: 1) knowing is achieved through action; 2) knowing processes produce tacit knowledge in the knower, who is shaped by a social context; 3) knowing is a result of the repository of skills and tacit knowledge the knower brings to a specific context; and 4) human beings know far more than what they can possibly say.

The workings of the natural world, conventional wisdom, common sense, and socially agreed upon rules are the bases for a person's tacit knowledge. These are structures and patterns of knowledge that are accepted as being the way things are or the way in which things are done. Language acquisition is probably the most significant form of tacit knowledge. Unreflective action, based on knowledge accumulated through experience, is tacit. Physical skills, language use, utilizing conceptual frameworks, interpretive reasoning, and reflexive actions are primary examples of tacit knowledge.

Polanyi does not speak directly of the body as a vehicle for personal knowing as Jennings and Bell do, yet it is clear from the examples he uses in *Personal Knowledge* and other writings that experiences in the body contribute directly to the processes of knowing. He asserts that personal knowledge is acquired through the performance of various kinds of skills.

> I regard knowing as an active comprehension of the things known, an action that requires skill. Skillful knowing and doing is [sic] performed by subordinating a set of particulars, as clues or tools, to the shaping of a skillful achievement, . . . practical and theoretical. . . . They are made to function as extensions of our bodily equipment and this involves a certain change in our own being. . . .[39]

The role of the body in the processes of knowing is seen most clearly in his discussion of subsidiary and focal awareness, where physical skillfulness is a significant dimension of knowing. Playing a musical instrument, typing, driving a car, using a hammer, running, writing, knitting, and the like, are examples of tacit knowledge that resides in a background or exists in a subsidiary way in a knower's consciousness and muscles. These bodily skills are the means or tools with which a knower can explore a situation with focal awareness. As soon as a knower begins to concentrate on the subsidiary skills required to accomplish a task, rather than on the focus of the task, the process of knowing breaks down.

> Subsidiary awareness and focal awareness are mutually exclusive. If a pianist shifts his [sic] attention from the piece he is playing to the observation of what he is doing with his fingers while playing it, he gets confused and may have to stop. This happens generally if we switch our focal attention to particu-

lars of which we had previously been aware only in their subsidiary role.⁴⁰ *skillfully known — over time becomes automatic.*

Even though subsidiary and focal awareness are distinct moments in
the knowing process, they merge at the point of action. One may say
that she has a subsidiary awareness of feelings in her hand that is
merged into her focal awareness of playing a piece.⁴¹

Personal knowledge parallels Jennings' claim that ritual knowledge comes through the body minding itself, discovering the fitting
action. In the case of hymn singing, once that fitting action is found, it
becomes part of the singers' tacit knowledge. This ever-increasing
body of tacit knowledge provides the means for the singer to engage
more deeply in the ritual, experiencing thoughts, feelings, intuitions,
and relationships with others more fully. Engagement in the ritual
action of music making in relationship with others is at the center of
the singer's focal awareness; the tacit knowledge acquired through
repeated experiences moves in the singers' subsidiary or secondary
awareness. Thus, ritual knowledge is acquired continuously over time.

Participants bring to a hymn singing event different levels of subsidiary and focal awareness, which affect their abilities to know in the
event. Those who cannot bring the tacit knowledge of reading music or
texts to bear may focus on imitating others or on listening to the sound
created by other competent singers. Those who cannot sense the
rhythm of the tunes or who cannot follow the tempos set will feel confused and frustrated. They may feel like the pianist who is suddenly
paralyzed when her attention fixes on a tricky fingering, shifting her
awareness from playing the entire phrase. Like the pianist, they will
have to fight to center their attention again. Leaders of hymn singing
events must be attuned to the skillfulness of the singers; this ability to
be aware of the singers' abilities is a dimension of competence required
in a leader. Singing many tunes that are technically beyond the reach of
the majority of singers will not yield a satisfying experience for anyone.

Singers who can concentrate their focal awareness on singing
while using their tacit knowledge might become aware of other
aspects of their experience. For example, they may recognize the different feelings the music evokes in them, the sense of being more than a
solo voice, the energy released in their bodies and in the atmosphere
through singing, the structure of the music, or perhaps a more vague
sense of pleasure or satisfaction. Singers who feel alienation from their
own bodies or the body of singers around them will likely not experience much satisfaction. Their focal attention is being constantly dis-
tracted by inadequate tacit knowledge.

In "Knowing and Being" Polanyi claims that knowing occurs within a milieu in which the knower integrates the experiences of 1) the stimuli that come from outside the body and yet can be known only through the body, and 2) a range of word or linguistic concepts based on past experiences that interpret specific aspects of the milieu (objects, relationships, actions, and the like). The tacit knowledge that results is integrated into conceptual structures that exist internally in the knower's consciousness. With these structures or frameworks, a knower can make sense out of the various aspects of experience. Polanyi says:

> To this extent knowing is an indwelling; that is a utilization of a framework for unfolding our understanding in accordance with the indications and standards imposed by the frame-work. But any particular indwelling is a particular form of mental existence. If an act of knowing affects our choice between alternative frameworks or modifies the framework in which we dwell, it involves a change in our way of being.[42]

indwelling

This indwelling framework may take the form of a ritual pattern or of a series of ritual actions. It orients the participant's actions in the ritual environment and reinforces understandings of the social relationships present within the environment. Yet, because ritual action is circular, the participant is continually experiencing new knowledge that shifts the framework of action.

Since this indwelling framework represents the totality of personal knowledge gained through experience, it is central to a ritual participant's sense of him or herself. Thus, any shifts in the ritual framework, large or small, will change the participant's personal sense of self within the action; it changes her or her way of being.[43]

People who have never attended a hymn sing do not have this ritual framework indwelling. They may leave with a description of what happens at such events based on their observations of the action sequence. They have no internal structure to orient their behavior toward it. The experience can tumble over them and may leave them feeling overwhelmed or indifferent. If their sense of self has changed at all, it is through the awareness that they are outsiders to the event; the power such ritual has for others may not yet be felt.

However, experienced singers, who can sense changes in the ritual, anticipate something new. The introduction of new hymns with unfamiliar rhythms and harmonies, different musical interpretations of familiar hymns, different types of vocal layering and vocal interactions, or even the season of the year when the event is held open possibilities for singers to know differently. They may come to know something that intensifies or changes their sense of who they are.

Whereas much more could be made out of Polanyi's work on knowing, it suffices now to have shown that his understanding of tacit knowledge, subsidiary and focal awareness, and indwelling can further explain some of the noetic processes that Jennings points to in his essay. Ritual knowledge is part of the tacit or unreflective knowledge that is necessary to know "how to act" in a ritual event; this is knowledge of the body and of the mind. Focal awareness centers on the action at hand, but also is the state in which ritual exploration and discovery occur in the context of the social body. The ritual action itself is the center of the singers' focal awareness. The indwelling framework provides a means for knowing and interpreting the world that singing creates and for the singer to know him or herself in that world. Polanyi's insights deal with the physical and mental competencies that are required to experience hymn singing ritual satisfactorily and with the changes in self awareness that result from knowing in the ritual context. His insights on self awareness are the connecting point with Douglas Hall's process of faith development. Although certain aspects of Polanyi's and Hall's epistemologies are similar, they are not overlapping approaches. Polanyi's work focuses primarily on social and cognitive aspects of knowing, whereas Hall's work focuses more directly on intersubjective aspects.

RITUAL AND LEVELS OF KNOWING

Hall's insights are particularly useful for getting closer to the experience of well-initiated singers for whom singing events have a sacramental power.

Hall identifies three sequential levels of knowing that are active in the development of faith. The first level, knowledge, is the acquisition of basic facts about the tradition, religion, group, or the like, that float independently of an individual. (In Polanyi's model, these facts would constitute a framework within which knowledge and experiences of knowing are organized. Such facts would constitute one type of tacit knowledge.) These facts need not be verifiable under rigorous scientific scrutiny, but simply are those essential elements that make life within a particular worldview, religion, or domain of experience intelligible.[44] There need not be any moral, psychological, nor religious commitment to these facts; thus a Christian may know facts about Buddhism without knowing them to have persuasive or orienting power in his or her life.

Acknowledgment, the second level, is an intermediary state in which some knowledge about the tradition takes on personal significance. The knower now allows these facts to be persuasive in personal interactions, daily actions, and decision making:

> . . . we need to recognize the difficulty of explaining precisely why certain information, which was formerly *only* information, became significant. Obviously it always has something to do with personal experience. Something happened to one, some new constellation of events and attitudes, and in the process what was previously mere fact became relevant fact. It helped to explain something.[45]

Hall does not mention explicitly the role that language plays in this transition from knowledge to acknowledgment, but this passage suggests that naming experience(s) in different ways is an important milestone in this transition.

In Polanyi's scheme, these personal experiences represent a context requiring focal awareness. Within that context the tacit knowledge of the faith tradition, which is part of the knower's subsidiary awareness, guides the knower's actions. As this tacit knowledge is used more, his or her understanding of the facts begins to shift the framework, and he or she discovers a new way of being in the world.

Trust is the final level of knowing in Hall's typology, which includes personal relationships, requires personal decision, and engages the will. The transition from acknowledgment to trust is rooted in the personal experience of living within the language and practices of a religious tradition over a period of time. Hall characterizes trust as a change of relationship.

> When I say that I know my friend, I obviously mean something quite different from either the possession of knowledge or the acknowledgment of certain ideas of truths. I mean that there exists between myself and this other person a certain *relationship*. . . . The relationship did not occur merely as a result of the information I possessed about her, or even as a consequence of the fact that some of that information became important or meaningful. . . . Something has to happen, some new dimension has to be introduced, if I am to pass from the state of acknowledging someone to the state of knowing him or her in this third, *interior* sense.[46] (italics added)

The first two levels of knowing that Hall describes are essentially cognitive. There are dimensions of knowing at the levels of knowledge and acknowledgment that remain independent of the knower's experience and outside of his or her desire to comprehend. The third level moves inward, reaching beyond the mind, though the direction of this movement is not clear. One might take the statement to mean knowing the interior, hidden nature or character of another person, or equally plausible, as the knower recognizing within him or herself a response to the nature or character of the other. In his discussion on decision Hall suggests that both senses are possible.

> . . . this third kind of knowing seems to occur in one as a matter of *decision*. I decided—but it would be better to say that *I find myself deciding*—that this other one has some kind of claim on me and, correspondingly, that I have some kind of responsibility for this other. . . . I use the word "decision" . . . to mean that whatever occurs when a person moves over into this kind of personal knowledge of someone else, it is something which involves not only *rational* activity but the activity of the whole self. This means in a specific sense that activity of what we call the *will*. . . . Willing . . . is a summing-up of the whole person, inclusive of thinking and inclusive of feeling, but transcending both. . . . It is the knowing of an encounter between persons who indeed know that they will *never* know each other fully in the fact-knowledge sense, and will *never* acknowledge in one another fully everything that really *is* significant about the other, but who nevertheless determine to commit themselves to one another.[47]

Marriage is Hall's recurring image for this kind of knowing, though he does not claim it exclusively. Any relationship in which another being is treated as a "thou" in Martin Buber's sense, is a trusting, knowing relationship. Knowing in this way is fundamental to the emotional and spiritual experience of human being.

The interior nature of trust and the knowledge that results from living in that state correspond with Polanyi's concept of indwelling. The knower grows in knowledge of the one known, whether it is one's parent, spouse, child, friend, or God. What is central to both epistemologies is the interior yet intersubjective nature of the knowing processes.

Everyone participating in a hymn-singing event must begin at Hall's first level of knowledge. A few examples of facts that participants find useful to know are 1) the significant place given to religious singing in the expressive life and faith of Christians; 2) the theological importance ascribed to the gathered community; 3) the hymn as an art form; 4) the significance of hymns as an expression of individual and/or corporate piety; 5) the unique possibilities of music for expressive behavior; and 6) fundamental concepts, images, and/or experiences that give form to Christian faith. (Notice that the skill of singing need not be an essential fact, since it is a form of tacit knowledge that contributes to a different kind of subsidiary awareness in the participant.)

Singers at the level of acknowledgment (the level where many regular hymn singers are found) would recognize that the experience of hymn singing plays some role in their expression of faith. They would recognize that participation in a group united in a common activity has significance for their sense of self; they might touch unacknowledged aspects of their personal experience through singing in verbal and/or musical languages or experience again a significant memory. At this stage, singers can remain skeptical of the singing ritual even while participating in it. These singers do not necessarily throw themselves into singing with abandon; their participation can be tentative and selective.

In contrast, singers who are in a state of trust are absorbed fully in the activity. Their attention is focused on the creation of sound with others and engagement in the action. Singing throws them into various kinds of interpersonal, cultural, and social relationships, some of which can be described, some which cannot be named. In singing they experience a way of knowing themselves and others and of being known that cannot be experienced any other way. A seminarian once told me that she experiences a sense of community in singing; another student recounted to me an experience she had of transcendence, of being lifted above this world. An evangelical church musician claims that the congregation can come to know itself as a priesthood of believers,[48] a theological claim about the nature of the church that is sometimes difficult to work out in practice. When melody, text, and harmonic structure have worked together and singers have willingly joined their voices in the ritual action, people have known joy, sorrow, healing, a sense of the past, or a sense of hope for the future. Knowing in this deep personal sense permits a singer to trust the experience as being authentic, to name its power though never fully describing its significance, and to be shaped by this experience of communal relationship, not unlike the way one is shaped by relationships with spouse, friend, child, or lover.

These last paragraphs have the tone of testimony; they spring from my experiences as a singer, as a leader, and as a friend and colleague with other singers and leaders. I have not experienced the depths of knowledge claimed above in every hymn singing event I have attended; far from it. Some events have been exhilarating; others downright boring or irritating. But I and other friends have had the experience of knowing and of being known in these ritual events. The task now is to move this work from testimony to a more systematic study of the interfaces between self, group, action, knowledge, and spirituality that exist through this ritual form.

Hall's work offers possibilities for getting closer to the spiritual and affective dimensions of hymn singing events. Trust is the dimension of knowing that needs more investigation in regard to ritual practice. The theoretical views offered by Jennings, Bell, and Polanyi are helpful for understanding this ritual form more fully, but it is the work implied by Hall's insights that will be most significant.

HYMN-SINGING EVENTS AS A RITUAL STRATEGY

People who sing regularly with others in hymn singing events feel deeply about the experience; they anticipate something of significance will happen when the words of their tongues mingle with the notes of others.

> There is a delight in and a feeling for this music that cannot be transferred. . . . At a *Sacred Harp* session when the singing reaches a certain level—when the singers respond wholly to the music—it is almost as if they are only receptacles, vessels for something age-old which lives again through them. As the old songs well up through and around them, the singers submit to the effects of the music with a kind of awe.[49]

Testimonies like this one are frequently found in the literature on hymn singing. For many modern and postmodern folks hymn singing is a quaint but sentimental practice for old ladies. For others, submitting to the effects of the music has also meant submitting to oppression and marginalization in their congregations, their families, or their communities. They can no longer submit. Awesome. Antiquated. Oppressive. All true.

The idea that ritual is strategic action is curious, considering the fact that the ritual form of hymn singing promises to accomplish so little. Many Christian denominations do quite well without using hymn-singing events to bolster congregational life. Why, then, do some religious groups regularly employ hymn singing events as a ritual strategy? Why would they choose to supplement their regular liturgical life with this ritual practice? I have hinted at two hypotheses throughout

this essay. First, singers can know only some dimensions 1) of their
social relationships in the physical world and 2) of themselves in relationship to the sacred (God) within that physical and social world of
hymn-singing events. Second, how singers know and the types of
knowledge they gain through this ritual practice could lead to a better
understanding of how the self changes through group interaction. The
following are starting points for a more methodic testing of these
hypotheses through interviews with singers and event leaders, through
participant observation, and through combing the descriptive literature of hymn-singing events.

1. Hymn-singing events establish a sense of order and move-
    ment. The medium of music itself, with its characteristics
    of rhythm, melodic progression, tonal center, and restruc-
    turing of time profoundly shapes the communal experi-
    ence of hymn-singing events, but how? What effect do
    these characteristics have on singers' experience of sing-
    ing? On their sense of self? What must a body know to be
    able to sing? What difference does it make that nearly all
    gospel songs are in major keys and that most *Sacred Harp*
    tunes are modal? How do such musical matters affect the
    singers' relationship to the sacred (God)?
2. Hymn-singing events can create a sense of communal
    unity, cohesiveness, or esprit de corps that is palpable.
    Knowing a sense of group unity is a common assumption
    about singing, and is well established in the literature on
    the social aspects of music. What actions in the ritual
    change the singers' awareness from "I" to "we" or from
    "we" to "I"? How does the experience of sound shape the
    singers' sense of relationship with others? How does the
    energy and movement of the acoustic world created by the
    group change the singers' self-perception? This point is a
    natural outgrowth of the first, but musical characteristics
    are rarely taken into account in discussions of the sense of
    unity that singing creates.

    On another plane, the relationship between group
    unity and the experience of the sacred needs examination.
    What musical qualities, forms of tacit knowledge, or previ-
    ous religious experience contribute to the sense of sacra-
    ment that some singers experience through singing? How
    does a common group action foster this sense of the

sacred? Under what conditions does the hymn singing ritual fail to unify?

3.   Hymn-singing events are a medium of communal expressiveness. Certainly the musical and poetic aspects of hymns contribute to the expression of some intent or purpose. In the Public Broadcasting System special "Amazing Grace," a song leader of a Sacred Harp singing convention reflected,

> . . . it's more than just the sound [of the singing], it's the fellowship and the love that we have for one another that makes us sing our hearts out for one another.[50]

What is there about the nature of hymn singing that allows it to be a means for expressing love and personal identification with other singers? How do trust, body mindedness, and indwelling contribute to the singers' ability to be expressive? How are singers known to each other through singing?

4.   Hymn-singing events are primarily celebrations, special events that connect the past and present. At least two significant characteristics of celebrations that apply here are memory and playfulness. Under what circumstances would hymn-singing events be a strategy to connect with the memory of past events or a past time? How do such events orient time in the present for singers? How do singers' experience the past through singing? How does memory affect the singers' sense of self in this ritual action?

Because each singing event is an end in itself and set apart from the regular liturgical routine, it has many qualities that characterize play.[51] This is what gives singing events their re-creational or creative sense. Do singers feel re-created through the event? What contributes to that sense of recreation? To what extent do singers experience these events as a form of play with the sacred (God)?

5.   Hymn-singing events can realign power relationships in a group; they can create, in Victor Turner's words, a sense of spontaneous *communitas*.[52] Song leaders and/or instrumentalists are recognized roles within the event; however, their power to lead depends entirely upon the singers' willingness to be led. Since hymn singing events are a ritual strategy frequently employed in groups with little or no

hierarchical clerical ordering (so-called "low church" groups), it is reasonable to ask how singers experience the relationship between leadership in this ritual action and other forms of leadership. How are leaders selected? How are the leader's power and authority recognized or negotiated? How does the alignment of power and authority contribute to the singers' sense of unity?

CONCLUSION

Noetic

Mapping the various aspects and dimensions of singers' noetic processes would constitute a significant work toward understanding this ritual as a social strategy. Hymn-singing events are an intersection of ritual action, social psychology, art, theology, and spirituality that deserves attention. Explorations of these events could help illuminate the noetic qualities of various types of relationships that are set in motion through ritual and the intersubjective nature of ritual action in general. Knowledge of the ritual participant as a social and interrelated self is needed to understand better how ritual action specifically changes his or her relationships, ideas, affections, and/or faith. We would know more fully how it is that a tongue refined by art of song could mingle (with all the richness this word implies) its notes with our own.

NOTES

1. From *Zion's Songster*, 1831.

2. This hymnal was published jointly by the Church of the Brethren, the General Conference Mennonite Church, and the Mennonite Church of North America. *Hymnal: A Worship Book* (Elgin, IL: The Brethren Press; Newton, KS: Faith and Life Press; Scottdale, PA: Mennonite Publishing House), 1992.

3. Further work on hymn-singing events would require careful attention to the different styles of "hymn sing" performance found among various groups of singers. In addition the relationship of hymn-singing events and other types of protracted singing in worship settings (e.g., praise and worship periods or "singing in the spirit") and other group singing situations (e.g., jam sessions, folk singing, or "hootenanny") would need to be explored.

4. Descriptions of hymn-singing events may be found in the following sources. These examples by no means exhaust the list of extant reports.

Lois S. Blackwell, *The Wings of the Dove* (Norfolk, VA: Donning Publishing Co., 1978); Buell E. Cobb, Jr., *The Sacred Harp: A Tradition and Its Music* (Athens, GA: The University of Georgia Press, 1978); George Pullen Jackson, *White Spirituals in the Southern Uplands* (New York: Dover Publications, 1965); Alan Luff, *Welsh Hymns and Their Tunes*: Their *Background and Place in Welsh History and Culture* (Carol Stream, IL: Hope Publishing Company, 1990); Ellen Jane Lorenz, *Glory, Hallelujah! The Story of the Campmeeting Spiritual* (Nashville, TN: Abingdon Press, 1980).

5. Ronald Grimes, *Ritual Criticism: Case Studies in Its Practice, and Essays on Its Theory* (Columbia, SC: University of South Carolina Press, 1990).

6. Theodore Jennings, "On Ritual Knowledge," *Journal of Religion*, 62:2 (April 1982), pp. 111–127.

7. *Ritual Theory, Ritual Practice* (New York: Oxford University Press, 1992).

8. Michael Polanyi, *Personal Knowledge: Toward a Post-Critical Philosophy* (Chicago: University of Chicago Press, 1958, 1962); "Knowing and Being," in *Knowing and Being*, edited by Marjorie Grene, (Chicago: University of Chicago Press, 1969); and *Meaning*, ed. Michael Polanyi and Harry Prosch (Chicago: University of Chicago Press, 1975).

9. Douglas J. Hall, *Thinking the Faith* (Minneapolis, MN: *Augsburg, 1989*).

10. Bell, p. 74. For comparison with Grimes' definitions see *Ritual Criticism*, p. 10.

11. One might argue that since they occur outside of the normal flow of liturgical activity, they could be considered a liminal state. However, I am not yet ready to concede that liminality is a useful way of understanding people's experience in these events.

12. Mircea Eliade's notion of the "eternal return," of experiencing an ancient past time in a mythic way, could offer a helpful way of understanding the experience of hymn-singing events. Singers have reported that the significance of an event is found in singing the "good old songs" that help them remember past experiences that have oriented their lives in great or small ways. Others associate certain hymns with people in particular situations (the funeral of a loved one is a frequent association); singing them again brings to mind people who may be far removed from the singing context. Remembering their personal history with these hymns helps singers reestablish their sense of place in the present (see quotation from Buell Cobb, p. 34). But this theory does not explain as much about the ritual as it might seem.

13. Richard Payne's insistence that ritual stands on its own and does not stand for something else must also be insisted on here. (See Payne's essay in this volume). The efficacy of singing events is found in their immediacy and in their independence from other ritual cycles and theological claims.

14. Grimes, *Ritual Criticism*, p. 9.

15. Ibid., p. 17. Grimes' list of ritual qualities also includes the following, which do not clearly serve the purposes of this essay:

- Patterned, invariant, standardized, stereotyped, ordered, rehearsed (not improvised, idiosyncratic, or spontaneous)
- Perfected, idealized, pure, ideal (not conflictual or subject to criticism and failure)
- Paradigmatic (not ineffectual in modeling either other rites or nonritualized action)

16. Hymn-singing events not only configure and reconfigure patterns of power, as Marty Stortz suggests in her essay, but also can configure and reconfigure social and cultural identity through singing hymns that have been part of "me and my people" and hymns that are not part of "me and my people."

17. Mary Oyer has charted a number of layers ("dimensions" is her word) of hymns in an unpublished paper presented to members of the Mennonite and Church of the Brethren Hymnal Project in October 1987. She identifies among others:

- Poetic: imagery, metaphor, rhythm, rhyme
- Musical: rhythm, pattern, harmony, repetition, tone
- Intersection of Poetic and Musical: Physical aspects of voice production, intellect and emotion joined, interpretive possibilities in union of text and music
- Heritage of ancestors: musical, religious, cultural
- Identification with a tradition
- Historical periods when music or text was written
- Polemics/Politics of the hymn (in its original setting or in the present)
- Didactic qualities
- Theological claims
- Social functions: as group activity, as mode of communication
- Ritual function in worship/liturgy
- Proclamation of intention/Commitments made through singing

- Memory: individual and group
- Associations: sentiments, insights, thoughts
- Connections with other cultures and traditions

18. Michael Aune's discussion of the subject in his essay in this volume intersects with this particular point. The self, or subject, singing with others is in the position to "see, feel, and understand their social reality and subjective identity." All the cultural and social markers of these events meet the personal history of the self, or subject, who is singing. This intersection creates the possibility for expansion in awareness of the self/subject and society or a contraction of awareness created by alienation, marginalization, or rejection.

19. Grimes, p. 14.

20. Establishing singing events as ritual activity is important not only methodologically for the sake of this essay, but for the sake of singers who do not recognize their behavior as ritual action. Given the cultural distrust of most ritual forms and the fear that ritual can become dead and lifeless, most singers in these events have refused to consider the ritual aspects of their behavior or have not reflected methodically upon their ritual action. According to Bell, these people mis-recognize their behavior as ritual. (See Bell, *Ritual Theory, Ritual Practice*, pp. 108–110.) Many of them would recognize Grimes' characteristics of ritual in their experience of singing events, but would be dubious of the thought that this behavior qualifies as ritual; they would not be able to see that the reason these events "work" is due in part to their ritual elements.

21. Jerry H. Gill, *On Knowing God* (Philadelphia: Westminster Press, 1981), p. 13.

22. Diana Raffman, *Language, Music, and Mind* (Cambridge, MA: The MIT Press, 1993), p. 41.

23. Cursory examples of this new focus used in this preliminary work include:

Gregory Bateson and Mary Catherine Bateson, *Angels Fear: Toward an Epistemology of the Sacred* (New York: Macmillan Publishing Company, 1987) [anthropology]; Mary Field Belenky, et al., *Women's Ways of Knowing: The Development of Self, Voice and Mind* (New York: Basic Books, Inc., 1986) [a popular press book in the area of women's studies and psychology]; Elliot Eisner, ed., *Learning and Teaching the Ways of Knowing: Eighty-fourth Yearbook of the National Society for the Study of Education* (Chicago: The National Society for the Study of Education, 1985) [education]; Jerry H. Gill, *On Knowing God* (Philadelphia: The Westminster Press, 1982) [theology];

Michael Polanyi, *Personal Knowledge* (Chicago: University of Chicago Press, 1962) [philosophy].

This list does not begin to touch the myriad of articles and books of a more technical nature that address issues of epistemology raised in the disciplines of anthropology, history, linguistics, philosophy, psychology, sociology, and theology.

24. Duane E. Huebner, "Spirituality and Knowing," in *Learning and Teaching the Ways of Knowing*, ed. Elliot Eisner.

25. Huebner, p. 169. Michael Aune's discussion of the subject in this volume also supports this claim.

26. At this point my interests touch on those of Michael Aune's work. Both of us are concerned about locating the "subject" within a social and cultural setting that gives rise to cognitive, affective, and, possibly, spiritual ways of being. My focus is on the knower and what he or she comes to know through experience in a particular context. Aune's focus is on the meaning-maker in the context and how he or she creates meaning. There are points where two endeavors overlap, and the line between knowing and meaning becomes obscured.

27. Jennings, pp. 115, 120–123.

28. Jennings, p. 115.

29. Bell's term is ritualization.

30. Bell, p. 98.

31. Ibid., p. 100.

32. Jennings, p. 115

33. It is not surprising that hymn-singing events flower in religious communities where strong prohibitions against dancing exist. Singing becomes an acceptable form of bodily expression that in other traditions and cultures is shared with dance.

34. Bell, p. 98.

35. Jennings, p. 121.

36. Bell, p. 99.

37. Roger Sessions, *The Musical Experience of Composer, Performer, Listener* (Princeton, NJ: Princeton University Press, 1950), p. 19.

38. George Steiner, *Real Presences* (Chicago: University of Chicago Press, 1989), p. 217. Steiner claims that the musical art form itself invites an experience of "real presence."

> Music and the metaphysical, in the root sense of that term, music and religious feeling, have been virtually inseparable. It is in and through music that we are most immediately in the presence of the logically, of the verbally inexpressible

but wholly palpable energy in being that communicates to our senses and to our reflection what little we can grasp of the naked wonder of life. I take music to be the naming of the naming of life. This is, beyond any liturgical or theological specificity, a sacramental motion.

39. Michael Polanyi, *Personal Knowledge: Toward a Post-Critical Philosophy* (Chicago: University of Chicago Press, 1958,1962), p. vii.

40. Polanyi, *Personal Knowledge*, p. 56. Gender-exclusive language his.

41. Polanyi's example here is of using a hammer ("Personal Knowledge," p. 33).

Jennings' uses the example of the Communion chalice to show that knowing how to handle it can be achieved only by handling it. Such knowledge cannot be achieved through contemplation or observation, but through the body. As the chalice is handled more frequently, one's movement becomes a form of tacit knowledge that contributes to one's subsidiary awareness of the communion celebration. As one's competence increases, one's focal awareness attends to other aspects of the eucharistic rite. (Jennings, p. 116).

42. Polanyi, "Knowing and Being," p. 134.

43. Much has been written about religious ritual and personal transformation. The general theme is: ritual agents in the presence of holy or sacred things (whose ontological status in the natural world has been changed) are transformed by their contact with these sacred objects. This is a foundational assumption in the *ex opere operato* belief of ritual efficacy. Jennings', Polanyi's, and Hall's work point toward an understanding of a ritual participant who is transformed by knowing more about the form and media of the event, about others present, and about themselves. Transformation through ritual comes from continually gaining more knowledge of how to be in the presence of other (holy or not) things and how to interact with them. This is knowledge that can be gained in no other way.

44. Hall, p. 373.

45. Ibid., pp. 379–380.

46. Ibid., p. 382.

47. Ibid., pp. 382–83.

48. Donald P. Hustad, *Jubilate! Church Music in the Evangelical Tradition* (Carol Stream, IL: Hope Publishing Company, 1981), p. 44.

49. Buell E. Cobb, Jr., *The Sacred Harp: A Tradition and Its Music*, p. 155.

50. Bill Moyers, "Amazing Grace," Public Broadcasting System Special (October 1990).

51. Cf. Josef Pieper, *In Tune with the World* (Chicago: Franciscan Herald Press, 1963); Gerhard M. Martin, *Fest: The Transformation of Everyday*, trans. M. Douglas Meeks (Philadelphia: Fortress Press, 1976); Johan Huizinga, *Homo Ludens: A Study of the Play Element in Culture* (Boston: Beacon Press, 1950).

52. Victor Turner, *The Ritual Process: Structure and Anti-Structure* (Chicago: Aldine, 1969), p. 132.

Part III

Clinical Explorations

Introductory Essay

VALERIE DeMARINIS

This third and last set of essays (Gay, DeMarinis, Driskill, Noonan) involves application and analysis of ritual processes in the actual contexts of psychotherapy or other therapeutic frameworks. Each essay is formatted as a dialogue between an approach to ritual process and a contextual application of that process. In addition, each essay investigates religious and social ritual functionally and phenomenologically. Thus, this section focuses on personal experiences of particular rituals and their resulting psychosocial consequences.

Although the essays are similar in format and function, their theoretical approaches to the study and analysis of ritual vary. These variations represent existing and emerging viewpoints in the theoretical and clinical arenas in each of the following areas: psychology of religion, depth psychology and psychotherapy, pastoral psychology and psychotherapy, feminist psychotherapy, and ritual studies.

The essays written by Gay, DeMarinis, and Driskill focus on different clinical contexts of psychotherapy in order to investigate the nature and function of religious ritual, memory, and meaning. Gay's essay focuses on the relationship, comparison, and contrast between ritual and psychotherapy. In his exploration of the topic, depth psychology concentrating on the intra-psychic process represents psychotherapy and Korean shamanistic practices represent the ritual component. Gay argues for the need to understand the normative component of religious ritual, one of the central differences between the ritual process and the psychotherapeutic process. DeMarinis' essay involves a case study of cross-cultural adjustment. It traces the psychological consequences of loss of ritual symbols, experience, the emergence of their meaning-making structure from culture and belief, and the pivotal role of access to and incorporation of ritual symbols and ritual experience within the psychotherapeutic process for assisting cross-cultural adjustment. DeMarinis' clinical context is that of pastoral psychotherapy, with an emphasis on a cross-cultural preventive

209

approach. Driskill's essay concentrates on presentation and analysis of a clinical case where traumatic ritual memory of childhood abuse plagues an adult female survivor. In the course of psychotherapy, ritual expression is used as a therapeutic tool for reconstruction and new meaning-making. Driskill's clinical context is also that of pastoral psychotherapy. Noonan's essay, through a case illustration, focuses on the importance of recognizing the symbolic and ritualistic dimensions of short-term hospitalization for surgery and the traumatic aspects arising when recognition of such is not present. He proposes a framework for recognizing the need for the development of clinical rites of passage in the hospital process and context.

These clinical essays are situated intentionally as the final section in this volume for three reasons. First, by their nature, they involve interdisciplinary endeavors whereby comparative and liturgical approaches to the study of religious and social ritual may prove to be a helpful background of reference. The essays of Gay, DeMarinis, and Noonan, for example, involve comparative ritual issues. Gay discusses the Korean shaman's ritual world and compares it to a North American ritual system. DeMarinis' clinical case involves a Brazilian student's process of cross-cultural adjustment to North American culture and meaning-making systems. Noonan's essay focuses on the clinical case of a Mexican-American woman using her social and cultural rituals in a North American hospital context. Liturgical concerns are also involved—that is, particular religious and/or social ritual practices and experiences of individuals in the context of their religious and cultural traditions.

Second, the comparative and liturgical concerns encountered in these clinical essays are explored by means of a psychosocial approach to ritual process. It can be argued that an intentional shift of focus occurs in this section from comparative or liturgical examination of religious rituals within specific traditions to what can be understood as a functional investigation of the psychosocial consequences of ritual participation. In this respect, all four of the essays proceed in their investigation of religious and social ritual in much the same way as Payne's essay does in the comparative section. That is, identification of an explanatory framework outside the religious tradition is involved. Such an etic approach analyzes the nature and consequence of ritual function, phenomena, and experience. (Since Payne's essay itself utilizes the psychological explanatory framework of analytic psychology to explore the ritual process in Shingon Buddhism, it might well be viewed as a methodological "cousin" to the clinical essays.)

Third, this functional and phenomenological investigation of ritual's psychosocial dimensions allows for and, of necessity, demands a somewhat flexible categorization system. A functional analysis of the nature of ritual and its effects, for example, encompasses a spectrum from health-producing to pathological. It is important to keep in mind the unique insider/outsider position (as discussed in this volume's introductory essay) of the clinician/researcher who is both participant and observer. Each of the four essays includes a discussion of the clinical vantage point through which the exploration of the topic of religious ritual is undertaken.

The reader may well feel, after reading the clinical essays, that he or she has no absolute idea of what ritual *is* precisely or whether it is categorically closer to health or pathology. And this is as it should be! If one investigates a topic from a functional and phenomenological standpoint, then the investigation will be dependent on how one is looking, what one is looking at, and the categories for recording what one sees. In this section there are four investigations underway, and their specific methodologies and results reflect significant variations. However, all four investigations point to the necessity to avoid thinking in absolute, fixed ideas and to focus, instead, on ritual's psychosocial functions and consequences in particular situations, to think of ritual more as a process and experience than as a static entity, and to avoid the theoretical and clinical mistake of a universal categorization system that is unconscious of personal, social, and cultural variables.

RITUAL, POWER, AND BELONGING

The initiating central theme for this volume as a whole—the interaction of ritual, memory, and meaning—emerged through a clinical therapeutic experience (See DeMarinis' essay). Though clinical therapeutic experience can be understood in different ways, it is used here to designate a particular type of process that involves intentional and specified engagement and interaction among participants for the purpose of addressing problematic or challenging areas in psychosocial function. Such a process will find expression through many forms and contexts and through diverse frameworks for interpreting the nature of the problematic, how such is to be understood, and what methods are to be used in addressing the problem. Despite the myriad of possible expressions, however, the process will nevertheless involve behavioral, cognitive, and symbolic dimensions.[1] The approach to and configuration of these dimensions in a given framework of interpretation shape the analysis of interaction between memory, meaning, and ritual.

The essays differ widely in their subject foci and means by which ritual, memory, and meaning-making are explicitly or implicitly approached and analyzed. However, there is an underlying thread that runs through them concerning the importance of understanding the intensity and power of ritual experience and its resultant memory formation in the construction of psychosocial meaning. The rituals dealt with in these essays cover a broad spectrum of type and design. Yet from a phenomenological perspective they can be understood as belonging to the same classification, which will be referred to as "religious."

Though not all deal with specifically religious content (concerned with traditional religious dogma), the rituals have a religious significance from a phenomenological perspective. That is, they signify that which functions as a meaning-making structure in the life of the individual or group.[2] Religious activity, understood in this way, coordinates movements of the symbolic dimension of existence with the cognitive and behavioral dimensions. At the heart of religious ritual experience lies the power of belonging, connection, or disconnection. Psychology of religion has dealt well with the effects of this disconnection, and has studied the effects of pathologic religious ritual. The essays in this section incorporate this necessary but, many would argue, not sufficient legacy of suspicion, and go a vital step further to the understanding and clinical documentation of the vital power of belonging, connection, and reconnection in religious ritual experience.

Theoretician and researcher Janet J. Jacobs provides a succinct description of this connection function through the religious ritual experience:

> As an interactive process, ritual engages the participant in behaviors that reinforce connection and attachment to significant others. The subject of such attachment may be a divine being, a spiritual leader, a religious community, or an entire society. However, it is the sense of connectedness that facilitates the cathartic response through which painful emotion can be brought to consciousness, and relieved or expressed for the first time.[3]

The themes of disconnection, connection, and reconnection in association with religious ritual experience and resulting memory are prominently featured and explored in these clinical essays. Though the explorations are undertaken independently and through diverse methodologies, each leads to the same essential findings concerning the nature of religious ritual experience. These findings, which are best understood as hypotheses generated for future testing, are as follows:

1. Religious ritual, in actual experience and through its resulting memory, belongs to a category of experience and of memory-formation that is psychologically powerful and which has a magnitude of function not easily paralleled by other types of experience or memory.

2. Ritual experience and resulting memory necessitate a containment system with both intrapersonal and interpersonal dimensions that can withstand the force of that which it hopes to contain, perhaps necessitating the experiencing or reexperiencing of religious ritual as a vital step in the containment process.

3. Religious ritual, as approached in life-cycle perspective, may be of use in the psychotherapeutic process, especially for the reconstructive work of understanding and assessing past traumatic experience, memory, and meaning-making, as well as for the formation of new ways of making-meaning.

4. A careful, ongoing, and culturally sensitive evaluative process of psychological function and dysfunction needs to be in place in order to distinguish between situations of mental health and illness related to ritual-like experience and expression.

These perhaps unexpected findings, or hypotheses generated, certainly are dependent on the frameworks of discussion and analysis through which they arise. Since each author has worked independently, each develops a framework through which these findings must be interpreted. To best prepare the reader for entrance into the essays' varied frameworks, however, a reference to psychologist of religion Paul Pruyser's "Illusionistic World," emerging from object relations theory, may be of assistance. Pruyser identifies the Illusionistic World as the domain in which orderly imagination, adventurous thinking, fantasy, symbols, play, creativeness, cultural needs, inspired connections, and the like[4] interact to create the necessary balance between the intrapersonal Autistic World and the interpersonal Realistic World. It is in this world where the experience and memory of religious ritual are negotiated between the symbolic, cognitive, and behavioral dimensions of human living. The Illusionistic World can be understood as the meaning-making domain through which containment of religious experience and memory takes place. It is, as are its contents, powerful and unparalleled. It is to this

Illusionistic World that we turn as we approach the four clinical essays.

Beginning from different starting points and focusing concerns in the broad area of psychosocial investigation, each of the authors develops theoretical and clinical questions whose answers involve numerous other disciplines and cross-disciplinary perspectives. This is significant to note for at least three reasons. First, these essays are illustrative of the clinician's need to deal with both theoretical construction and practical method and application. He or she approaches the clinical context as a resource to apply, refine, and/or generate theory. Yet such a context can also raise critical questions about the sufficiency of a particular theoretical approach. Second, this challenge can be approached as an opportunity to augment disciplinary and theoretical knowledge through the quest for clinical wisdom, which often demands a broader field of investigation and methods for analysis and interpretation. Third, these essays point to an immense need for further psychosocial, psychotherapeutic, and therapeutic explorations in the area of ritual studies so as to incorporate and translate the insights from and approaches to other fields into the clinical contexts of care.

MOVING THROUGH THE CLINICAL SECTION

The essays by Gay, DeMarinis, and Driskill are concerned with different psychotherapeutic contexts, the function and use of ritual in those contexts, and analysis of the psychotherapeutic context itself as a ritual-like experience. The essays can be understood as moving along an imaginary continuum from a more prevention-centered approach to a more pathology-centered approach to psychotherapy. There is also a correlated movement in the development and understanding of the relationship between psychotherapy and ritual.

Noonan's essay can be approached as tackling the issues of prevention and pathology in terms of the Western hospital context. If both patient and institution could approach hospitalization for surgery as being like a rite of passage, with all the psychosocial dimensions and consequences involved, preventive measures could be taken to identify patient resources and to address patient fears at the beginning and throughout the process. An inability to understand the rite-like dimensions of hospitalization can be understood as having an iatrogenic effect, whereby the institution itself adds significant stress and trauma (pathology) to an already stressful process, while the patient's own personal and cultural resources for coping and adapting are left out.

Finally, a note needs to be added on the way to read these essays in relationship to the umbrella field of ritual studies. Noonan's essay involves the clearest example of and fit with the objective of ritual criticism—interpretation with a view to the improvement of practice.[5] The essays by Gay and Driskill fit partly into the area of ritual criticism as well as that of ritual application. These different relationships to the field of ritual studies do not in fact imply, however, a more or less critical or selective approach to either ritual or ritual theory. Rather, it is because the intentions and objectives of the essays in this section are different.

NOTES

1. Exploration of the cognitive and behavioral dimensions can be assisted by the work of William L. Hathaway and Kenneth I. Pargament, "The Religious Dimensions of Coping: Implications for Prevention and Promotion," in *Religion and Prevention in Mental Health: Research, Vision, and Action*, Kenneth I. Pargament, Kenneth I. Maton, and Robert E. Hess, eds. (New York: The Haworth Press, Inc., 1992). The symbolic dimension can be explored through Arthur Kleinman *Patients and Healers in the Context of Culture. An Exploration of the Borderland Between Anthropology, Medicine, and Psychiatry* (Berkeley, CA: University of California Press, 1980).

2. Psychologist of religion Jan van der Lans argues convincingly for a broader functional definition of religious activity in his essay, "Meaning Giving Behavior. A Neglected but Urgent Research Task for the Psychology of Religion," in *Religionspsykologi Nu*, ed. Owe Wikström, (Uppsala, Sweden: Uppsala University Press, 1987).

3. "Religious Ritual and Mental Health," in *Religion and Mental Health*, ed. John F. Schumaker (New York: Oxford University Press, 1992), p. 291.

4. "Forms and Functions of the Imagination in Religion," in *Religion in Psychodynamic Perspective: The Contributions of Paul Pruyser*, H. Newton Malony and Bernard Spilka eds. (New York: Oxford University Press, 1991) p. 177.

5. Ronald L. Grimes, *Ritual Criticism: Case Studies in Its Practice, Essays on Its Theory* (Columbia, SC: University of South Carolina Press, 1990), pp. 16 and 34.

7

Ritual and Psychotherapy

Similarities and Differences

VOLNEY P. GAY

INTRODUCTION: RITUAL AND PSYCHOTHERAPY

What counts as "psychotherapy" and who performs it are issues much changed since the days in which psychiatry, a medical specialty, dominated the delivery of mental health care. Now persons with psychiatry, psychology, social work, ministerial, and nursing backgrounds, as well as those trained in "Recovery," "Twelve Step," "Inner Child," and similar programs claim expertise in some or all domains of the treatment of mental disturbances. Prior to these modern professions, even prior to psychiatry, whose European history is no more than a few hundred years old, was ritual. Looking backward at the central rituals of the Christian church, for example, we find root metaphors, such as salvation, forgiveness, mourning, recognition, listening, communication, and the transformation of the self that reappear in the professions that provide contemporary psychotherapy. It may be with ineluctable nostalgia that we look back to the "prescientific" ages when the vast majority of Europeans experienced themselves as part of Christendom. Even if this is false history and nothing but nostalgia it illustrates the usual problem of comparing contemporary psychotherapy and ritual.

Ritual in its fullest sense refers to a communal activity. I prefer to define "ritual" as I do in my study of Freud and ritual (Gay, 1979); ritual is activity that is patterned, meaningful, symbolic, and normative.

(See also Lukes, 1975.) This definition effectively rules out defining psychotherapy derived from the medical and scientific paradigms of nineteenth century Europe as "ritual." I therefore discuss "ritual-like" aspects of psychotherapy because I wish to preserve a normative definition of ritual and similar activities, like liturgy, distinct from psychotherapy.

To amplify this distinction I compare a full-fledged ritual that employs altered states of consciousness to a highly personal use of an altered state of consciousness. Using this comparison I describe psychoanalytic psychotherapy that is rule-based, but not ritualistic. The ritual I have cited elsewhere derives from contemporary Korea.[1] S. N. Kim (1989) documents how many Korean shamans use their trance states to recall political violence and murder that the state has declared "did not occur." She describes how shamans on the Korean island of Cheju recount, using the voice of the dead, the actual story of the seventy thousand civilians who died in a civil war that raged between 1948 and 1957. In this war, called the "April 3 Uprising," communist insurgents evoked immense destruction from the Korean military. Official Korean histories do not document this war. Based on field work in 1984–85, Kim suggests that shamans have preserved the memories of the dead and address the suffering that persists among the survivors. These suppressed memories reemerge in the shaman's altered states of consciousness (ASC). Also, through private, individual dreams, relatives of the dead recall the fate of their loved ones. Officials who wield state police powers deny such histories and punish anyone who recounts them. In the face of such power Korean shamanism has adapted its ancient traditions of trance state "pronouncements" to preserve the collective memory of these atrocities and to recount them. One cannot but think of the holocaust museums in Europe and North America that preserve the memory of the Nazi war against the Jews. In place of these officially sanctioned memorializations, shamanism has provided a vehicle that permits recollection which cannot be altered by political authority.

Similar public rituals, such as baptism, Communion, festivals, and the like, which are explicitly public and symbolic, are also "empty" and therefore open to new meanings and new formulations. A seasoned pastor in Alaska describes how the Lutheran liturgy was flexible enough to deal with the Exxon Valdez disaster in 1989, whereas a newly concocted "celebration" fabricated by city officials fizzled in comparison (Houglum, 1990). Lutheran pastors do not enter ASC, nor do their parishioners reveal the raucous and dramatic experiences of the Korean shamans. Therefore, their "affect" and psychology appear wholly dissimilar. Yet structurally, especially in their appeal to transcendent powers, their utility is very much alike and both are clear instances of ritual repair and restorations.[2]

A second use of ASC similar to that of the shamans comes from a radio call-in show on which I was the guest-expert on "occult experience." A woman somewhere in the Midwest told me about her great aunt, whom I'll call Alice, a woman in her nineties now. Just before World War I, Alice's older sister married a young man with whom Alice worked in a local grocery store and after whom Alice pined. Shortly after her marriage, the older sister died. Following her sister's death and funeral, Alice had a remarkable dream: "Her sister appears to her. She seems calm and at peace. With much feeling the older sister pleads with the younger woman to marry the grieving widower, Alice's brother-in-law." The younger woman felt this was an uncanny sign sent to her from beyond the grave. Responding to her sister's ghost and its petition, Alice married her brother-in-law, perhaps sooner than custom and propriety would usually allow.

This account resembles the story of the Korean shamans. First, both events require the existence of an altered state of consciousness; the shaman enters a trance, the young woman sleeps and enters a dream. Second, while in this altered state, both persons can express wishes and recount facts that are officially denied. The Korean shaman recounts atrocities of which everyone knows but no one can speak. The young woman's dream recounts her love for her brother-in-law, competition with her sister, and perhaps her guilt over her sister's death—an event that permitted her to realize her fondest wish. Although Alice may never have wished for her sister to die, upon hearing that tragic news, she might well have thought, "This removes a barrier to my love." Her dream overcomes these obstacles and reverses the dreamer's guilt by transforming her wish to marry her brother-in-law into a duty: she must obey her sister's ghost with its uncanny claims of authority. What gives it this authority? Even if there were such entities as ghosts, that would not grant them special powers per se. If human beings persist in an altered state beyond death, in the form of spirits or ghosts, that hardly qualifies them for a higher status than the neighbor down the street whose opinions on marriage and duty one may ignore. Does not the "power" of the ghost reside in its actual origins, within the woman's deepest feelings? Having evolved from those feelings the ghost's pronouncements accrue an "uncanny" sense of rightness since they echo what she had denied herself.

Third, the Korean ritual and the visionary dream counteract the demands of official powers who deny unsavory truths. These forms of memory do not challenge the legitimacy of the official powers. The shamans do not confront directly the police state. The young woman, Alice, did not directly challenge the mores that deny sexual attraction between relatives. Nor could she confront, in 1914 America, the established rules of mourning and propriety which required that a "decent" length of time pass before any new intimacies could take place.

Yet Alice's private story differs dramatically from the Korean public story. Precisely because it was private and idiosyncratic, Alice's dream had no publicly validated form of "normative" behavior. Like all dreams, it is replete with latent "symbolic" flexibility. As Sperber (1974) says, all symbolic processing reveals this quality of variability: there is no dream and no other symbolic entity that cannot be stretched to meet any given tendentious demand. Her dream was not normative; it appealed to no public, validated mode of interaction, nor to a publicly held consensus about value hierarchies. In contrast, the Korean shamans, drawing upon an identical psychological capacity, "work" by employing normative claims about the spirit world provided them by Korean folk culture and folk religion.

RITUAL-LIKE ASPECTS OF PSYCHOTHERAPY

Setting the Frame

I find it valuable to document both the similarities between ritual actions and therapy and the differences between them. To sharpen differences between concepts of ritual enactment and well-framed therapy may seem elitist. I find it helps clarify what I do and why I do it.[3] By being constant and predictable in my behavior I can better gauge my patients' responses to me: hence they can help me improve my performance. I favor the possibility of progress of technique and skill in delivering psychotherapy. A danger in pursuing this is that I may seem to claim exhaustive knowledge for "my" school and therefore denigrate the claims and aspirations of other schools. This is not my intent. A discipline that claims scientific lineage cannot advance all at once. In a complex enterprise that claims validation and "progress" one must hold some things constant, including some key concepts. These key concepts—such as the idea of "frame" and "unconscious process"—are *not* equivalent to theological opinions or ideologies. I am not persuaded that every clinical encounter or every clinical theory rests upon more foundational theological, political, or ideological claims.[4]

Given the variety of "therapies" it is helpful to delineate how they differ from one another and to delineate errors common to all forms. Like other authors in this volume I note common ground between forms of ritual and some types of psychotherapy, especially those influenced by psychoanalysis. I agree that there are "ritual aspects" of well-handled psychoanalytic psychotherapy. Agreeing with the major premise of the editors of this volume, I find it helpful to assess the degrees to which bona fide rituals are also therapeutic. However, I suggest that these are two distinctive experiences and two distinctive tasks for the practitioner. True, many pastoral moments may be both "ritualized" and "therapeutic." Here the word *therapy* has coopted the dignity of other words, like "spiritual," "healing," "accepting," and, in some contexts, "saved." These latter terms derive from theology, which is far older than psychotherapy and need not yield over to "therapists" all discourse about the psyche. By distinguishing between therapy—a ritual-like transaction between two persons conducted within a well-grounded frame and all other modes of relationship—we can avoid the rampant psychologizing that dominates American television and American life. If a person trained in the ministry carries out frame therapy, that person is not also doing "pastoral therapy." So, too, a psychiatrist, trained in medicine, who carries out a well-framed therapy, is not also doing "medical therapy." When a competent minister counsels a bereaved family, and does *not* do so within the confines of a well-framed contract, that is not "therapy." It is competent ministering and an essential part of the grieving process facilitated by the believing community.

Ritual-like Rules of Psychotherapy

Psychoanalysts and psychoanalytically oriented therapists place themselves under the umbrella of science and medical practice. This umbrella may cover psychoanalytic values, training, and theory. It does not cover fully psychoanalytic or psychotherapy practice. Within the techniques of psychoanalysis and its offshoots, as opposed to its theories, are basic rules of conduct. These rules include ethical guidelines and generally accepted professional mores, such as confidentiality, the protection of patients, and other such rules. (See Browning, in press.)

Another set of rules, those that establish the "psychoanalytic frame" (Langs, 1985), is ritual-like.[5] For example, the following are some basic rules of good therapeutic or therapy technique as defined by major figures in the field.

1. The analyst (by this I mean the analytically oriented therapist) does not advise the patient.

2. The therapist does not touch, seduce, or woo the patient.

3. The therapist does not vary the time and space and general rules of the relationship. One tries to:
   a. Retain the same hour and same length for sessions.
   b. Retain the same fee and billing.[6]
   c. Retain patient responsibility for all sessions. (Hence, patients are expected to pay for missed sessions.)

4. The therapist listens primarily, and asks questions, (or comments) rarely.

5. The therapist focuses on the "here and now" features of the actual events transpiring in therapy.

6. The therapist works from the surface of the patient's experience down into preconscious feelings and ideas.

7. The principal goal of therapeutic work is to find linkages between these conscious, manifest experiences and the patient's behavior and actions that seem "unconscious," that is, not under the patient's control.

8. The principal mode of analytic listening is empathic immersion in the patient's inner world and inner feelings.

9. The principal goal is to permit the patient to speak without hesitation; to permit "free association" from which the total picture of the neurosis will emerge; to create a stage in which "formlessness" can occur and from it the authentic self emerge. (See D. W. Winnicott, 1971.)

10. From an empathic immersion in the patient's experience and feelings the therapist seeks to uncover defenses against free association, against the state of formlessness. (The therapist seeks to uncover resistances to the deepening of the therapeutic relationship.)

11. After discovering the source of these resistances, patient and therapist together discover moments of formlessness in which sources of the patient's suffering emerge.

12. These insights make possible interventions or interpretations that link current, transference feelings with genetic precursors, and with the patient's symptoms.

13. Following these requirements of the "frame" does not obviate the delicate tasks of discovering appropriate-

ness. To keep the fifty-minute hour, for example, does not mean that the therapist clangs a bell exactly at fifty minutes even as the patient is in midsentence. The actual "frame" resides within the therapist's emotional and intellectual capacities to regulate affects without dominating them.[7]

A typical example: a patient pays his bill compulsively because he is sure his therapist will respond to late payment with rage, the way his father responded when the boy challenged dad's perfectionistic demands. By following the rules of the game, by not demanding payment but inquiring why the patient always pays on time the therapist makes possible otherwise unavailable insights about the patient's life. This leads to further insights about the patient's perfectionism.

Many books on technique and the basics of therapy amplify these basic rules. They differ in particulars; they share a common goal. That goal is to permit the patient to experience "transformative" moments. Pursuing these goals, which are common to transformative rituals in all contexts, produce shared anxieties. Like bona fide rituals of transformation, such as puberty rituals Eliade described in his classic text (1962), analytic "rules of containment" induce common anxieties. These include the fear of suffocation, the fear of bodily harm (castration), claustrophobia, the fear of going crazy, the fear of shame and guilt reaching overwhelming proportions, the fear of abandonment. (See Brenner, 1982.) The latter is especially painful. By revealing hidden truths about oneself, truths that one is sure will disgust everyone, the patient is vulnerable to the therapist's rejection in turn. As in modern teenager "slasher" films, variations on these anxieties are endless.[8]

Langs (1985) documents how the well-maintained psychotherapy frame elicits precisely the same anxieties, since the frame denies to both patient and therapist opportunities to escape the buildup of intrapsychic tensions. Because the frame restricts the range of action (action discharge) it evokes in *both partners* archaic images of suffocation, constriction, and the like, against which many people and much of our culture battles.

Ritual Studies and the Transforming Moment

Many authorities on ritual testify to the value that ritual actors place on the transformation of the self. In detailed and voluminous studies scholars describe the nuances of ritual actions, modes, symbols, and the like, directed toward the transformation of the ritual actor. The most obvious examples might be puberty rituals that have as their central task the conveyance of the child into adulthood. Rituals of the forbidden, including Dionysiac rituals and other hypersexual modes, clearly promise similar transformations. In a less spectacular way, evangelical rituals in this country, with their appeal to emotional depths, also promise transformation of the self. (See Chasseguet-Smirgel, 1985.)

Transformation can also occur in the safety of the well-maintained frame. In this frame, made possible by psychoanalytic rules, unconscious convictions emerge full-fledged into the transference. For example, a common unconscious conviction in many neurotic patients is that they must make their parents healthy. In turn, the healthy parent can then help raise the child. Many discussions of the co-dependent personality in alcoholic families focus on this aspect of childhood. Yet a more pervasive conviction many children have is that they can or should do away with their parents' deficits no matter what the source. Using other terms for the same event, good, ritualized technique permits pathogenic ideas to emerge with force and therefore conviction. (See Weiss and Sampson, 1986.)

The parallels between psychoanalytic "ritual-like" rules and those of medicine experts in other cultures are well known, and the comparison of psychoanalysts with "modern day witchdoctors" is as old as psychoanalysis itself. Lévi-Strauss (1958) suggested a generation ago that psychoanalysts function like modern day medicine experts. He amplified this theme in his recent book (1988). There he reduces Freudian discoveries to simple variations on great themes available in myths, which, since they are older, are therefore superior to those Freud offers. Before Lévi-Strauss, many other scholars documented similar parallels between traditional healing rituals and those of modern Western psychiatry. I suggest a similar parallel when I compare rituals that express the forbidden with the ritual-like aspects of the "good frame."

Most patients in my practice, like most people in my culture, experience their troubles as if they were thrust upon them by outside forces. Though we may quote Hamlet and say that the fault lies not in the stars but in ourselves, we usually choose to believe that it is our spouse, mother, father, boss, god, or "the system" that produces our unhappiness. They are at fault: they caused this problem and we can show this awful truth with many illustrations.

When a patient did have an especially horrible childhood the goal of therapeutic work is to strengthen the patient's ego, the patient's internal capacities. It is not to gain revenge against the perpetrators of the patient's suffering. (A successful therapy might issue in a patient who decides to pursue legal claims against those who wronged him or her.) Our fundamental goal is to find ways to reduce the patient's *current* external struggles and conflicts to their ultimate source in *current* intrapsychic conflicts. By solving those intrapsychic conflicts patients gain crucial strengths; they no longer are their own worst enemies, they no longer sabotage themselves. In schematic form we work from top down in the following fashion:

> External conflicts with boss, spouse, parent
> reduced to
> Interpersonal conflicts with the therapist
> reduced to
> Intrapsychic conflicts within the patient

These technical goals differ from those of pastoral care and other "transformation" in ritual contexts. In those contexts one is supposed to "act" and to "change." Only in action can one validate that a new self has been born. "Intrapsychic" change need not (and probably cannot) occur. Dramatic actions, like those carried out in ritual transformations, alter self-understandings by adding to one's original repertoire "new" images of oneself. The "old person" is dead only because new understandings of "person" supplant those associated with the past. Intrapsychic change, according to frame theory, can occur only when the patient is free enough to examine the actual contents of intrapsychic self- and object representations. These original structures are what drive neurotic patterns. Ritual transformations work, sometimes. Thousands of authors and millions of practitioners, in all the world's religions, can rightly attest to the power of specific traditions to effect real change in human personalities. Frame theory and its parent theory, psychoanalysis, represent alternate values to those offered in religious theories of change (Gay, 1988).

None of the rules of "frame therapy" is central to other forms of treatment, such as drug interventions or reeducation. Indeed, the general mood of many forms of popular therapy, such as group work or cognitive therapy, amplifies the public nature of the symptom. For example, to focus on "my eating disorder," or "my agoraphobia," in a group setting devoted to that symptom is to treat these behaviors as if they were discrete entities, rather like one might treat a sprained knee as a discrete part of the body on which one "has to work." So, too, many forms of drug treatment for "symptoms" of depression occur in a mundane, one might say, secular frame where a "chemical imbalance" is corrected by adding more chemicals to the patient's system.

Note that it is not their content nor "language" that defines these forms of therapy. A charismatic group leader, especially the public and popular versions, might employ a psychoanalytic vocabulary. But the group process remains public and therefore contradicts key parts of the rules of frame therapy. Group therapy and other forms of treatment might work as well or as better than psychoanalytic forms. Some authors cite well-marshalled evidence that Alcoholics Anonymous, for example, is unexcelled in the treatment of character disorders that typify many alcoholic persons (Khantzian and Mack, 1989). Such issues are matters of empirical proof and validation. My point is to compare the rigorous demands of the analytic frame and note its central task is to effect change at an intrapsychic level.

According to "frame theory," nonframe therapies may permit patients to escape momentarily their superego's burden of shame for being sick, needy, or the like. If public forms of treatment reduce such burdens for patients they may be beneficial. A cost of such "normalization" of symptoms is that the patient loses access to the actual, hidden roots of his or her internal story. By losing access to altered states of consciousness, like the dream or free-floating fantasy, we cannot gain access to forbidden wishes. Drawing upon Freud's value system and Freud's metapsychology, frame therapy holds that forbidden wishes are also our deepest wishes. They are the wellsprings, the sources of energy and power or "libido" that make us animate creatures.

The ritual vision, which I ascribe to the Korean shaman, values the possibility of linkages between one realm and another. To gain access to the "realm beyond this one" the shaman finds ways to induce a preliminary state of "formlessness" (or what Victor Turner [1969] and others call the "liminal state"). The shaman typically speaks of these realms as if they were distinct spaces; therefore the shaman's vocabulary speaks of flying, diving, exploring, searching, and the like, leaving this mundane realm and finding the answer in the "other" realm. Psychoanalysts share a similar vision, except they consider these realms to be within the person's psyche. The psyche is not identical with the person's brain. Like Erikson (1963) and later Gregory Bateson (1979), most psychoanalysts locate the mind within the matrices of body, family, and cultural systems. Familiar to all therapists is a similar play within the play, the transference. It is real and holds within it the possibility of new freedom, yet it is also artificial, induced by the ritual-like qualities of the analytic hour and space. This new freedom includes a deeper sense of living in the moment, that one is less compelled to repeat the past, that one can forgive one's parents and that one can leave the never-never land of the analytic relationship.

CONCLUSIONS: DISASTERS OF THERAPY AND SOME COMMON ERRORS

In arguing for a distinction between therapy proper and ritual proper I may seem an elitist. I am elitist only to the extent that doing psychotherapy, especially with more disturbed persons, requires a good deal of rigor, training, and circumspection of one's limitations. Academic training, in both M.D. and Ph.D. programs, typically gives one very few of these skills. Being privileged to teach in doctoral programs (Ph.D.) and a residency program (post-M.D.) and having made many errors myself, I suggest the following issues typify mistakes generated out of amalgamating therapy with ritual action.

1. Loving the patient and offering that love as curative.
2. Identifying with the patient.
3. Feeling a "mission" to save the other person.
4. Evoking "occult" validation of one's interpretations.
5. Recruiting the other for the "movement."
6. The antiphenomenological effects of theology.
7. Misdiagnosing or failing to diagnose severe mental illness.

These first three modes occur especially in naive therapists fascinated by the intensity and power of listening to another person's deepest mental anguish. To "love" the patient, in all the myriad ways one can define that term, means to act toward the other with compassion, commitment, and urgency. To identify with the patient is to dwell on the ways in which one shares a common reality. In moodier moments, to identify and love another is similar to watching one's child perform some difficult task; one uses a kind of emotional "body English" to help the kid get through the recital piece, for example. To "save" the other is to take on the other's struggles. In many nuanced ways these three modes occur daily, and necessarily in relationship to people important to us. They typify an urge to help another human being and are therefore normal and part of the expectable environment of therapy in our culture. They also run the great danger of making one's encounters unempathic. In a strict sense, empathy is the capacity to put aside our impulses, feelings, and urges—including the urge to love and rescue others. Empathy is the accurate and detailed comprehension of other persons' sense of their emotional landscape, of the ways in which the world offers them emotional sustenance (Kohut, 1971; Gay, 1992). The unhappy fact that therapists may "fall in love" with their patients typically derives from the excitement the patient's profound hunger and idealization evokes in the therapist. Sexual contact with patients and other disasters of therapy (such as having a patient move in with the therapist) often begins "innocently" enough in these dramatic moments when the therapist abandons the frame in favor of a higher good, like loving the patient.

A much cited article (Buckley et al., 1979) conveys the results of surveying twenty expert teachers of psychotherapy. The most common mistakes cited by these teachers were wanting to be liked by the patient, an inability to tune in to the patient's unconscious communications, and premature interpretations (p. 1579). The authors hold that this clustering derives from the novice therapist's efforts to establish a professional identity, to be seen as competent and therefore eliciting from the patient affirmations of the therapist's skills. Identity theory is helpful, but we also may note that each of these common errors correlates with the burdens of establishing the frame. By needing the patient to like him or her, the novice therapist places the therapist's emotional deficit centermost in the relationship.[9] To "need" something from the patient other than a fee, or professional recognition, or the fulfillment of one's commitment, is to use the patient, commonly as others have also used the patient.[10] The consequences of botching psychotherapy range from neutral to poor therapy outcomes, to precipitous terminations, to suicide attempts on the patient's part, and acute depression in the therapist. Identical efforts by a ritual expert, such as a priest or minister, in a bona fide ritual space guaranteed by a believing community, need *not* produce negative outcomes.

Like many persons whose parents failed to validate the deep sense that life is worth living, patients *in therapy*, as opposed to parishioners *in church*, do not need zealots, nor do they need another person to "fill the room" with that person's feelings. Typically, neurotic level patients and those with character disorders present stories full of drama, battles, and such, in which they compete with others about who among them will be tended. "Tending" means actions and reactions, such as sexual favors or money or glorification of the self: it never means a genuine experience in which another person listens.

The therapy frame, especially in its ritual-like forms, promises a respite from the pressures of the other, even if well intentioned and genuine. The well-framed therapy gives the patient explicit instruction not to "take care" of the therapist, not to validate the therapist's beliefs, and not to make the therapist feel better by taking on and enjoying the therapist's answer. Many religious experts claim to have found a way of healing themselves and, they claim, others, too. This may be true. Yet even if these healings take place, they do not do so out of an empathic frame. The ecstasy and delight promised by some religionists—even if valid—is not empathic listening.

In the same way, evoking intense "occult" experience in the other person, whether through ritual techniques, like drumming, dancing, singing, drug states, and the like is common in many ritual performances. It is also highly unempathic since, again, it is the product of manipulation and technique, rather as good acting and other modes of drama manipulate the audience. By "occult experience" I mean experiences in which a long held wish is suddenly gratified by a hidden and transcendent power (Gay, 1989). So, too, recruiting the other for the "movement" is common and expectable within many religious traditions but antithetical to the basic values of the well-framed psychotherapy.

By the "antiphenomenological" effects of theology I refer to the ineluctable fact that many traditional theological claims, such as folk religious claims about the Virgin Birth in Christianity, say, or doctrines of transubstantiation in Hindu thought, are explicitly otherworldly. No matter how brilliant the exposition, in these clear cases of transcendental claims, they require the proselyte to forgo immediate reality testing in favor of something "higher." Students and parishioners must be "educated" into doctrine, that is, they must be brought out of their immediate thought world and led forward and "upward" into that of a religion's intellectual constructs. It may be true that Jesus is risen and that God requires us to be Christian (or Jewish or Hindu). Even if one could make philosophic sense of these claims, which appear highly nonrational and "symbolic," it does not also make these empathic communications. On the contrary, the very fact that many religious faiths require memorization, training, and other highly ritualized forms of indoctrination underscores how "unnatural" they are. Here we note, again, that "unempathic" does not mean hateful or wrong. These latter terms obtain in the domain of morality and judgment: empathy refers to a psychological capacity to comprehend the internal, subjective experience of the other. Some clever salespeople are skillful, empathic in this technical sense, and manipulative and coercive.

Finally, an obvious and very real consequence of failing to distinguish ritual performances and promises from psychotherapy is that severely ill people may go misdiagnosed and undertreated. Ritual experts, like a well-trained rabbi or a mature minister or a mature Yoga instructor, will soon learn that they must act as front-line mental health officers, distinguishing between spiritual yearnings and the consequences of major thought disorders. Most experienced religious experts will recall the parishioner whose religious zeal went hand in hand with a mental disorder. Naturally, one may find mixed cases, questionable diagnoses, and gray areas where psychiatry and spirituality differ, such as the notion of "cults" and brainwashing (Shinn, 1993). There are also many clear cases of overt pathology that, if left undiagnosed and untreated, create havoc, not renewal. These evoke immense distress within the parish and a new task for the religious expert.

One of the lessons of "frame therapy" is that when one attempts to understand the most complex entity in our universe, the human mind, one ineluctably feels pulled toward making claims that are grandiose and presumptive. The rules of frame therapy are self-imposed restrictions upon the *therapist's* urges to absorb the patient's demands for immediate and permanent cure. In the idiom of frame therapy, a "well-analyzed" patient should neither abjure religion and religious ritual (as Freud might say) nor should the patient find his or her personal myth (as Jung might say). As therapists we are fortunate when everything works well and when a patient summons up the courage needed to effect change. Then we enjoy the privilege of aiding human freedom. That is a sufficient reward. We do not also have to supplant the great traditions and rituals of religious heritage.

NOTES

1. The distinction between private and public, or personal and cultural, is common to religious studies and accompanies a demand that "cultural forms" not be reduced to their origins. Yet someone invented shamanistic rituals. True, rituals typically evolve over many years and many generations, but that does not alter their primary status as inventions.

2. I noted another place (Gay, 1992) that the ghost in Hamlet has a task identical to the shaman's task in folk cultures, especially the Siberian circle traditions in which the shaman or medicine expert speaks out for justice that has gone awry (as cited above, S. N. Kim [1989]).

3. That we find, sometimes, two camps about the "value" of ritual suggests both that the issue is murky and that either/or demands reflect primary process response to anxiety provoking stimuli. To "attack" ritual processes per se, as Freud sometimes did, seems to me irrational. To "celebrate" ritual per se seems to me irrational and

unjustified. With religionists I find myself critical of those social scientists who dismiss all ritual activities. With psychoanalysts I find myself critical of rhetoric that admires rituals in themselves as if they were art forms and does not see also their consequences.

4. Many sophisticated people push psychologists to reveal their hidden agendas, their implicit anthropologies, and the metaphysics upon which their psychological theory rests. Marxist theoreticians have always done this—often to interesting and illuminating effect. Yet it is extreme and ideological to claim that all clinical practice rests upon these articulated or unarticulated metaphysics. First, if these metaphysics are "hidden" from view of the practitioners themselves, then the theologian (or other practitioner) must discover, show, and convince one of these depths. Second, the metaphor of "rests" and its variations is an overt truth claim about the derivation of clinical theories and behaviors. As a theory of such it must yield some validatable and refutable propositions about specific instances. It is not sufficient to claim merely that this is so, or that everyone knows, but to show how an actual practice is itself ideological. Third, either this claim is universally true or it is not. If universally true, then all clinical theories and actions "rest" upon ideological underpinnings. Hence they are hidden, and in that sense irrational. Hence "true change" must be revolutionary and political, not merely academic and scientific. Some extreme versions of Marxist epistemology seem to make this claim fundamental to their arguments. Like any other universalizing claim, this becomes self-referential, and the Marxist or feminist or Freudian metaphysics must submit itself to its own critique. (Cf. Gouldner's well-known study of the "the sociology of sociology" [1970].) If these claims are not universal, then the task becomes more interesting: to develop a criteriology for distinguishing ideological from nonideological discourse.

5. Robert J. Langs is the most visible and most prolific of contemporary authors writing on this topic. I find his textbooks on this subject (1985) essential in all respects. I have used them for eight years to train residents in psychiatry (post-M.D.) and Ph.D. candidates in psychology and religion, for whom they provide a foundational sense of the unique features of the bona fide therapy relationship.

6. A pastor colleague objected to my emphasizing money, as if it were essential to psychotherapy. It is not essential. Rather, the essential aspects of money in many therapy contexts is that the patient and therapist agreed to a certain fee (whether five dollars or a hundred and five), and not paying that amount violates one's word. Not to keep one's word is to denigrate one's self. The therapist who first agrees to a

fee and then "kindly" overlooks the fact that the patient has not paid as agreed, joins with the patient in denigrating both the patient's social reality testing (for *did* the patient promise to pay?) and complicitly agrees that the patient is not competent to keep his or her word. Yet an essential part of self-esteem is honoring one's commitments and one's ego ideal, that is, doing what one said one would do.

7. Expertise in psychotherapy is like expertise in many other fields: one begins with the basics and the rules and then gradually learns better how to adjust them given the details of an actual story and actual patient in an actual moment. The "frame" is the set of goals, values, skills, and restrictions the expert therapist imposes on the patient and the therapist, *both of whom* seek to flee the therapy process and to substitute actions for genuine insight. If "following the frame" were simply a matter of following behavioral rules, then an efficient robot could carry out "good" therapy. But the goal of therapy is to help patients develop their own internal guidance systems, their internal repertoires of self-governance, just as a person learning to swim develops tacit knowledge of myriad ways water affects that person's body and how the two interact.

8. Are these anxieties pan-human? That is, are the anxieties which the frame elicits typical only of European and North and South American psyches? That they are common to these contexts seems likely. Propagandists of all types often elicit these anxieties in attempts to evoke support for their cause. For example, in their efforts to halt the American practice of slavery, the Boston abolitionists of the mid-nineteenth century found that the most effective protests included empathic and forceful renditions of the claustrophobic conditions that obtained on the slave ships. Reilly (1993) reports that the Boston abolitionist movement of the 1830s and 1840s found that among the most effective means to convey their disgust with slavery and to build popular support was to reprint numerous copies of visual renditions of the crowded slave ships. "The sense of dreadful confinement was developed further in pictures of the face masks, gags, manacles, and irons diagrammed with care in Samuel Wood's broadside *Injured Humanity* (pp. 61–62). On the other side of the ledger see Nazi war propaganda efforts, documented in R. Taylor (1979) and S. Taylor (1983).

9. Other errors cited frequently, such as an inability to tolerate aggressive affects in the patient, an inability to tolerate silence, and the avoidance of fee setting, pertain directly to the well-managed frame as established in the initial interviews.

10. Denial of psychic pain occurs in many ways. One is to focus on an irrelevant aspect of the situation. Another is to seek larger and larger abstract renditions of the situation and its suffering, so that only formula remains. Lévi-Strauss accomplishes this feat in his recent book, *The Jealous Potter* (1988) when he reduces the oedipus complex to a "variant" on the idea of procreation. Even if we find the death camps fascinating and horrible we do not wish to empathize with Nazi criminals. We rebel against this assignment and find reasons to end it. When we read accounts of the death camps we stop understanding at some point. The story is too upsetting, too dark, and too dreary a set of facts to keep together in mind all at once. Stalin remarked that the death of one is a tragedy, the death of thousands a statistic. This describes ordinary people's inability to comprehend the suffering of more than a few people close to themselves and within their narcissistic realm.

REFERENCES

Bateson, Gregory. (1979). *Mind and Nature*. New York: Bantam.

Brenner, Charles. (1982). *The Mind in Conflict*. New York: International Universities Press.

Browning, Don S. (1993). "Moral Psychology and Moral Philosophy: Theoretical and Professional Perspectives." *Religious Studies Review* 19/4: 317–320.

Buckley, P., et al. (1979). "Common Mistakes in Psychotherapy." *American Journal of Psychiatry*, 136, 12:1578–1580.

Chasseguet-Smirgel, J. (1985). *Creativity and Perversion*. New York: Norton.

Eliade, M. (1962). *The Forge and the Crucible*. New York: Harper & Row.

Erikson, E. H. (1963). *Childhood and Society*. New York: Norton.

Gay, Volney P. (1979). *Freud on Ritual*. Missoula, Mont.: Scholars Press.

Gay, Volney P. (1988). "Philosophy, Psychoanalysis and the Problem of Change." *Psychoanalytic Inquiry*, 9:26–44.

Gay, Volney P. (1989). *Understanding the Occult*. Minneapolis, MN: Fortress.

Gay, Volney P. (1992). *Freud on Sublimation: Reconsiderations*. Albany, NY: State University of New York Press.

Gouldner, Alvin W. (1970). *The Coming Crisis of Western Sociology*. New York: Basic Books.

Houglum, Mark D. (1990). Pastoral Care and Play: Revisioning the Distinctiveness of the Care by Parish Pastors in Transitional Times. Unpublished Ph.D. dissertation, Vanderbilt University.

Khantzian, E. J., and J. E. Mack (1989). "Alcoholics Anonymous and Contemporary Psychodynamic Theory." *Recent Developments in Alcoholism*, 7:67–89.

Kim, S. N. (1989). "Lamentations of the Dead: The Historical Image of Violence on Cheju Island, South Korea." *Journal of Ritual Studies*, 3, 2:251–286.

Kohut, H. (1971). *The Analysis of the Self*. New York: International Universities Press.

Langs, Robert (1985). *Workbooks for Psychotherapists*. Emerson, NJ: New Concept Press.

Lévi-Strauss, C. (1958). "The Effectiveness of Symbols." In *Structural Anthropology*. New York: Doubleday, pp. 181–201.

Lévi-Strauss, C. (1988). *The Jealous Potter*. Chicago: University of Chicago Press.

Lukes, S. (1975). "Political Ritual and Social Integration." *Sociology* 9/2, 289–308.

Reilly, Bernard F. (1993). "The Art of the Antislavery Movement." In Jacobs, Donald M. (ed.), *Courage and Conscience: Black and White Abolitionists in Boston*. Bloomington, IN: Indiana University Press, pp. 47–73.

Rowse, A. L. (1973). *Shakespeare the Man*. London: Macmillan.

Shinn, L. (1993). "Who Gets to Define Religion? The Conversion/ Brainwashing Controversy." *Religious Studies Review*. 19/3: 195–207.

Sperber, Dan (1974). *Rethinking Symbolism*. Cambridge: Cambridge University Press.

Taylor, R. (1979). *Film Propaganda: Soviet Russia and Nazi Germany*. London: Barnes and Noble.

Taylor, S. (1983). *The Rise of Hitler: Revolution and Counter-revolution in Germany, 1918–1923*. New York: Universe Books.

Turner, Victor (1969). *The Ritual Process: Structure and Anti-Structure*. Ithaca, NY: Cornell University Press.

Weiss, J. and H. Sampson (1986). *The Psychoanalytic Process: Theory, Clinical Observation, and Empirical Research*. New York: Guilford Press.

Winnicott, D. W. (1971). *Playing and Reality*. London: Tavistock.

8

A Psychotherapeutic Exploration of Religious Ritual as Mediator of Memory and Meaning

A Clinical Case Presentation of the Therapeutic Efficacy of Incorporating Religious Ritual into Therapy[1]

VALERIE DeMARINIS

OPENING NOTE

With an essay such as this where two central concerns are being brought together, psychotherapy and religious ritual, it is important to identify the nature and direction at work. Though this identification process is explored in the course of the essay, I can provide a brief frame of reference here to avoid unnecessary confusion for the reader. The central focus is psychotherapy, with a discussion and application of religious ritual taking place in the larger psychotherapeutic context. Therefore, this essay cannot be classified as an essay focusing on ritual criticism, but rather on ritual application in a specific and delimited arena of human interaction. It is perhaps accurate to classify the essay as being in the area of psychotherapy criticism based on clinical data concerning the use of religious ritual in psychotherapy.

Since my interest in the relationship between psychotherapy and religious ritual emerged through my clinical work, especially my work in cross-cultural settings with immigrant individuals and families, it seems fitting that the clinical case discussion included here has its focus on the very case through which the idea of religious ritual as mediator of memory and meaning emerged. The case involves Anna, a young woman from Salvador, Brazil and the religion and culture of Macumba, experiencing distress in her diminished ability to function psychosocially in the midst of her cultural and religious experiences in the United States. This case involves several of the issues and problems raised in both the comparative and liturgical sections of this volume. As with the characters Beret and Per Hansa in Ole Rölvaag's *Giants in the Earth*, discussed in Aune's essay in this volume, Anna, too, is struggling to find a way to belong in a new cultural context. Though it is a long way, at many levels, from Norway to Brazil, the psychological process of belonging is functionally the same. For both the literal person Anna and the literary characters Beret and Per, the liturgical experience provides a way of entry and the beginning of the belonging process in a new cultural context.

The concerns raised by Payne's essay in this volume concerning the problems raised by different interpretative cultural and intellectual frameworks are relevant here. In psychotherapeutic contexts where the therapist and client are from different cultures and where those cultures make meaning differently, the anthropological explanatory systems of "etic" (outside the tradition) and "emic" (inside the tradition) both come into play. Like Payne's, my focus in this essay is primarily on the etic level, concentrating on an analysis of the function of religious ritual in the psychotherapeutic context, using psychotherapy's explanatory system. Neither space nor intention allows for a primary focus on Anna's Macumba framework of religious ritual and culture in and of themselves. In focus here is the function of Anna's religious and cultural framework in and for the psychotherapeutic process. However, it needs to be made clear that in the psychotherapeutic process itself, an understanding of the client's emic framework must be part of the shared therapeutic world between therapist and client in order for communication to take place at any significant level. Likewise, the client needs to have some basic understanding of the emic framework of the psychotherapeutic system with which he or she is involved if the therapeutic communication process is to lead to a specific goal.

RITUAL EXPERIENCING

Human beings live with ritual action every day. There are rituals of various kinds, but for each person, through the contexts of culture and community, certain rituals appear to hold both special power and significance. This simple and functional approach to ritual experience in human life finds support in Ronald Grimes' understanding of ritual as a way of human activity. Certain qualities characteristic of this activity include but are not limited to the collective, symbolic, functional, religious, performed, and patterned.[2] From a functional perspective, these experiences of ritual seem to create their own powerful memories and to serve as unique markers of time and space. Quite simply, their function can be understood as marking experiences that have had an impact upon us. As powerful memories, such ritual experiences may in turn become more than just memories. They can become a source of influence on thoughts and actions. They obtain a significance, consciously or unconsciously, that functions to envelope persons and psychosocially influence them at the same time as persons may hold onto and work with these memories of ritual.[3] In this functional sense, these rituals and their memories are meaning-filled. These ritual experiences and their subsequent memories may help persons to mediate between events of the past and present, and to negotiate meaning for the future.

The significance of these ritual experiences and memories makes them markers of what is of concern. They do not exist as isolated units of physical or emotional experience. They are bound to a person's world of symbols and symbolic meaning, and play a significant part in the interpretative structure. In this sense, that of binding one back to symbolic meaning and simultaneously pushing one forward toward translating meaning into behaviors and decisions, such rituals can be understood as having religious significance. They can be approached as markers of that which is of highest concern for the persons involved, the essential in life and how life is organized. "Religious" as used in this essay, is approached from a functional and phenomenological perspective, distinct from a theological perspective. In other words, that which functions as the symbolic meaning-making system is that which is here designated as religious. The content of the symbol system is distinguished from its function as a symbol system.[4] Rituals that serve this function of binding and shaping concerns will, in this essay, be designated as religious.

Beginning from this vantage point of approach to religious ritual experience and the formation of subsequent ritual memory, it could be argued that a person's life consists, in part, of a series of religious ritual experiences and related memories which can be traced throughout his or her development. These religious ritual experiences serve as signifiers and mediators of past memory, present activity, and future meaning. From such a functional perspective, questions such as the following would need to be addressed. How might mental health, healing, and illness be related both theoretically and clinically to such religious ritual experiences? How would an understanding of psychotherapeutic process be influenced? How could religious ritual and ritual memory be engaged in the psychotherapeutic context? These questions will begin to be addressed in this essay, which includes a brief theoretical overview, clinical approach, case application, and a discussion of emerging hypotheses on the use of religious ritual in the clinical context of psychotherapy.

I. BRIEF THEORETICAL OVERVIEW[5]

The essay's title indicates that a connection is being made between religious ritual and psychotherapeutic exploration. Such a connection might be approached through any number of disciplines or fields. It is undertaken here by a clinician and researcher in psychology of religion and not by a professional whose discipline lies directly within the broad field of ritual studies. My interest in religious ritual has sprung primarily from my clinical interaction with and observation of the multilevel function religious ritual can serve in the psychotherapeutic process. Though my context for psychotherapy has been through pastoral psychotherapy, the foundational issues raised here may be applicable to different contexts and schools of psychotherapy.[6] Each context will undoubtedly shape its own approach to and possible incorporation or deliberate avoidance of incorporation of religious ritual in accordance with its interpretative framework of and clinical approach to the therapeutic process. (See the essay by Gay in this section for a somewhat contrasting viewpoint to the topic.)

Prior to my direct interaction with religious ritual in the therapeutic context in the way to be discussed here, my psychological and psychotherapeutic orientations had positioned me, if I may consciously overstate the case for the sake of emphasis, to approach "religious ritual as publicly validated obsessive behavior."[7] In other words, there existed a critical suspicion about the nature and effect of ritual in general and religious ritual in particular. Such suspicion was most certainly not unfounded, since exposure of ritualized experience emerging in the clinical context most often focused on situations of psychopathology or disturbance in which religious dimensions and religious ritual frequently played active roles.

My experience clinically, however, especially when working across cultures, led me to the point of raising questions of sufficiency about these assumptions concerning the nature and function of religious ritual. As a result of raising such questions, I found myself needing to become acquainted with theoretical positions from a variety of disciplines concerned with the topic of ritual and its significance for understanding human nature and meaning-making.

Anthropologists and those working in other areas in the field of ritual studies often engage in ritual research on a societal and cultural level, carefully describing and analyzing the way in which and means by which a culture's religious rituals serve to contain and generate cultural memory and meaning. Depth psychologists, especially those influenced by the Freudian legacy, have engaged to a large extent in examining religious rituals from another vantage point, focusing on pathological consequences of religious ritual experience for particular individuals in a given cultural context.

A constructive and responsible theory of the therapeutic cannot afford to be without a way to critically assess the impact of ritual experience on and for a person's way of making meaning, as well as aspects of health and illness. Psychologist of religion Paul Pruyser offers a perspective cognizant of these different vantage points. He cautions against an extreme Freudian legacy, seeing it instead as being a necessary but not sufficient approach to the analysis of the nature and consequences of ritual experience. "But the pairing of rituals with compulsions and obsessions gives rituals short shrift—it fails to do justice to those many other rituals which we may call celebrations and which call for joyous spontaneity rather than laboriously upheld defenses."[8]

The approach to psychotherapy used in this essay, emerging from my clinical work in cross-cultural contexts, is referred to as "cross-cultural–preventive." Though remaining in a depth psychology orientation, the emphasis here is on understanding the cultural dimensions and resources in the client's system of making meaning, including the religious ritual dimension, and constructing a therapeutic context that allows for the identification and incorporation of these resources in cross cultural context. The term *preventive* is used to stress the emphasis on early intervention and therapist-client cooperation in the therapeutic relationship.

II. TOWARD A THEORETICAL FRAMEWORK
FOR APPROACHING RELIGIOUS RITUAL IN A
CROSS-CULTURAL-PREVENTIVE FRAMEWORK

The space of this essay permits only an initial attempt at a theoretical framework for approaching religious ritual within a psychotherapeutic context. In the next section of the essay a clinical approach will be discussed. However, a clinical approach, it can and has been regularly argued, rests upon a theoretical and philosophical foundation or, at the very least, framework of interpretation, whether articulated or not.[9] This foundation will be introduced through the brief presentation of five theoretical points.

Point 1. Human meaning-making is relational.

Human meaning-making and memory-making are done in the context of culture and community. Meaning-making systems, religions,[10] and religious rituals are a necessary part of human meaning-making and of human experiencing. Human life begins and is sustained through relationship. Order and meaning are established for the individual person through the communal and cultural system in which she or he lives. An important part of that system is religion. When using this term I am relying on the definitions of religion and faith used by Clifford Geertz and Paul Tillich, respectively. Geertz understands religion as a system of organizing symbols, "(1) a system of symbols which acts to (2) establish powerful, persuasive, long-lasting modes and motivations in men [sic] by (3) formulating conceptions of a general order of existence and (4) clothing these conceptions with such an aura of factuality that (5) the moods and motivations seem uniquely realistic."[11] Geertz' definition offers a way to understand that religious belief is constitutive; it constitutes the framework through which symbols are understood and meaning is made.

Tillich's definition of faith is centered around the term *ultimate concern*, which unites the subjective and the objective side of the act of faith. It brings together "the centered act of the personality, . . . and that toward which this act is directed, the ultimate itself, expressed in symbols of the divine."[12] Tillich's understanding of faith offers insight on the functional nature of belief and the religious system through which the ultimate concern is named and understood. A person's religion is therefore that which functions as a person's ultimate concern.[13] It is the system through which a person comes to make meaning, and this system is cultural and communal in its construction. Religious ritual is kept alive through the symbol system of culture and community. Space does not permit discussion here of the multilevel dimensions of a meaning-making system. However, it is important to understand that the ultimate questions and concerns exist in relation to the questions and concerns of everyday existence. These levels of meaning-making interact in various ways, and this interaction is especially tested in life's "limit-situations."[14] In situations such as severe illness, family death, or an experience that disrupts the patterns established in daily life, the different levels of meaning-making will be tested. Interaction between ultimate concerns and daily functioning will be brought to the conscious level of awareness. How resolution occurs or does not occur will depend on the nature and function of the meaning-making system, understood in its entirety. Concern for approaching the function of meaning-making leads to the following question: How is this meaning-making system to be understood and analyzed in terms of a clinical psychology of religion perspective?

To raise this question is to move from a focus on culture and community (interpersonal) to a focus on the inner workings of an individual person (intrapersonal). This shift in focus does not indicate a shift in philosophical or theoretical foundation. Just as a context of meaning-making in cultural and relational perspective is central to understanding the inter-personal nature of human existence, so too is it central for understanding intra-personal function as well. There is a working relationship within the individual person among memory, present experience, and meaning-making function. Object-relations theory assists with understanding the workings of this relationship. The object-relations theory at work here is influenced by the work of Ana-Maria Rizutto, who explores interaction among object-relations, God-representation, and memory formation. Central dimensions of her framework include an understanding of human development which assumes that "each individual produces an idiosyncratic and highly personalized representation of God derived from his object relations, his evolving self-representations, and his environmental system of beliefs."[15] That psychic equilibrium must be understood in relation to past events and memory recall; "multiple memories of the most varied nature and level of complexity of our relevant objects are available—or unconsciously available—to us in the ceaseless process of keeping ourselves in psychic equiblirium."[16] Past memories that appear to contradict present wishes, needs, or self-representations "come to conscious memory whenever we try to deal with aspects of ourselves linked historically with the original object."[17] And, the psychological function and space for understanding God-representations in theistic religion occurs in transitional space. "That is the space for illusion, where art, culture and religion belong. That is the place where man's life finds the full relevance of his objects and meaning for himself."[18] A theoretical framework built from an understanding of human nature as relational and as meaning-making, religious, both interpersonally and intrapersonally, needs to appreciate that the substantive and functional dimensions of religious symbols and religious ritual deeply affect the individual person at the psychological level. Exploration of this effect is essential for understanding not only what symbols and beliefs inform meaning-making for a person, but also what the consequences are psychologically of these beliefs and symbols.

Point 2. These contexts shape the assessing process and value patterns
that influence the present through the function of memory
and the structure of meaning-making.

Culture, community, experience, and rituals of meaning-making work together in shaping a person's memory, in the naming and cultivating of values, and in the shaping of strategies for meaning-making in the present and future. The world outside and the world inside come together to shape reality. The work of Arthur Kleinman in medical anthropology provides a useful model for approaching the multidimensional nature of a person's system of reality. Kleinman's model of reality is described as symbolic reality, "a bridging reality that links the social and cultural world with psychological and biological reality."[19] Symbolic reality "enables individuals to make sense out of their inner experience. It helps shape personal identity in accordance with social and cultural norms. In this view, symbolic meanings influence basic psychological processes, such as attention, state of consciousness, perception, cognition, affect, memory, and motivation."[20]

Starting from the cultural context of symbolic reality, Kleinman is able to formulate a critical distinction between illness and disease. *Disease* refers to a malfunctioning of biological and/or psychological processes, whereas the term *illness* refers to the psychosocial experience and meaning of perceived disease.[21] The cultural category of disease likewise has its parallel in a cultural category of health. The individual person and his or her illness or health needs to be placed in the cultural context of the interpretation and valuation of symptoms and means for healing.

Point 3. The experiencing of religious ritual can be traced
developmentally through the life cycle. Each ritual
experience shapes memory, and each new ritual
experience adds memory. Ritual allows for the
necessary rhythm of movement between
chaos and order in life.

Just as life needs to be understood as a relational process of meaning-making at the intrapersonal and interpersonal levels, so also does it need to be understood rhythmically as a process involving transitions. Victor Turner's focus on ritual and the nature of liminal experience offers a concrete way of understanding not only the function of ritual and the movement to, through, and from the liminal, but also presents a metaphor that may be used to describe the cyclical return to ritual throughout the life cycle. The appreciation of liminality as a critically important component of and for change and development allows for an understanding of human nature which can comprehend that, as Turner notes, "liminality may be described as a stage of reflection."[22] Gerald Arbuckle interprets the movement to and from liminality through the sequence: separation, liminality, and reaggregation.[23] Arbuckle's movement sequence provides a helpful way of imagining the developmental process as a life-cycle of transitions from aggregation to and through separation, liminality, and, finally, a reaggregation of the person within a community. This sequence provides a way of thinking about how change takes place and the normalcy of movement and chaos in the ordering and reordering processes. This happens not only in the ritual process; it is a paradigm sequence in life itself.[24] Change and growth necessitate an embracing of separation, the feeling of isolation; liminality, moving through undifferentiated and nonhierarchical chaos; and finally, reaggregation, the movement to incorporation.

Point 4. Religious ritual can be understood to function
as a conduit for meaning and memory's interaction.

At whatever stage in the life-cycle a person may be, religious ritual experienced in the present can be used to help mediate between memory and meaning. Progression through the life-cycle can be understood as the adding of ritual experience and ritual memory and the consequences of such on the meaning-making process. [25]

Insights from those working in the broad field of ritual studies offer clues to the psychosocial function of ritual activity and ritual memory. Theodore Jennings' work contributes an understanding of ritual experience, especially efficacious rituals, as an opportunity for engagement in action that may lead to a special kind of knowing and further understanding. "Ritual action is a means by which participants discover who they are in the world and 'how it is' with the world."[26] Ritual activity works to engage motion and movement, thereby providing a vehicle and resource for knowing unduplicated by other forms of knowing. "Ritual action does not primarily teach us to see differently but to act differently. It does not provide a point of view so much as a pattern of doing."[27] Jennings' work stimulates the theoretician to entertain important questions about the role of activity, motion, doing, and being in the nature of healing. This naturally leads to further thoughts about the points of intersection between mind and body, thought and activity, observing and doing. Richard Schechner's explorations in ritual and theatre provide a resource for further thinking in these areas. "The future of ritual is actually the future of the encounter between imagination and memory translated into doable acts of the body."[28] The constructions of Schechner are supported by the research of Eugene d'Aquili on biogenetic structure and neurobiology in relation to ritual activity. [29]

Point 5. Religious ritual experience may be analyzed in reference to a continuum whose respective end points are psychological health and psychological illness.

The cultural understanding of ritual experience and the interpreted position of the person in that culture will need to be assessed before the effects of a ritual experience and its impact on memory and meaning can be understood. Ritual, and especially religious ritual as discussed here, can be understood as a basic part of human activity, a necessary part of human meaning-making. As such, ritual and ritual experience are in themselves not to be approached as signs of health or pathology. The cultural, social, and personal contexts need to be analyzed in order to understand dimensions of health and illness. The work of Volney Gay on Freud and religious rituals can offer much to the design of psychological evaluation process in terms of ritual experience and consequences. Gay argues for a critical distinction to be made between the containment process of religious rituals through repression that unconsciously leads a person to an unhealthy denying of meaning and memory, and that of a conscious process of suppression by which a person can contain meaning and memory, developing a strategy of organizing and containing.[30] The type of containment brought to and brought about by religious ritual can be a significant assessment tool of the ritual experiences in a person's life.

The fundamental nature of religious ritual as a human function, coupled with the importance of a cultural assessment of ritual experience, and the need for understanding the effects and consequences of religious ritual for the containment of memory and meaning are among the central theoretical and operational concerns upon which the following clinical approach is built.

III. CLINICAL APPROACH TO INCORPORATING RELIGIOUS RITUAL IN A CROSS-CULTURAL–PREVENTIVE PSYCHOTHERAPEUTIC PROCESS

In light of the theoretical and operational concerns given, we can begin a clinical approach to incorporating religious ritual in cross-cultural– preventive psychotherapy. Perhaps it is not unwise to begin an approach by considering that the psychotherapeutic process can itself be understood, with very defined limits, as a ritual context in the sense that it is here that a person, through a safe space and trustworthy interaction, can enter into a three-stage therapeutic process that parallels the ritual process.[31] Robert Moore discusses psychotherapy as ritual process through his interpretation of the three-stage process of therapy as submission, containment, and enactment.[32] The therapeutic process can provide the opportunity for safely entering the liminal dimensions of the present in order to discover the impact of the past and to identify resources in approaching decision making for the future. As Moore notes, this orientation to the therapeutic process permits a person to "experiment with new images of both self and others and with new behavioral modalities which the world of structure may require."[33]

If the psychotherapeutic process itself is approached as having the potential to be a ritual-type experience, an experience through which responsible growth and transformation may take place, then the incorporation of religious ritual into the work of psychotherapy can be viewed as a natural and necessary phenomenon. The psychotherapeutic process would appear as a macrocosm of ritual process in which would be set microcosms of particular ritual memories and ritual experiences. In this macrocosm the religious rituals of the past and their memories can be encountered safely. These rituals and their memories are powerful, and need to be properly contained. Encountering and containing these rituals can be done effectively through the experiencing of present-day religious rituals coordinated through the therapeutic process. The design of such rituals varies as to the nature of the past ritual and the meaning-making dimensions of the person's life and with all necessary evaluation and caution concerning issues of safety and readiness. However, as researcher Janet Jacobs notes, the importance of these rituals is not least the function they provide. "Cathartic rituals . . . raise the emotional consciousness of those who participate, providing an outlet for emotional responses in a society that is prone to repression and denial."[34] The rhythm of movement between ritual macrocosm (psychotherapy itself) and ritual microcosm (particular ritual experience and memory) would serve as a potential conduit for new ritual experiencing, new naming, new meaning-making, and for the formation of new memories. The attention to the ritual-type experience of psychotherapy and to the macro- and micro-levels is not done with the intention of understanding psychotherapy as a substitute for religious ritual experience in the context of culture and community. Such is absolutely not the intention here for that would be both professionally irresponsible and therapeutically dangerous. Rather, the intention here is to underscore the need for access to and understanding of a client's multilevel system of communication and meaning-making, which includes his or her ritual experience as well.

The rhythm of the movement between macrocosm and microcosm and its possibilities in the psychotherapeutic context are dependent on the creation and maintenance of a therapeutic space and relationship that can responsibly contain this process. Insights and research within the broad field of feminist psychological theory have raised vital issues about participation, containment, strategy, and empowering procedures in the psychotherapeutic context. Such issues are important in themselves and especially so when we approach the psychotherapeutic process as a macrocosm for ritual process. These include:

- The therapeutic process involves a partnership where strategies can be designed and tested.
- Personal experience needs to be examined in light of social context.
- Internal experiencing of reality needs to be distinguished from external experiencing.
- Survival strategies developed to cope with difficult and often unjust situations need to be named, explored, and validated.

- Therapeutic emphasis where and when feasible and possible needs to be on responsible change rather than adjustment to a problematic status quo situation.
- The therapeutic process needs to encourage self-nurturing and empowerment.
- A full range of emotions needs to be recognized, including the expression of responsible anger.[35]

The ritual macrocosm and microcosm image of the psychotherapeutic process working together with the orientation built through feminist insights provides three central objectives for this process:

1. Understanding the present therapeutic relationship as a joint process for developing strategies for memory recall and containment through development of a person's language of meaning-making.
2. Working to name and assess the dimensions of past religious ritual experience and related memory.
3. Providing the necessary context(s) for creating and recreating religious ritual experience and memory formation.

Meeting these objectives can be done through recognition and incorporation of the following movements[36] in the therapeutic process:

Cross-cultural–preventive therapeutic process movements

- Creation of safe therapeutic space and development of containment strategies
- Way of entry into meaning-making system(s), access to symbolic reality
- Identifying through life-cycle perspective, central religious rituals experienced
- Assessing impact of religious ritual experience on memory and meaning in cultural context
- Incorporating religious rituals into therapeutic context
- Creating strategies for new religious ritual experiences and new ritual memory formation

IV. CASE APPLICATION

At the time of our first meeting, Anna was a young woman in her early twenties. Her home was in Salvador, Brazil, and this was her first extended time away from her home and her culture. She was an exchange student at a large university in the midwestern area of the United States. Though she had prepared herself intellectually for her time in North America, she had not anticipated needing to prepare herself emotionally or psychosocially for this transition. Consequently, Anna found herself unable to focus energy on her studies, unable to sleep, unable to understand why she felt so isolated from her new friends. She sought therapeutic help hoping to identify and work to solve the cause of her adjustment problems.

Anna appeared as a bright and engaging young woman. In the initial meetings Anna spoke openly about her current situation but stopped abruptly when she found herself beginning to talk about her family and community in Brazil. Anna revealed that twice before she had tried to talk about this with two of her friends, but that they did not understand, or seemed distant. Anna felt overwhelmed by her friends' world, and especially by their Christian religious rituals to which they invited her. In general, she felt that there was no way to feel at home or at peace in this new place. She experienced increasing anxiety attacks, with shallow breathing and dizziness.

Work was done in the therapeutic context to make the space and the therapeutic relationship safe and as trustworthy as possible. This discussion and activity helped Anna to relax, although she found herself yet unable to talk about her family and community, or at least about a special dimension of her life she called "the secret."

At our fourth meeting Anna was able to reveal the secret through a special religious ritual. The ritual was from her culture and religion in Brazil, that of Macumba. From a psychosocial viewpoint, the following dimensions of Macumba culture and religion are important to bear in mind. Macumba, an Afro-Brazilian religion that came into contact with Portuguese Catholicism and Amerindian spirituality, has its roots in the Yoruban tradition. Small group and community gatherings are common. The community context of decision making is central. Music, drumming, and movement are central to Macumba liturgies. The gods or spirits, *orixás*, deliver messages through specially initiated mediums through a trance-possession process. Theological focus is often on the present world and on the use of energy and resources to improve conditions in the present. Many Macumba followers in Brazil often use both Christian and Macumba symbols in religious rituals and community life.[37]

Anna's Macumba ritual involved a sacred dance performed within a circle. It needed to be engaged in or witnessed by at least one other person for the sharing and containing of energy generated through the ritual. Anna became totally involved in the dance as I watched from outside the circle. She began to chant and utter a variety of different sounds and words. After about ten minutes, Anna fell to the floor and gradually rose. She carefully gathered her ritual objects and found her resting place in one of the comfortable chairs. I moved to my chair and conversation began. Anna said,

> "I have shared my secret because I trust you and this place. This is the dance of my childhood from my people. I have not been able to dance this before in this country. It feels good to have danced this now. This is the dance I learned as a child, the way to bring things all together to help people make decisions."

The ritual provided for Anna a means to bring her way of making meaning and her decision process into the therapeutic context. Throughout our nine months of work, Anna often called upon the memory of this religious ritual and engaged in further ritual activity in therapy when she needed to concentrate energy on a particular and difficult task.

Anna's world of Macumba culture, religion, and language, was relatively unknown to me. What was known was her urgent need to try to find a way to bring her past into her present, to bring the resources of her past to bear upon her present situation of alienation, of not belonging, of feeling lost. Anna had attempted previously to bring her past, her Macumba rituals, into her present but had not been able to do so. Once she felt able to experience and talk about these religious rituals in the present, Anna was able to trust that she could find a way to make it through the challenges of her present situation.

Each time Anna engaged in Macumba ritual activity, a visible change would follow the experience. She would become more relaxed, better able to communicate, able to focus energy on developing a particular strategy, and would refer to herself and her belief in her own ability to create and test strategies in a more positive manner. Talking about the rituals clearly did not have the same effect as actively engaging in them or in actively remembering them. The ritual activity itself and the powerful memory that it created permitted Anna to gain access to energy, or so it appeared, not available to her through other means. The ritual activity allowed for a different kind of energy release and access to resources for Anna.

At first, based more on intuition than conscious deliberation, the dimension of containment of the religious ritual became our primary focus. Anna's own words concerning these rituals indicated that they were not to be engaged in alone; someone needed to be there to witness and contain energy, as coparticipant or as trusted observer. As we moved through the therapeutic process, the conscious work of containing the "special energy," as we termed it, became more natural. Through the course of the nine months, Anna began to feel comfortable sharing her religious rituals with a few of her friends. This allowed Anna to feel more connected to her present community through its positive response to and respect for the religious rituals of her home community. Likewise, Anna began to be more comfortable with and better understand the religious rituals of her friends. At the same time that Anna was assessing how and with whom to share her past and her religious rituals, I encouraged her to let her family and community know how she was doing and the difficulties she was having. She debated within herself about this, but finally decided to write to one of her sisters and to one of the religious leaders of her Macumba community. Anna was delighted and strengthened to read that the community had anticipated her difficulties and had organized a special time in their religious rituals to, as her sister wrote, "send energy and spirit to you so you feel us there with you and can call upon us."

After Anna completed therapy and her course of studies she returned to Brazil. She has periodically written to me reflecting upon the value of having been able to use her religious rituals to get energy to help with her problems. She has reported that this experience helped her understand things better when she returned home, witnessing both the political and social struggles at work there. It was through my work with Anna that the connection between ritual, memory, and meaning was brought to consciousness. She described her first ritual dance as being, in her words, "the link between my past memory and my way of making meaning."

DISCUSSION AND ANALYSIS OF THERAPEUTIC PROCESS MOVEMENTS

Anna, at the time of our first meeting, was virtually a stranger in a strange land and a strange symbolic reality. She was transplanted from another culture, another way of making meaning, another community of accountability. Though it took time and trust to gain understanding of Anna's symbolic reality, it was evident at our first meeting that different symbolic worlds were operating for Anna. Anna realized that she was experiencing herself as being caught between them.

Diagnosis of illness and health issues in Anna's situation naturally needed to be set in the symbolic-worlds and cultural-worlds conflict. The symptoms of anxiety Anna was experiencing intrapersonally were related directly to this present conflict of worlds. This does not mean that intrapersonal diagnostic categories were not used or that such were not helpful. However, this does mean that the intrapersonal symptoms needed to be explored in light of the symbolic and cultural conflicts taking place for Anna. Understood through this context, her anxiety was natural and more existential than pathological. Analyzing Anna's situation without recognition of the symbolic and cultural dimensions would in itself be a "pathological" methodology. Anna's illness was therefore diagnosed as a kind of existential anxiety brought about by the collision between symbolic and cultural worlds and by an absence of a strategy to navigate these worlds. Likewise, the therapeutic plan for Anna had to be placed in the symbolic and cultural context as well. The goal of the therapeutic process was to help Anna understand, approach, and identify the dimensions of conflict between these worlds and to identify or develop resources through which she could create a strategy of navigation between these worlds.

If I as therapeutic partner were to work responsibly to help Anna explore these worlds and create strategy to navigate them, it was imperative that I become at least somewhat conversant with her primary world of meaning-making. Therefore, I needed to be an active learner in order to be a competent partner in this therapeutic process.[38]

It was my professional responsibility to familiarize myself to the degree possible with the meaning-making dimensions forming Anna's world, if that symbolic and cultural world was to be invited into the therapeutic context. Three dimensions of Anna's world became indispensable reference points for the therapeutic process.

These three dimensions of Macumba culture and religion were experienced in her childhood and had become central to her adult way of making meaning: 1) the communal way of life and of decision making; 2) the importance of music, rhythm, and movement in her way of communicating and collectively as a level of communication; and 3) the importance of religious and community rituals for social and individual stability. Anna's earliest experiences and memories were shaped by a way of making meaning in which the individual person is contained in and has his or her identity formed by the community. In the context of a Macumba community each person and family finds place and direction. Decisions are made and strategies are planned communally. The individual person is never alone. Joy and pain are shared in the community context. Body and soul are understood to be connected in the same way as are community members. Movement, dance, and rhythm are natural parts of life and an essential part of the communal meaning-making process. A cooperative mentality and collaborative model are descriptive of life and also of thinking patterns.

Distinctions are recognized, but they are used toward an end of gaining communal wisdom. Wisdom is understood to be more than just the tabulation of diverse areas of knowledge. Wisdom is that which inspires a better life for all. Wisdom's inspiration is thought to come most often during communal gatherings and religious rituals. Rituals are a part of daily and community life. Inspirational energy enters into the religious rituals and is contained through the community presence. This energy is later translated into words and actions in the community context through community wisdom.

Community, dance, and religious ritual through her Macumba culture formed the interlocking triad of Anna's symbolic reality, her way of making meaning. Access to this powerful triad had been essential for Anna throughout her developmental stages. It had provided a way of positive containment for the different crises of her development. It gave her a working strategy. Blocking access to this triad meant blocking Anna's access to her symbolic reality, to her way of making meaning and strategy for coping with situations encountered in daily life.

When Anna encountered the symbolic reality of North America through her interaction with her university friends and their worldviews, she found that her path of access to her own symbolic reality became blocked. This manifested itself in the development of symptoms related to anxiety. Anna's awareness of and wisdom in realizing that something important was not able to function led her to seek therapeutic assistance.

Therapeutic Process Movements

Creation of Safe Therapeutic Space and Developing Containment Strategies.   In any therapeutic encounter, a process is begun. There is a coming together of persons and their symbolic realities. In the case of Anna, there was also the coming together of different cultures. Issues of trust and safety were recognized as important from the very first session. Anna's mention of having a special secret, in the opening session, was significant. Though Anna did not at that point know how to tell her secret, she did know that the time must be right, that somehow trust and safety must be established. My encouragement of Anna not to share her secret until she felt it safe to do so helped to build the necessary trust. This encouragement empowered her to trust also in herself and her ability to make judgments as well as to develop needed strategies.

In such cross-cultural contexts where therapist and client are from different cultures and where same-culture resources for a client are scarce or unavailable, safety and trust may take time, and this needs to be respected. In significant ways it helped both Anna and me to consider ourselves to be, in her words, "like two cultural refugees who go on a trip together." It was important for Anna to understand that I was also a "refugee" struggling to get glimpses of her meaning-making world while assisting her to live in the new world around her.

Way of Entry Into Meaning-Making System(s), Access to Symbolic Reality. Entering into Anna's meaning-making system and symbolic reality was aided by two factors. First, Anna and I discussed dimensions of the therapeutic process and issues of safety and trust. She understood my encouragement to go at her own pace as a sign of respect. Second, once Anna experienced this respect and felt the therapeutic relationship trustworthy, she was eager to talk about her world and have me experience it through her.

Visual tools can be of immense help in the entry process. When Anna expressed interest in drawing, this was included in the process. Anna began to visually and vocally express her situation of being caught between the world she knew and her new world. She had tried to find a bridge between her known world of Salvador and her new world in the States. However, she had been thus far unable to do so and understood that her anxiety symptoms were related precisely to this caughtness, unable to access the resources in either world.

This visual mapping process helped Anna to identify the source of the tension she was experiencing and to begin to identify the different parts of the present symbolic reality that resulted in her feeling alone and isolated even when she was with other people. As this identification process continued Anna found herself more and more able to identify certain resources from her Macumba world. She began to trust that there might be a way for a bridge to be built between her known world and her present reality.

Identifying Through Life Cycle Perspective, Central Religious Rituals Experienced. At the end of the first month of therapy Anna was able to share her special secret, the religious ritual of her Macumba community. Her ability to bring this and other religious rituals into the therapeutic space were evidence of the trust and safety built in the therapeutic relationship. This relationship allowed for the therapeutic space to become space for ritual process and enactment. The religious ritual of her sacred dance provided a means for unblocking what had been blocked, a means of access for Anna and for me into her symbolic world. The ritual dance brought about a visible change in Anna. The ritual objects used during the dance remained living symbols that we made use of in the therapeutic work. These became in themselves transitional objects that we made use of in the therapeutic process.

Assessing Impact of Religious Ritual Experience on Memory and Meaning in Cultural Context.   The power and impact of ritual experience is evident at four levels in Anna's case. First, religious ritual from her childhood held a central place in the Macumba symbolic worldview and meaning-making structure. Ritual experience was vital to community and individual stability. Second, Anna's experience of relationship and of religious ritual in the United States led her to encounter a symbolic reality foreign to her own, and one through which she found it impossible to gain access to her own. As ritual system encountered ritual system, Anna found herself trapped helplessly between them. She temporarily was blocked from access to her own symbolic reality's resources and unable to access those of the new cultural environment. Anna's caughtness was as a kind of "ritual hostage."

Not by design but nevertheless as a consequence of new ritual exposure, Anna experienced distance from and rejection of her own cultural rituals in the new culture. The cultural construction of order and separation of body and spirit in the new culture's rituals had the symbolic effect of labeling the Macumba construction of body and soul integration and the use of dance and movement as illness-related, rendering Anna as a member of that culture as foreign and ill. Being isolated and experiencing the impact of such a label, Anna became isolated from the symbolic systems of both cultures.

Third, feeling caught, labeled, and unable to access her sacred triad of Macumba meaning-making, Anna's present and future felt trapped and suspended. The therapeutic experience became for Anna a third level of ritual engagement as it became a ritual context that could contain her caughtness in a safe context which then allowed her a means for access to her meaning-making system. The therapeutic relationship and environment functioned as a trustworthy container in a foreign environment, a container that allowed Anna to step beyond the present time in order to gain access to the liminal, religious rituals of her symbolic reality. Fourth, as the therapeutic context provided Anna a way of access to her past memories of religious ritual, other memories surfaced as well. Anna uncovered one particular traumatic memory from her childhood that had been blocked from consciousness prior to this. Examination of this will come in the next section. The point here is that Anna was able to use her symbolic reality and its way of containing not only to address her present situation but also to address disturbing memories from her past. Religious ritual served to contain, through conscious naming and renaming, what had been repressed through unconscious containment before.

Incorporating Religious Rituals into Therapeutic Context. The ritual dance described above was the first of four central rituals that took place during the therapeutic process. This first ritual experience allowed Anna to unblock the path of access to her religious ritual memories and symbols. It also allowed her to feel connected spiritually despite the geographical distance. The second religious ritual took place at the beginning of the fourth month. This ritual involved, as did the first, forming a sacred circle from her beads and stones, chanting and dancing in the circle with the figure of Yemanja. At the end of the dance Anna knelt down and said a final prayer. Anna invited me into the circle. This was a ritual for protection. In the therapeutic sessions Anna had been working on interpreting the world around her and testing strategies for carefully sharing her world of Macumba with a few of her friends. Things in the present were somewhat calmer for Anna as she was beginning to successfully negotiate situations in her present world. Yet, Anna found herself having unsettling dreams, nightmares that made no sense to her. She sensed that there was something in her past which she did not remember and which was coming to her consciousness now. I asked Anna if there were a ritual from Macumba that could help her approach her dreams more safely. She thought of the protection ritual.

Over the next month, Anna recalled enough scattered memories to reconstruct a traumatic mosaic of a past event that had been blocked from memory. The event was of her being beaten and raped when she was nine years old, and living for a time with relatives when her father was away and her mother was ill. According to Anna, such things were not that uncommon in the childhood world in which she was raised. Anna, recalling this childhood memory in the present, found it difficult to understand how this newly recalled memory could have been kept inside her all these years. Conversation about this kind of traumatic memory recall helped her. She felt certain that something in her present had triggered her remembering. We approached her present world for clues. This kind of investigative approach was useful. Anna found that she could direct energy in the present toward the specific goal of understanding and containing this past memory.

Anna's investigation of her present world helped her to see a connection between the present and her memory recall of this past event.
In the present she was experiencing an emerging relationship with a
young man from the university. This relationship brought her into a
closeness with her body that she had not experienced before. Though a
cause and effect analysis in such cases can never be absolute, the connection between the present and past seemed to be supported. Her present experiencing of her body appeared to have disturbed a physical
and psychic balance surpressing this memory and to have brought it to
consciousness. This recovery of memory and Anna's naming of what
had happened allowed Anna to better understand what had happened
and what was happening in her present. However, this understanding
was not enough for her to contain the memory. The memory of rape
could not be contained by her understanding alone. In her words: "This
memory is very full of power. It is so strong and I need to build a wall
around it somehow. I don't want to forget it and I can't anyway. But I
need to find a place for it."

Anna's words incorporate an instinctive wisdom concerning the
power of such memory. It was of a nature and kind that needed to be
specially contained. Though space does not permit a full exploration of
the idea, it could perhaps be argued that this kind of traumatic experience and its resulting memory were of ritual-level magnitude. In other
words, the experience of this trauma brought about the creation of
traumatic memory. This kind of memory, when surfaced, demands a
special kind of containment, a containment equal in kind and degree
to the original experience. Following this line of thinking Anna's traumatic experience and traumatic memory, of ritual-level magnitude,
would require new experience and memory of ritual-level magnitude
for containment.

The need for containment led us to the third ritual, which was in
important respects different from the preceding ones. This ritual
needed to have more than one participant, more than Anna herself.
Anna planned this ritual with the idea that I would join her, in a limited way, in the process. She designed the ritual from memories of
Macumba cleansing and purifying rituals. During the ritual I sat with
Anna in the middle of a circle of beads. All the ritual objects used previously were brought into the circle as well. Anna's special cup was
filled with water and a fragrant oil. Anna sang a particular chant and
then we chanted together. Then Anna anointed me on the head, hands,
and feet, and I did the same to her. More chanting followed and then
Anna anointed herself. After a brief silence we quietly picked up the
objects and returned the room to its original condition.

Though this ritual of cleansing and purifying did not eliminate Anna's nightmares, it did reduce their number and frequency. Anna found herself more able to concentrate on other things for longer periods of time. We discussed the way in which ritual containment functioned. Anna herself noted that whenever she thought of the rape memory, the new memory of the transported Macumba ritual in the therapeutic context also came to mind. As past, traumatic ritual memory encountered present, transforming ritual memory containment began to take place.

Over the next months Anna became more comfortable and able to test strategies for finding support networks for herself in the American context. She joined a support group for women of African and Afro-American heritage. Anna found it a relief to talk openly, in this group, about her Yoruba heritage. Anna became friends with one of the group members whom we shall name Anda. At the same time Anna's relationship with Tom, an Irish-Italian American student at the same university, was growing stronger. Anda and Tom were representatives of two support systems for Anna. Anna felt that it was important to bring Tom and Anda, who had both expressed interest, deeper into her symbolic reality. Anna could think of no deeper way than through the sharing of a ritual with them.

This idea led to the fourth ritual, which took place in the beginning of the eighth month. Anna discussed this with Tom and Anda, who both were eager to plan a ritual together with Anna. This ritual took place in the therapeutic context, the context that had become Anna's ritualizing space. As with the first and second rituals, my function was that of special participant-observer. The three ritual participants each brought special symbolic objects. Anna brought all her ritual objects. Tom brought a crucifix and candle. Anda brought a statue of an African goddess and anointing oil. Toward the close of the ritual I joined them in the circle of beads and "brought" the therapeutic space itself into the circle. Spontaneously the group sang, prayed in different languages, and joined Anna in a dance. In the two months of therapy following this ritual Anna referred to it often, as it clearly formed a vital ritual memory for her. This ritual memory helped Anna to regain a more calm perspective when she felt tense or stressed.

Creating Strategies for New Religious Ritual Experiences and New Ritual Memory Formation. Anna brought with her to therapy a culture and symbolic reality rich in ability to understand the importance of the link between memory and meaning, between ritual and reality, and between individual and community. These understand-

ings had made the idea of working on strategies a self-evident enterprise for Anna. Her culture and symbolic reality provided unlimited
resources for the therapeutic dimension of creating and testing strategies once issues concerning trust and safety had been identified and
addressed.

Anna began creating and testing strategies from the beginning of
the therapeutic process. The four rituals in the therapeutic context
themselves created new memories that Anna used to help restore and
create meaning in her life. Anna, from the beginning of the therapeutic
process, had some awareness of the connection among memory, meaning, and ritual. As Anna experienced the connection in the therapeutic
context she desired also a framework for better understanding these
experiences.

Our strategy in the final two months of the therapeutic process
concentrated attention on Anna's building her framework. Carefully,
Anna used her ritual objects to create first a musical and dance framework for understanding. Anna knew herself well enough to know that
she approached understanding first with her senses and then with her
mind. Through this multilevel process, Anna built a framework of
understanding which led to her formulation that ritual functioned for
her as a mediator between meaning-making and memory. The four rituals experienced in the therapeutic context and their consequent ritual memories each served different functions in the mediating process.
Anna worked intensively on identifying and exploring these functions:
testing the safety of a context; creating a safe context; solidifying and
strengthening a relationship; containing traumatic memory; and
restoring a calm perspective in the midst of stress. Anna's framework
of understanding, which included all of her resources and herself,
helped her to trust that she had the power to call upon the transforming ritual memories from the therapeutic context and to create new ritual experience and ritual memory in the future.

*Final Notation on the Nature and Function of Religious Ritual
with Anna.* Anna's case involving the confrontation of cultures and
initial dysfunction in relation to access to meaning-making resources
can be understood as a limit-situation. In such a situation, Anna's
meaning-making balance systems, both internal and external, were no
longer in psychic equilibrium. In Anna's situation clinical intervention came at a relatively early point in the disequilibrium process, contributing to the prevention of a more serious escalation of symptoms.

Clinical intervention paying primary attention to the nature and
function of Anna's meaning-making system and resources available

through it or related to it, incorporated the use of religious ritual in the psychotherapeutic process in the following ways:

1. The psychotherapeutic process itself was approached as a container for ritual discussion and a conduit for ritual experiencing, as discussed previously.
2. Discussion of the psychotherapeutic process as ritual-containing process became a dimension of the therapeutic process itself.
3. The clinical method incorporated discussion, analysis, assessment, and engagement of the client's past and present ritual experiences and consequent memories.
4. Such discussion, analysis, assessment and engagement in turn created the context for the experiencing of new rituals and their subsequent memories.

There are three considerations concerning ritual experience related to Anna's case that need to be raised. First, there are several levels of ritual experience that took place in Anna's case. These are: central religious rituals from her Macumba culture, the psychotherapeutic context as a ritual container and its own process of ritual-like experience, and the rituals that were created by Anna and her friends in the new cultural context. These levels of ritual experience are not of the same order or magnitude. What is important is that these levels worked cooperatively in the therapeutic process and Anna, with a central focus on her Macumba religious rituals, was able to experience a way into her new cultural context.

Second, Anna's experiencing of her Macumba religious rituals in a North American context certainly needs to be understood as a different experiencing than if in Salvador, Brazil. Through my work with Anna and many other immigrant clients, the process of experiencing religious rituals from one cultural context in another cultural context can be understood as a "transplanting" process. The transplanting of a ritual from one cultural context to another needs both to preserve and adapt simultaneously so that the two cultural contexts can cooperate in the adjustment process. As with the process of agricultural transplantation of plants, where adjustments to soil, nutrients, sunlight, and water demand careful attention (which in the best conditions will result in a plant that can thrive in its new surroundings), so also with the delicate process of religious ritual transplantation.[39] In Anna's case, the psychotherapeutic context provided the initial "new" cultural context through which Anna could transplant her Macumba ritual. Since other contexts in the new culture had proven unhelpful or daunting, it was fortunate that the psychotherapeutic context, with its attention to issues of safety and containment, proved a helpful one.

Third, the process of evaluation concerning safety and containment needs in the use of religious ritual in the therapeutic process was essential. Evaluation was a part of the process from the very beginning. Working in this way is not suitable for every case, and even when it can be argued that it is suitable for a particular case, serious evaluation of safety and containment needs to be done at every step of the process. In Anna's case, prior work had been done to talk about the therapeutic process and to address issues of safety and containment. Work proceeded at Anna's pace, and she decided when and if her religious ritual world could enter into the therapeutic process. The initial and subsequent entry of her religious ritual world into the therapeutic process was planned through the process, and this planning provided a carefully constructed safeguard. Had Anna felt an internal or external pressure to bring her religious ritual into the therapeutic process before it was safe to do so, the results would have been devastating and psychologically damaging. Caution and extreme care are needed in the therapist's ability to evaluate the situation. In many cases of psychological illness or dysfunction the incorporation of religious ritual in this way would be inappropriate and should not be attempted.

It can be argued, in conclusion, that access to religious ritual experience and memory in the therapeutic context with Anna led to the following consequences: aiding in the identification and use of resources in the client's meaning-making system in the therapeutic context; clarifying the client's reality of being psychosocially caught between cultural meaning-making systems; providing a successful intervention strategy in the disequilibrium process and thereby serving a preventive function in pathological development; permitting the reexperiencing and containing of earlier traumatic memory; and serving as a preventive psychological resource for the client's future use. The relative therapeutic success with Anna in working in this way needs to be understood through the safeguards of therapeutic evaluation, limits, procedures, and cautions about the use of religious ritual in the psychotherapeutic process.

V. EMERGING HYPOTHESES CONCERNING RELIGIOUS RITUAL AND THE THERAPEUTIC PROCESS

Area 1. The Relationship Between Psychotherapy and Religious Ritual

Psychotherapy, as understood through the cross-cultural–preventive approach presented here, stands in relationship to the topic of ritual in general and religious ritual in particular in three ways. First, it needs to be understood that religious ritual and psychotherapy are distinct entities. Psychotherapy is not the same as or a substitute for religious ritual experience. Psychotherapy's goal, in relation to religious ritual, is to assist the client in understanding the nature and function of his or her world of meaning-making and to identify resources and strategies emerging from that world. If religious ritual is one of those resources, then it can create opportunities within the therapeutic process. Second, it can be argued that the nature and function of the psychotherapeutic process can be thought of as being in itself a ritual-type process, where the client, in a controlled and safe context, takes part in his or her own liminal-resembling transformation sequence. Third, the psychotherapeutic context can be an appropriate context in which the client is able to understand and explore the religious rituals that have been a significant part of her or his developmental process. This understanding and exploring may, under the right conditions, include the contained experience of religious ritual within the therapeutic context for the explicit purpose of assisting the client to gain access to the resources of his or her culture and meaning-making system.

Area 2. Religious Ritual's Psychosocial Aspects in Cross-Cultural Contexts

Religious ritual involves both individual and social dimensions, understood through a cultural meaning-making system. In situations of a cross-cultural nature, access to religious ritual may provide a way into a client's meaning-making system and may make access possible to the different dimensions of his or her communication process. Insofar as the psychotherapeutic context represents, in the immigrant person's case, one of the new culture's meaning-making systems, attention to and inclusion of the person's religious rituals and cultural ways in the therapeutic process can serve as a literal and symbolic first step in the cultural transplantation process.

Area 3. Religious Ritual and the Creation of Ritual Memory

Religious ritual experience and resulting memory involve the range of human perceptual, cognitive, and sensual dimensions, and therefore cannot be subsumed under conscious, rational analysis. Religious ritual experience leads to the creation of ritual memory. Religious ritual memory requires special psychological containment because of its nature and psychological force. Traumatic ritual experience and memory require extreme care in the containing process and in the reconstructive work of the therapeutic process. Psychological containment of religious ritual memory can be accomplished by the experiencing of new religious ritual, and consequently the creation of new religious ritual memory. Access to and involvement of religious ritual experience and memory in the therapeutic process requires careful attention to issues of therapeutic safety, containment, and psychological evaluation.

NOTES

1. A word of appreciation needs to be expressed to my colleagues Professors Owe Wikström, Uppsala University, Sweden; Volney Gay of Vanderbilt University, United States; Halina Grzymala-Moszczynska of Krakow University, Poland; and to the outside readers at SUNY Press for their insightful critiques and suggestions for the manuscript.

2. *Ritual Criticism: Case Studies in Its Practice, Essays on Its Theory* (Columbia, SC: University of South Carolina Press, 1990), p. 14.

3. For further discussion of the nature and function of memory formation during ritual experience see my book: *Transitional Objects and Safe Space: Insights from a Dialogue Between Clinical Psychology of Religion and Ritual Studies* (Uppsala, Sweden: Uppsala University Press, expected 1996). See also the classification of different types of remembering developed by Ana-Maria Rizutto, *The Birth of the Living God. A Psychoanalytic Study* (Chicago: University of Chicago Press, 1979).

4. The distinction here between functional and phenomenological on the one hand and theological on the other by no means indicates that these different approaches to exploring a meaning-making system are not both significant for a complete investigation of a meaning-making system. The distinction is made to highlight the need for understanding the difference between these approaches. When the approaches are properly distinguished, they can work cooperatively by examing a system in perspective from outside and within. In analysis of the case here, some attempt is made to use this multiperspectival approach, though attention is primarily given to the functional and phenomenological approach as necessary for the topic's objectives.

5. I am appreciative of the fact that clinical theories can be developed apart from attachment to particular philosophical frameworks. Volney Gay's essay in this volume discusses this point. However, since clinical theories are used in particular contexts that lead to par-

ticular consequences, articulation of the interpretative framework being used seems a worthwhile and perhaps necessary task for clinical discussion and case application.

6. Clinical colleagues working in the respective contexts of neo-Jungian, feminist, and humanistic frameworks of psychotherapy have found the approach and model discussed in this essay to be of use in their different clinical settings.

7. Volney Gay, *Freud on Ritual: Reconstruction and Critique* (Missoula, MT: Scholars Press), 1979 p. 5.

8. Paul Pruyser, *Between Belief and Unbelief* (New York: Harper & Row, 1963), p. 206.

9. See especially Susan Sturdivant, *Therapy for Women: A Feminist Philosophy of Treatment* (New York: Springer, 1980). Psychologist Sturdivant makes the point that there is no psychological or psychotherapeutic theory that is purely objective, purely scientific. Theories are built on a philosophical foundation, and therapeutic techniques are built on theory. In order to gain a responsible understanding of a clinical approach one must be able to understand the philosophical and theoretical claims upon which it is built.

10. For a convincing approach to the understanding of meaning-making systems as an area of investigation for psychology of religion, see Jan van der Lans' "Meaning Giving Behaviour. A Neglected but Urgent Research Task for the Psychology of Religion," in *Religions-psykologi Nu*, ed. Owe Wikström, (Uppsala: Uppsala University Press, 1987).

11. "Religion as a Cultural System," in *Anthropological Approaches to the Study of Religion*, ed. Michael Banton (London: Tavistock, 1978), p. 4.

12. Paul Tillich, *Dynamics of Faith* (New York: Harper & Row, 1957), p. 10.

13. There are two additional points to be made. First, not every person's system of ultimate concern need be theological, formed in relation to a divinity. Whatever it is that becomes the central image in the system functions as the "god" of the system. Second, it is possible and often is the case that a person has different systems of meaning-making functioning simultaneously, or is situated in a context that sets systems in tension. More on this will be discussed in the clinical case used in this essay.

14. This much-employed term is first discussed by Mircea Eliade, *Images et symboles: Essai sur le symbolisme magico-religieux* (Paris: Gallimard, 1952). Generally, in the social sciences it has been and continues to be anthropologists and sociologists who have offered frame-

works for exploring meaning-making systems. For an initial discussion of progress in this area from psychology of religion, see Jan van der Lans' "Meaning-Giving Behaviour."

15. Ana-Maria Rizutto, *The Birth of the Living God: A Psychoanalytic Study* (Chicago: University of Chicago Press, 1979), p. 90. Gender-exclusive language Rizutto's.

16. Ibid., p. 55.

17. Ibid., p. 81.

18. Ibid., p. 209. Gender-exclusive language hers.

19. Arthur Kleinman, *Patients and Healers in the Context of Culture: An Exploration of the Borderland Between Anthropology, Medicine, and Psychiatry* (Berkeley, CA: University of California Press, 1980), p. 41. See also Kleinman, *Rethinking Psychotherapy: From Cultural Category to Personal Experience* (New York: The Free Press, 1988).

20. Kleinman, *Patients and Healers*, p. 42.

21. Ibid., p. 72.

22. "Betwixt and Between: The Liminal Period in Rites of Passages," in *Betwixt and Between: Patterns of Masculine and Feminine Initiation*, Louise Carus Mahdi, Steven Foster, and Meredith Little, eds. (LaSalle, IL: Open Court, 1987), p. 5. See also Victor Turner and Edith Turner, *Images and Pilgrimage in Christian Culture: Anthropological Perspectives* (New York: Columbia University Press, 1978).

23. Gerald Arbuckle, "Communication Through Everday Life," *Human Development 9* (Summer 1988), pp. 22–23.

24. For a discussion of the sequential rhythm between chaos and order in developmental perspective, see William R. Rogers, "Order and Chaos in Psychopathology and Ontology" in *Dialogue Between Theology and Psychology*, ed. Peter Homans (Chicago: University of Chicago Press, 1968).

25. Developmental psychologist Erik H. Erikson's incorporation of ritual as an important activity for transition between stages in the life cycle is an important reference point. See especially his *Toys and Reasons: Stages in the Ritualization of Experience* (New York: W. W. Norton, 1977).

26. Theodore Jennings, "On Ritual Knowledge," *The Journal of Religion* 62 (1982), p. 113.

27. Ibid., p. 117.

28. Richard Schechner, "The Future of Ritual," *Journal of Ritual Studies* 1,1 (Winter 1987), p. 34.

29. Eugene d'Aquili, "A Biogenetic Structural Analysis," *Zygon: Journal of Religion and Science* 18 (September 1983), pp. 247–269; Eugene d'Aquili, "Myth, Ritual and Archetypal Hypothesis," *Zygon: Journal of Religion and Science* 21 (June 1986), pp. 247–269; Eugene d'Aquili and Charles Laughlin, "The Neurobiology of Myth and Ritual," in *The Spectrum of Ritual: A Biogenetic Structural Analysis*, Eugene d'Aquili, et al., eds. (New York: Columbia University Press, 1979).

30. See Volney Gay, *Freud on Ritual*.

31. Time and space do not permit discussion of the limits and boundaries of the therapeutic process and the importance of examining ethical concerns related to such. The emphasis given here to the deliberate creation of a safe therapeutic space and therapeutic relationship will, it is hoped, express the author's concern for these issues.

32. Moore, "Contemporary Psychotherapy as Ritual Process: An Initial Reconnaissance," *Zygon: Journal of Religion and Science* 18 (September, 1983), pp. 292–293.

33. Ibid.

34. Janet Jacobs, "The Effects of Ritual Healing on Female Victims of Abuse: A Study of Empowerment and Transformation," *Sociological Analysis: A Journal in the Sociology of Religion* 50, 3 (Fall 1989), p. 276. See also Jacobs, "Religious Ritual and Mental Health," in *Religion and Mental Health*, ed. John F. Schumaker (New York: Oxford University Press, 1992).

35. This listing is the author's own, influenced especially by the ideas contained in the following resources: Lucia Albino Gilbert, "Feminist Therapy," in *Women and Psychotherapy: an Assessment of Research and Practice*, Annette Brodsky and Rachel Hare-Mustin, eds. (New York: Guilford, 1980); Miriam Greenspan, *A New Approach to Women and Therapy* (New York: McGraw-Hill, 1983); Doris Howard, ed. *A Guide to Dynamics of Feminist Therapy* (London: Harrington Park, 1986).

36. The choice of the word "movements" is used here to indicate the active and multidimensional nature involved. The movement can be done in the sequence appropriate for the situation involved. For a discussion of these movements in another format and presentation please see my *Critical Caring: A Feminist Model for Pastoral Psychology* (Knoxville, TN: Westminster/John Knox Press, 1993).

37. For further information on Macumba see my, "Movement as Mediator of Memory and Meaning: An Investigation of the Psychosocial and Spiritual Function in Religious Ritual," in *Dance as*

Religious Studies, eds. Doug Adams and Diane Apostolos-Cappadona. (New York: Crossroad, 1990).

38. In this case the learning took place in listening to Anna, reading about her culture, and finding academic and clinical resources that could help with this process.

39. For a discussion of this transplantation process see my forthcoming *Transitional Objects and Safe Space.*

9

The Significance of Ritual in the Case of Joanne

Insights from Depth Psychology

JOSEPH D. DRISKILL

INTRODUCTION

In the contemporary academic context ritual studies is emerging as a distinct field within the discipline of religious studies.[1] This increased attention to ritual can be found in a number of fields, including social anthropology, psychology, liturgical studies, and comparative religion.

From these various disciplines many definitions and approaches to ritual have emerged. In this paper I will use a definition of ritual that is informed by Robert H. Ayers'[2] definition of myth. Ritual is a value-charged, patterned action that expresses to some degree the life orientation of a group and/or individual. This definition furnishes four salient features: human activity, patterned, meaningful, symbolic.[3] It provides a framework that is useful for describing the salient features of both unique personal rituals and rituals engaged in by collectives. Concurrently, it is broad enough to permit, from a functional perspective, an experimental approach to both the theory and therapeutic use of ritual or ritual-type activity in the clinical setting.

In this work I will use the case study of Joanne to explore the significance of ritual or ritual activity for understanding the nature of the incestuous sexual abuse she received as a child. This abuse, it must be noted—though involving ritual or ritual-type activity—does not involve cultic sexual rites. The destructive meaning-making structure provided to Joanne by the abusive ritual or ritual-type activity, however, makes it incumbent in this case also to explore the role of ritual in the therapeutic processes of the clinical setting. An analysis of this case from a functional perspective on ritual provides implications for a general theory of ritual as well as implications for the clinical setting.[4]

The theoretical framework that informs the practice of therapy is guided by the understanding of pastoral counseling provided by Howard Clinebell.[5] Clinebell recognizes that clergypersons often interact with their clients in settings outside the therapeutic hour. These may include formal worship and other social gatherings associated with the life of a congregation. In this case the client attended chapel services for a significant period of time while she was receiving therapy. As a result, I served as both pastoral counselor and priest/minister to Joanne in my capacity as college chaplain.[6]

Clinebell's model of relationship-centered pastoral counseling recognizes a need for supportive, confrontational, and action-oriented elements in pastoral care. His appreciation of the variety of counseling situations that confront the minister leads him to see the need for an eclectic approach to pastoral care. Among the various types of therapy that he contends may have a role in pastoral care, one-to-one depth counseling may be useful for those who minister in settings where such therapy is possible and appropriate. It was used in this case.

The nature of the therapeutic relationship is guided by qualities Carl Rogers[7] contended a therapist must communicate to a client: for example, trustworthiness, caring, acceptance, sensitivity, respect. The work of George Gazda[8] informs the therapeutic responses employed— for instance, empathy, concreteness, confrontation, and three stages of therapy: self-exploration, self-understanding, and action. This pastoral counseling framework draws upon depth psychology for an understanding of the nature of both human growth and human pathology.[9] Of particular interest in this paper is the mother-child relationship for the life of a child, and the psychological defense mechanisms of repression and suppression.

The understanding of ritual, central to this work, is informed by depth psychology. In this case study one discovers the way in which ritualized behavior may assist in shaping the memories and self-esteem of a client in both destructive and constructive ways. The discipline of reference for the theoretical understanding of ritual used in this paper is, therefore, depth psychology, especially as it has been influenced by social anthropologist Victor Turner's work on rites of passage[10] and Ronald Grimes' findings that the body "remembers" through rituals.[11]

Within the discipline of depth psychology one finds highly diverse views of ritual. If one can say in general that Freud's work illumines the negative aspects of ritual behavior and Jung's work its positive significance,[12] it is also important to recognize that several contemporary depth psychologists, such as Volney Gay,[13] have been developing and elaborating the importance of ritual for clinical practice. Given the nature of the case study being examined, it will be useful to draw from these diverse points of view. Such a work suffers the lack of a comprehensive theoretical frame[14] from which to draw insights. In an emerging area of interdisciplinary dialogue, however, the dialectical relationship between different theories, and between theory and practice may lead ultimately to a unified, new theoretical construction. This work's much more modest aim is to further the general discussion by providing a clinical case study in which several aspects of ritual behavior are present. It is hoped that such insights will be useful for the larger theoretical scheme yet to emerge from ritual studies.

A brief introduction to the case will include an orientation to the counseling context, brief biographical material about the client, and a description of the presenting issues. Following this, ritual as an expression of pathology will be considered by analyzing the way in which ritual behavior functioned in the lives of those who abused the client. The third section of the paper will examine the way in which the understanding and use of ritual assist the therapeutic process. The paper will conclude with some general observations about ritual that emerged from this case study.

1. INTRODUCTION TO CASE

Therapeutic Context, Biographical Material, and Presenting Issues

Joanne was a 19-year-old woman who had left her home in a rural area of the nation to attend college in a large metropolitan area. During her second semester a classmate of hers who was seeing me for pastoral counseling at the college chaplain's office,[15] encouraged her to talk with me about her "problems." The friend said to me that Joanne, "was 'down' a lot of the time and seemed to have a lot of issues around her family life that she didn't talk about openly."

Joanne came to see me some three or four weeks later. She reported having had a teacher in high school who befriended her and supported her through a troubled time. This relationship had ended when the teacher felt Joanne was becoming "too dependent" on her. A psychologist in a town near her parental home had met with her two or three times; she reported having told him she was having trouble feeling "down." Her perception was that he did most of the talking. She said he told her to "forget about her problems" and that "they would go away." He believed the things she worried about were normal issues connected with "growing up" and "things would be fine." She said they weren't fine and she felt she needed help. She was now away from home for the first time and could take this step on her own.

In the first session she said she felt there were two issues that needed attention. She spoke about a boyfriend whose ethnic origin differed from hers and who had taken her out a number of times when they were in high school; she had been disillusioned when the relationship ended. She said that she also had unresolved issues around the death of her sister Laura. Laura, two years older than Joanne, had died in a freak accident when Joanne was 7 years old. Joanne said she had not been able to resolve her feelings around her sister's death. She indicated that she would like to begin by discussing the loss of her boyfriend.

Issues Addressed in Therapy

In the course of three and a half years of therapy, three major issues were addressed: a) the responsibility she felt for the death of her sister;[16] b) sexual abuse by her grandfather; and c) physical and sexual abuse by her mother. After dealing with the issue of the boyfriend she decided to approach the topic of the abuse by her grandfather. The feelings of guilt associated with her sister's death followed this. Last, her troubled relationship with her mother was examined. Psychoanalytic theory's concept of repressed emotional material contends that the issues most deeply buried in the unconscious are those with the greatest emotional impact. Its understanding of the fundamental importance of the primary love object (the mother) suggests that disorders in this relationship would be most repressed and thus the last to emerge in counseling.[17]

2. RITUAL AS AN EXPRESSION OF PATHOLOGY

Sexual Abuse by Joanne's Grandfather

Description. Joanne first surfaced the issues around her grandfather's sexual relationship with her through fleeting and fragmentary flashbacks. Her style of working with this issue involved sitting in silence for up to the first twenty minutes of a session. Suddenly she would spontaneously move to a corner of the room, lie on her back, writhe on the floor, and cry or whimper. Frequently she would repeatedly say, "He is coming at me again," and "Please stop him."

The grandfather's sexual relationship with her began after the death of her older sister Laura.[18] The sexual abuse by the grandfather assumed the form of ritualized rape, inasmuch as the sexual encounters followed a routine pattern. When the pattern was initiated, Joanne quickly recognized what was expected of her. Two scenes repeatedly provided the setting. During the summer months when she was visiting her grandparents' cottage, he would ask her to go for a swim. She quickly learned that this meant he would have sexual intercourse with her in the secluded section of the lake near the cottage.

Her grandfather's aggression and coercion assumed a "gentle" form verbally; he repeatedly told her what a good girl she was. Once he had removed her swimming suit, however, and sexual intercourse had begun, he would inflict physical pain by pinching her nipples. She reported this as one of the most physically painful aspects of the sexual encounters.

During other times of the year the seduction involved sitting on his lap in his favorite chair. He would tell her how much he liked her; and that she was his favorite granddaughter because she was "nice to him." Then he would take her by the hand to the guest bedroom on the second floor of the grandparents' home. He would continue to compliment her while he removed all of her clothing and took off his pants. Sexual intercourse followed.

Ambivalent feelings accompanied the incestuous acts because of her strong desire to feel loved. She hated him for what he did to her, and yet she wanted desperately his kindness and affection. Inasmuch as she described her mother as cold and her father as caring but remote, her grandfather was one of the few people who offered her positive regard in an emotionally expressive way.

Analysis.   We see first in the grandfather the pathological nature that ritual behavior can express. Freud's work suggests that sexual perversion occurs when the "sexual instinct has to struggle against certain mental forces which act as resistances, and of which shame and disgust are the most prominent."[19] Freud contends that if these forces acting to restrain the sexual instinct develop before the sexual instinct has reached its full strength, "it is no doubt that they will determine the course of its development."[20] When the sexual instinct gets thwarted, the libido behaves like a stream that has been dammed up. Positive[21] or negative reactions can occur at this point. In the case of perversions the individual acts out from the energy center cut off from normal sexual development, and therefore the objects to which one attaches sexual impulses are inappropriate.

Hanns Sachs made an important contribution to the understanding of dysfunction. He concluded that the afflicted individual does not simply permit her or himself, owing to lack of conscience, what the neurotic represses because of her or his inhibition. Instead the conscience permits one part of the forbidden tendencies to be acted out in order to escape from other parts, which seem even more objectionable to the superego. "What it rejects are desires belonging to the Oedipus complex, and the apparent absence of inhibition in the pervert is only the effect of a super-ego not less strict, but working in a different way."[22]

In the case of Joanne's grandfather the rape was conducted with positive verbal affirmations and physical tenderness alternating with painful touch and verbal warnings not to tell their secret or he would kill her. The oedipal issues in this context are related to power and control. Sexual gratification was achieved in this context not by relating to a mature adult object, but by overpowering an object (the child) that did not have the power to refuse or reject the advances.

The disgust or shame that may have been directed against the grandfather's sexuality when he was a child blocked his libido. Through the ritualized rape some of his repressed energy was released, while most of it remained in the unconscious. His pattern of abuse was not victim specific. Joanne later learned that her grandfather had had a sexual relationship with her mother when her mother was young, and with her sister Laura until the time of her death. At age 7 Joanne became the next, most available target for the acting out of his infantile sexuality.

It is significant, however, that the seduction and rape were expressed in patterned behavior which reflected the unresolved sexual issues of Joanne's grandfather. Although Freud did not address the ritual nature of dysfunctional sexual behavior, he wrote at length about the ritual nature of obsessive behavior.[23]

Freud notes that prior to the work done by Breuer and himself, those who suffered from obsessive behaviors were labeled "degenerates." The various patterns of their repetitive behaviors had been noted, but connections between these symptoms and the source of the illness were unknown. Freud and Breuer changed that by concluding in 1893[24] that neurosis could be equated with a traumatic illness which would occur because of a person's inability to deal "with an experience whose affective colouring was excessively powerful."[25]

In his *Introductory Lectures on Psycho-analysis* (1917) Freud noted that those suffering from obsessional neurosis often engage in actions which are repetitions or ceremonial elaborations of activities in ordinary life. For the neurotic, however, the actions are extremely tedious and exhausting. Although the obsessional actions themselves are available to consciousness, the psychical predeterminants remain in the unconscious. Repression, the process or mechanism by which an impulse or wish is denied access to consciousness,[26] occurs around an emotionally charged event or impulse. Some persons respond by displacing the repressed content with obsessional thoughts and actions. By means of analysis, however, the connections between the external behavior and interior states can be made.[27] The repetitive, ceremonial nature of these activities generated by repression and displacement is described in detail in Freud's "Rat Man" case study.[28]

By recognizing the ritual nature of the rape from the perspective of the grandfather it seems apparent that the patterned behavior expresses a repressed sexual dysfunction which no doubt emerged from the inability to move beyond infantile sexual gratification. In this sense the ritual serves as a mediator of a deeply held, unresolved emotional issue. The pathological manner in which this dysfunction is expressed is not an arbitrary pattern of behavior; it serves a symbolic function revealing something of the meaning of the sexual dynamics that have been repressed. In the case of Joanne's grandfather we find a paradigmatic example of the way in which ritual can mediate pathological and repressed memory and meaning.

Physical and Sexual Abuse by Joanne's Mother

Description.   Immediately following her sister's death Joanne also began to experience physical and sexual abuse from her mother. This abuse was a patterned form of behavior that was repeated about twice each week. The actual intervals between episodes of abuse varied from two to three days. Joanne remembers walking home from school and feeling terrified that her mother might have found something out of place in her bedroom or some chore (such as washing dishes) not completed to her mother's satisfaction. On days when this occurred her mother would start to scream loudly at Joanne when she opened the front door; she would berate her for what she had not done properly and tell her she was a "bad girl." The verbal abuse would escalate until the inevitable physical abuse would begin. This took the form of slapping and punching. Ultimately Joanne would be forced into a corner and hit repeatedly until she would wet her pants.

At that point her mother would tell her again what a bad girl she was, drag her into the bathroom and undress her. Once Joanne was naked her mother would take her to the nearby bedroom, put her on the bed, spread wide her legs, and very aggressively wash her genitals with a wash cloth. Joanne remembers the pain of the washing and repeatedly saying, "Mommy, please stop hurting me." Her mother would explain, "This is what happens to little girls who are bad and wet their pants."

Analysis. As discussed in the analysis of the grandfather's abuse pattern, these ritualized patterns of physical and sexual abuse by the mother are not merely random expressions of sexual dysfunction. They are in fact clues that link the current behavior to previous maladaptive experiences. Although the mother was not the client in this case, it seems likely that the physical abuse she received from her own mother and the sexual abuse she received from her stepfather were in some fashion combined in her abuse of her own child, Joanne. The shame and guilt she experienced from her own past blocked the normal flow of sexual energy. As a result of this blockage she split off part of her own sexual feelings. The inability to gain normal sexual gratification through mutual pleasurable relations required that she have a reason for touching the genitals of another person. In this case the person "could not refuse" her advances, advances that were "justified" by issues of cleanliness.

This form of abuse could well be considered from the vantage point of ritual purification.[29] Forbidden acts are permitted under another guise; the ritualized action allows for the release of psychic energy, and for a time a certain level of equilibrium is maintained.

As in the case of the obsessive-compulsive persons treated by Freud who consciously wished to avoid their ritualized activity, many parents who abuse their children report the desire to stop. In spite of this strong conscious desire to alter their behavior patterns, however, the abuse almost always continues unless there is therapeutic intervention. An understanding of ritual will shed light on this recurrent though consciously undesired behavior.

Ronald Grimes argues that rituals are the way in which the body itself "remembers." In other words, memory, as Grimes understands it, is not limited to cognitive processes associated with recall and recognition. An essential aspect of being human is having a body that, through patterned action, comes to "remember" its past. Grimes uses the descriptive metaphors of "bank" or "library" to posit the bodily effect of ritual activities on memory. Through ritual activities the cognitive dimension of memory is expanded; the body also has the ability to remember.[30]

In order to more fully explore the functioning of ritual in human behavior, Grimes directed a ritual laboratory where students were involved in experimentation with ritual behavior. Grimes has found that the body often responds to symbolic activities in which it does not cognitively believe. This example of an emotional response from the body to something not adhered to cognitively reveals the body's ability to operate at a level beyond the cognitive process.[31]

In the example of Joanne's mother, we find a woman whose ritualized physical and sexual abuse of her daughter lies largely outside her conscious control. Her own experiences of ritualized abuse received from her parents "act" themselves out in her own life in spite of any conscious desire to alter her behavior. It seems plausible to argue that where repression is symptomatically expressed through ritualized behavior there is a memory at the level of the body which, if not treated, will continue to exert a powerfully destructive influence.

3. THE CONTRIBUTION OF RITUAL TO WHOLENESS AND HEALING

Joanne's Response to Therapy

Joanne's response to the therapeutic setting illumines three important aspects of the interaction between therapy and ritual studies. Here we will focus on a) ritual as therapeutic; b) therapy as ritual container; and c) spontaneous ritual in the context of therapy.

Ritual as Therapeutic

Description. When Joanne came for pastoral counseling she had not yet affiliated with a church in her new college location. Her parents did not participate in organized religious activities; they were not hostile to the church, merely indifferent. During her high school years Joanne had begun attending a church in her home town. She told me that she felt God did not like "who she was," but "he did love everyone and cared for those who were down and out."

Although few of my clients attended a weekly campus worship service for which I had ongoing responsibility, I routinely let them know of its existence. Although the service was open to the college community, it was composed largely of first- and second-year students living in a particular dormitory. Several weeks into the counseling process Joanne decided to attend.

Her participation in the campus worship group for about two and a half years seemed to parallel her own growth in therapy. She had never taken Communion prior to these worship experiences; she was not pressured to participate, and declined the first few times it was offered. As a result of reading and reflection with other students, however, she decided to participate fully.

For several months she was quiet and reserved in the group; by the end of the first year, however, she began to assume a leadership role in the community that continued throughout the second year. In the community she was a strong but not aggressive advocate for social justice concerns.

In the final six months of therapy it was clear to me that she had outgrown the group. She was now a third-year student, and although the group still affirmed her leadership she decided, without any input from me, to ease gradually out of these positions. Eventually she stopped coming.

Analysis.   What did participation in the formal liturgical ritual of a worshipping community mean to Joanne? How did it function in her life? Was it merely another expression of her psychological dysfunctions, or is it possible that it served a positive role in the healing process?

In the case material related to Joanne's grandfather and mother we observed the way in which ritual activity expressed pathological disturbances through its patterned symptomatology. Freud's attention to the ritualized activities of those suffering from obsessive-compulsive disorders led him to conclude that psychic disorders undergird *all* ritual activity. Near the conclusion of *Moses and Monotheism* he writes, "Perhaps the preceding chapter has succeeded in establishing the analogy between neurotic processes and religious events and thereby in pointing to the unexpected origin of the latter."[32] That, however, is not the only point of view of depth psychologists or even necessarily representative of Freud's early position.

Recent scholarly work on Freud's 1907 essay "Obsessive Actions and Religious Practices"[33] has challenged the basis upon which he drew these conclusions. Gay's analysis of Freud's 1907 essay finds that Freud distinguished the mechanism of *repression*, which he says operates in the formation of obsessional neurosis, from that of *suppression* or renunciation, which he ascribes to religious behavior.[34] According to Gay these two processes suggest very different realities: "As I have tried to show above, these two terms designate quite distinct processes; the former entails or implies the presence of psychopathology, the latter only implies the presence of instinct control."[35] Had Freud maintained the distinctions he postulated in the 1907 essay, it would be possible to argue that at least some religious rituals emerge not from repressed (thus unconscious) impulses, but from a conscious decision to engage in instinct control. Such control can, in many circumstances, make a positive contribution not only to the individual but to the social order. Thus one can find in Freud's early work the recognition that not all rituals "must" be pathological.[36]

This theme was further elaborated by Carl Jung, an early follower of Freud. Although Jung accepted many of Freud's assumptions about human development and repression, he broke with him over, among other things, the nature of the libido. Their differences are unquestionably apparent in their respective treatments of religious rituals. Whereas Freud throughout his life essentially argued that all ritual was pathological, Jung found that rituals can in fact express and thereby contain the powerful forces of the unconscious. Jung's conclusions were based on his discovery of common themes in his patients' dreams and in the mythological stories of primitive people.

> Primitives are afraid of uncontrolled emotions, because consciousness breaks down under them and gives way to possession. All man's [sic] strivings have therefore been directed towards the consolidation of consciousness. This was the purpose of rite and dogma; they were dams and walls to keep back the dangers of the unconscious, the "perils of the soul."[37]

Jung observed that primitive rites consisted of the "exorcizing of spirits, the lifting of spells, the averting of the evil omen, propitiation, purification, and the production by sympathetic magic of helpful occurrences."[38] In the contemporary context the Roman Catholic Mass serves the believer by appropriating fundamental existential fears of meaninglessness and death.

> The Mass is an extramundane and extratemporal act in which Christ is sacrificed and then resurrected in the transformed substances; and this rite of his sacrificial death is not a repetition of the historical event but the original, unique, and eternal act. The experience of the Mass is therefore a participation in the transcendence of life, which overcomes all bounds of space and time. It is a moment of eternity in time.[39]

Jung makes a similar point about the healthy dimension of ritual when he speaks of the mythological mother and daughter, Demeter and Kore. He contends that they extend the feminine consciousness both upward and downward.

> They add an older and younger, stronger and weaker, dimension to it and widen out the narrowly limited conscious mind bound in space and time, giving it intimations of a greater and more comprehensive personality which has a share in the eternal course of things. . . . Every woman extends backwards into her mother and forwards into her daughter. This produces an experience of being outside of time, which brings with it a feeling of immortality. The individual's life is elevated to a type—the momentary individual is a bridge passing to the future generations. An experience of this kind gives the individual a place and a meaning in the life of the generations, so that all unnecessary obstacles are cleared out of the way of the life-stream that is to flow through her. At the same time the individual is rescued from her isolation and restored to wholeness. All ritual preoccupation with archetypes ultimately has this aim and this result.[40]

In the works of Jung we find a positive appreciation for the way in which rituals may connect persons individually or collectively to deep sources of meaning; this connection brings with it a type of psychological integration that both expresses and contains the various forces of the unconscious. Such rituals may contribute to the general well-being of both individuals and the society.[41]

To return specifically to Joanne's situation, it would appear that her participation in the liturgical life of a student community was therapeutic. The community became a safe place where she could try out new behavior. As she made strides in the counseling sessions there was another safe setting that allowed her to experiment with new behaviors. She developed friendships and shared talents which her previous isolation had not permitted. If the ritual had been reflecting and reinforcing her pathology rather than her growth, it seems unlikely this would have been the setting of choice for reinforcing and augmenting therapeutic advances.[42]

Therapy as Ritual Container

Description.   When Joanne started to gain access, in the therapeutic process, to her repressed emotional material, the intensity of these emotions was expressed in a variety of ways. Frequently she would begin the sessions by sitting in silence for periods of time ranging from ten to thirty minutes. As her style changed from verbal to a more physical, bodily acting out, it was apparent that many of these feelings could be spoken of only once they had been physically expressed. Crying, punching a large, overstuffed pillow, hitting the sofa with her clenched fists frequently followed the period of silence.

The intensity with which her emotions were expressed verbally and enacted physically gave me, as the counselor, a heightened awareness of the therapeutic session as a special location where emotions could be surfaced, expressed, and contained. The session was in fact a container. It was as if when the door to the room closed she used the silence to move into an altered sense of space and time. I often had the feeling of entering a special territory or zone where emotions Joanne found frightening could be released in safety. A few minutes before the hour ended I would remind her that we would be stopping soon. At that point she would begin the reentry process; we would interpret and summarize what had occurred during the therapy session. By the time the interpretation was completed she was ready to move back into "regular" space.

Joanne's personal working style in the clinical hour highlights and dramatizes the notion of therapy as ritual container.[43] This understanding of therapy, which has emerged from the dialogue between depth psychologists and social anthropologists, reveals the importance of transitional or liminal space for growth and healing.[44]

Analysis.   In *The Future of an Illusion* Freud asserts that one day the human race will be able to do without religion. He contends that ultimately religious beliefs will fall; "In the long run nothing can withstand reason and experience, and the contradiction which religion offers to both is all too palpable."[45] Freud believed psychoanalysis contributed insights important to the advance of science; a gradual rise in the general level of rational explanation would one day eliminate the need for religion. It would surely come as a surprise to Freud to learn that some psychoanalysts today use ritual theory to explicate some of the dynamics of the psychoanalytic container. Such interpretations suggest that psychoanalytic treatment may share some of the dynamics of religious rituals that promote healing and wholeness.

Social anthropologist Arnold Van Gennep's *The Rites of Passage*[46] noted that all rites of transition are marked by three phases: separation, margin (or *limen*), and aggregation. In the first phase there is some form of symbolic behavior that signifies the detachment of the individual or group from some earlier fixed point, for example, from a social structure or state. During the liminal period the state of the ritual subject is ambiguous; the person "passes through a realm that has few or none of the attributes of the past or coming state."[47] In the final phase the passage is consummated and the ritual subject (individual or group) has the rights and obligations commensurate with the new status or condition.[48]

Turner's work on liminality,[49] the phase of transition, has been most fruitful in shedding light from a ritual perspective on the therapeutic process. In ritual processes the neophytes are withdrawn from their structural positions. The values, norms, sentiments, and techniques associated with their former status or condition are suspended; the process itself helps divest them of their previous habits of thought, feeling, and action. In such a state the neophytes are alternately forced and encouraged to think about their society, cosmos, and the powers that sustain them. Understood in this way, "liminality may be partly described as a stage of reflection."[50] Liminality breaks the traditional patterns and customs and enfranchises creative speculation. This speculation permits the initiate to explore both cognitively and affectively aspects of the world previously taken for granted or accepted solely on the basis of someone else's experience.

Three crucial elements of the therapeutic process that reflect the liminal phase of a rite of passage are identified by Robert Moore: submission, containment, enactment.[51] Moore contends that the temporary surrender of autonomy by the client facilitates some degree of deconstruction of the individual's personality. Orientation and organization during this unsettled and painful period is maintained through the psychosocial container or vessel provided by the therapeutic context. Through the establishment of the "rules of therapy"[52] a special time and space are provided for the client's personal exploration. Confidentiality, acceptance, reflection, and interpretation provide a psychosocial context of liminality. In this context the client can "experiment with new images of both self and others and with new behavioral modalities which the world of structure may require."[53]

If it is acknowledged that various liminal states involve varying degrees of deconstruction and emotional pain, it follows that the container needs to be stronger in certain situations than others.[54] In this case the severity of Joanne's abuse and the amount of repression required for her to maintain a degree of normalcy through childhood and adolescence[55] meant that she needed a therapeutic container where the space-time dimension of reality had rules which permitted behavior not sanctioned in the ordinary world. Her use of silence at the commencement of most sessions; her willingness to express verbally and physically her outrage, hurt, guilt, pleasure, and shame; and her own reentry process at the conclusion of the sessions, dramatized the sense in which the therapy functioned as a ritual container in the service of health and wholeness.

Spontaneous Ritual in the Context of Therapy

Description.   Often in the therapy sessions, after sitting for many minutes in silence Joanne would suddenly begin to enact the trauma she was remembering. During the months she explored the sexual abuse by her grandfather she would often go spontaneously to a corner of the counseling room, lie on the floor on her back, and writhe in pain. This was always accompanied with tears and anguished verbal expressions, such as, "He's coming at me"; "Don't, it hurts so much"; "Don't let him do it again." Her body movements left no doubt that she was acting out the ritualized pattern of rape she had experienced many times.

In response to the intensity of her emotions I would often sit on the floor beside her and at times hold her hand. This was accompanied by responses that not only reflected her emotional state, but also reminded her that she was in the counseling room with me, not with him. These reminders seemed necessary; she often spoke of experiencing the terror as if he were present in the room. She said the terror and pain were so strong that she would "almost forget" that she was in the counseling room.

Later, when Joanne was working on the memories associated with her mother's physical and sexual abuse, the ritualized activity involved sitting in the corner in silence and staring at me with a hostile and violent gaze. When she could at last verbalize she said, "I am bad. I am an evil person." It was only later that she was able to say, "I hate her."

Analysis.   Joanne's spontaneous method of expressing her repressed emotions involved repeated displays of the rituals to which she had been subjected. The reenactments seemed to express her body's deep memories. The intensity of her negative experiences appeared to require this ritual reenactment in a safe context in order to overcome the power of the pathological rituals.[56] Only when the ritualized memories had been expressed physically could she verbalize, reflect upon, and reinterpret the experiences.

The repression of emotionally charged material has a bodily component that may not be addressed if therapy is limited to affective and cognitive mental activities.[57] In Joanne's case the power of the emotions that were remembered through and carried by the ritual seemed to have the power to completely pull her into its energy. Verbal reassurances and empathic responses, in my judgment, were not strong enough to resist the negative forces. The physical contact of holding her hand seemed necessary to assist her as she neared being completely overpowered by the surfacing of the repressed material. If ritual is the way the body remembers, it appears that containing and healing at times may require some bodily contact.

The ritualized therapeutic container allowed formerly destructive rituals to be reenacted, deconstructed, and reinterpreted. Through this process, however, Joanne was able not only to reappropriate her split-off memories from the past but also to reconstruct her self-esteem.[58] This latter process was crucial if she was to overcome her sense of being "bad." The oft-repeated, overt message from her mother that she was a bad girl was one of the last issues to emerge in the therapy.

Gay argues that self-esteem is ritualized particularly in the mother-child matrix.[59] Actual failures in a parent's empathy toward the infant or young child can create a condition in which narcissistic self-regulation cannot occur. The immature ego cannot constrain the organism's natural tendencies toward the extremes of grandiosity and self-abasement.

> Narcissistic wholeness, a feeling of self-worth and confidence, is not an intrapsychic skill. Rather it is the reflection of adequate relationships and an adequate capacity to find in one's environment the persons and experiences which will serve self-regulation.[60]

In the therapeutic context her relationship with me provided an alternative source of insight and support to that which had been given by her mother and grandfather. Through the transference/countertransference matrix Joanne had an opportunity to reconstruct her own self-image.[61]

In summary, through the years of counseling the repressed, split-off emotions that resulted from the terrorizing she received from her mother and grandfather came to the surface through spontaneous rituals performed in the ritual container of the therapeutic hour. In addition, the empathic and interpretive processes constrained the self-abasement and supported the building of her self-esteem.[62]

4. CONCLUSIONS

The findings from the dialogue between depth psychology and ritual studies connect the therapeutic process to a religious dimension not envisioned by Freud. It challenges assumptions about the human being's ability to move "beyond" religion. Whereas this dialogue does not suggest abandoning the insight and clarifications depth psychology has gained by using the scientific method, it does suggest that such an approach will be augmented usefully and, perhaps, corrected by under-standing more fully the dynamics of ritual. Toward this end and from this paper the following implications have emerged for a general the-ory of ritual and for the impact of ritual in a clinical setting.

Implications for a General Theory of Ritual

1. Human beings both define and are defined in part by rit-ual activities, for instance, self-esteem rituals of the mother-child matrix.
2. Rituals tap unconscious as well as conscious levels of meaning and provide a way for the body to remember and speak.
3. That which the ritual expresses (remembers) is meaning-ful whether it be affectively negative or positive, for it has shaped the individual.
4. The vulnerability of young children makes it virtually impossible for them to resist adult sanctioned rituals, even if the rituals are destructive to the child. Adults, on the other hand, are generally capable of making more con-scious choices about the rituals in which they will partic-ipate. Where the adult has been ritually abused, however, the pathologies created by the experience are often con-tained only by the power of another, healing ritual.
5. Rituals can create a liminal, transformational space that can contain strong emotions.
6. Rituals that promote wholeness can be constructed to contain rituals which have created pathology, for exam-ple, using the therapeutic setting.

Implications for the Clinical Setting

1. If the clinical setting is viewed as a "sacred," liminal space with a numinous quality, there is a recognition that

both the therapist and the client may be transformed through the experience.
2. When the body's memory is being expressed through ritual an important aspect of therapeutic containment may require some body contact, e.g. holding the client's hand. The clinical therapeutic frame will need to permit and account for the use of responsible touch.

NOTES

1. See *The Encyclopedia of Religion*, M. Eliade, ed. (New York: Macmillan, 1987), s.v. "Ritual Studies," by Ronald L. Grimes. This article notes that in 1977 the American Academy of Religion called for a consultation on ritual studies. By 1982 the consultation had attained official status and was named the Ritual Studies Group.

2. Robert H. Ayers, "Religious Discourse and Myth," in *Religious Language and Knowledge*, ed. R. H. Ayers and William T. Blackstone (Athens, GA: University of Georgia Press, 1972), pp. 76–95. Ayers defines "myth" as "a value-charged story expressing to some degree the life orientation of a group and/or individual." The "life orientation" dimension suggests that myth involves the whole person and not simply the intellect (and its search for explanations); the "expressing" character of myth indicates that the individual and/or group is participating in what is believed; "value-charged" speaks to the profound meanings of the myth for the believer(s) without raising the truth/falsity issue.

3. Volney P. Gay, *Freud on Ritual: Reconstruction and Critique* (Missoula, MT: Scholars Press, 1979), p. 41. Gay uses a definition of ritual by S. Lukes that includes the four features I have used in my definition, and a fifth characteristic, a normative feature, which I have omitted.

4. For additional material on the clinical approach to religious ritual in psychotherapeutic processes see the chapter by DeMarinis in this work, "A Psychotherapeutic Exploration of Religious Ritual as Mediator of Memory and Meaning," especially her discussion in the section "Clinical Approach to Incorporating Religious Ritual in a Cross-Cultural–Preventive Psychotherapeutic Process."

5. Howard Clinebell, *Basic Types of Pastoral Counseling* (Nashville, TN: Abingdon Press, 1966), Chapters 2 and 15.

6. In the North American context of the 1970s and 1980s it was not uncommon for a college chaplain to serve in the dual role of pas-

toral counselor and minister/priest of a college or university worshipping community.

7. Carl Rogers, *On Becoming a Person: A Therapist's View of Psychotherapy* (Boston: Houghton Mifflin Company, 1961), pp. 50–57.

8. George Gazda, Frank R. Asbury, Fred J. Balzer, William C. Childers, and Richard P. Walters, *Human Relations Development: A Manual for Educators* (Boston: Allyn and Bacon, Inc., 1977), p. 23.

9. Although this work draws upon depth psychology for understanding human growth and human pathology, it does not in all instances adhere to the rules for therapeutic intervention practiced by most depth psychologists. For a psychoanalytic theoretical frame see Gay's work in this volume, "Ritual and Psychotherapy: Similarities and Differences." He lists some basic rules for good therapeutic technique.

10. Victor W. Turner, *The Ritual Process: Structure and Antistructure* (Chicago: Aldine Publishing Company, 1969); *The Drums of Affliction: A Study of the Religious Processes Among the Ndembu of Zambia* (Oxford: Clarendon Press, 1968).

11. Ronald Grimes, *Research in Ritual Studies: A Programmatic Essay and Bibliography* (Mctuchen, NJ: Scarecrow Press, 1985); Grimes, ed., *Ritual Criticism: Case Studies in Its Practice, Essays on Its Theory* (Columbia, SC: University of South Carolina Press, 1990).

12. *The Encyclopedia of Religion*, s.v. "Ritual," by Evan M. Zuesse.

13. Gay, *Freud on Ritual: Reconstruction and Critique.*

14. Fred Clothey, "Toward a Comprehensive Interpretation of Ritual," *Journal of Ritual Studies* 2 (2), 1988. Clothey speaks of the "groping for a comprehensive hermeneutics of religious phenomena" by highlighting some of the issues that have emerged from the use of his field method. His work represents a current attempt to address the issues involved in constructing a comprehensive theoretical frame.

15. The college provided a small office that was shared by six chaplains, appointed by their respective denominations. I used for counseling sessions both the college office and an on-campus office provided by the denomination. In this setting the chaplain's office was one branch of student services. Psychiatric and psychological counseling also occurred in other student services. Consultations as well as referrals were frequent among the various types of counselors.

16. Revealing the details of the freak accident that took her sister's life would be tantamount to breaking confidentiality. Joanne did fear, however, that she was in some way responsible.

17. Sigmund Freud, "Repression" in *The Freud Reader*, ed. Peter Gay (New York: W. W. Norton & Co, 1989), pp. 568–572. The psychoanalytic notion of repression and the emotionally charged nature of the material in question would account for this ordering. A hierarchy of the layers of guilt and shame would suggest that those associated with feared responsibility for the death of one's sibling would be at a deeper level than those associated with incest, as painful as those would be. In the clinic the issues with her grandfather were gradually raised to consciousness more quickly than those associated with her sister's death. Psychoanalytic theory would suggest that the physical and sexual abuse by her mother, the primary love object, would be the deepest layer to uncover.

Nancy Chodorow describes the profound and enduring effect the mother/child relationship has on the child. Nancy Chodorow, *The Reproduction of Mothering: Psychoanalysis and the Sociology of Gender* (Berkeley, CA: University of California Press, 1978), p. 78.

> In a society where mothers provide nearly exclusive care and certainly the most meaningful relationship to the infant, the infant develops its sense of self mainly in relation to her. . . . Insofar as aspects of the maternal relationship are unsatisfactory, or such that the infant feels rejected or unloved, it is likely to define itself as rejected, or as someone who drives love away. In this situation, part of the infantile attention, and then the infantile ego, remains preoccupied with this negatively experienced internal relationship. Because this situation is unresolvable, and interferes with the ongoing need for love, the infant represses its preoccupation. Part of its definition of self and its affective energy thus splits off experientially from its central self, drawing to an internal object energy and commitment which would otherwise be available for ongoing external relationships. . . . The infant's mental and physical existence depends on its mother, and the infant comes to feel that it does.

18. Joanne later learned that the grandfather had previously had a sexual relationship with Joanne's mother and her older sister Laura. The sexual abuse of Joanne began after Laura's death when Joanne was 7 years old. For a discussion in this volume of ritual and the complex nature of dominative power see M. E. Stortz, "Ritual Power, Ritual Authority: Configurations and Reconfigurations in the Era of Manifestations."

19. Sigmund Freud, "Three Essays on the Theory of Sexuality," in *The Freud Reader*, ed. Peter Gay (New York: W. W. Norton & Co., 1989), p. 254.

20. Ibid.

21. Sigmund Freud, "Civilization and Its Discontents," in *The Freud Reader*, Chapter 3. Freud's descriptions of sublimation offer an understanding of the positive aspects of inhibited sexual impulses.

22. Otto Rank and Hanns Sachs, *Die Bedeutung der Psychoanalyse für die Geisteswissenschaften* (Wiesbaden, Germany: Bergmann, 1913); quoted in Melanie Klein, *Love, Guilt and Reparation and Other Works 1921–1945* (New York: The Free Press 1975), p. 184.

23. Freud's interest in religious behavior focused around what he contended was its obsessive, neurotic nature. His 1913 work *Totem and Taboo* discusses the prohibitions against murder and incest, which originate in totemism. In this work Freud examines the relationship between the father complex and a person's helplessness and need for protection. The helpless child, whose first love object is the mother, soon decides that the father is the stronger figure. The child then fears the father while at the same time longing for him and admiring him. The growing individual, however, finds that one always needs protection from superior forces. In *The Future of an Illusion*, his 1927 work on wish fulfillment and religion, he asserted the formation of religion grows out of the adult's reaction to the feelings of helplessness characteristic of childhood. Each person "creates for himself the gods whom he dreads, whom he seeks to propitiate, and whom he nevertheless entrusts with his own protection" (Gender-exclusive language Freud's). Sigmund Freud, *The Future of an Illusion*, trans. and ed. by James Strachey (New York: W. W. Norton and Company, 1961), p. 30.

In *Totem and Taboo* Freud suggests that religious ideas include not only the wish-fulfillments noted above, but also historical recollections. He contends that the son's conflict with the father is not merely a psychic conflict; it is also an historical recollection based on the actual death of the original father by violent means. The ambivalent emotional reaction of primitive people to this death resulted in a desire to obey both the will of the father and the commandment "Thou shalt not kill." In *Totem and Taboo* Freud makes two significant claims about the relationship between private obsession and public taboo. He believed 1) a comprehensive understanding of obsessions will explain exhaustively the psychological nature of taboos; and 2) taboos that persist among us are displayed in the actions of obsessive neurotics. Gay, *Freud on Ritual: Reconstruction and Critique*, pp. 25–26.

Later, in a 1934 work, *Moses and Monotheism*, Freud forthrightly contends that religious ritual was based on the same repressive mechanisms that characterize neurotic behavior. Gay, however, contends that Freud drew this conclusion not on a careful application of his own clinical and theoretical work, but from his belief that religious beliefs (illusions) would one day be replaced by rational thought. Gay, *Freud on Ritual: Reconstruction and Critique*, pp. 18, 30–32.

24. Sigmund Freud and J. Breuer, "On the Psychical Mechanism of Hysterical Phenomena: Preliminary Communication," in *On the History of the Psycho-Analytic Movement, Papers on Metapsychology and Other Works*, vol. 14; trans. James Strachey in *The Standard Edition of the Complete Psychology Works of Sigmund Freud*. Collected Papers, 1, 24; Standard Edition, 3, 9. (London: The Hogarth Press and the Institute of Psycho-Analysis, 1957).

25. Sigmund Freud, *Introductory Lectures on Psycho-Analysis*, Trans. and ed. James Strachey (New York: W. W. Norton and Company, 1989), p. 341.

26. Gay, *Freud on Ritual: Reconstruction and Critique*, p. 5.

27. Freud, S. *Introductory Lectures on Psycho-analysis*. Lectures 17 and 18.

28. Sigmund Freud, "Notes Upon a Case of Obsessional Neurosis (Rat Man) and Process Notes for the Case History," in *The Freud Reader*, ed. Peter Gay (New York: W. W. Norton & Co., 1989), pp. 309–350.

29. For a discussion in this volume of purification rituals in Shingon Buddhism see R. Payne, "Realizing Inherent Enlightenment: Ritual and Self-Transformation in Shingon Buddhism."

30. Ronald Grimes, public lecture at Pacific School of Religion, February 22, 1990. See also Paul Connerton, *How Societies Remember* (New York: Cambridge University Press, 1989). For a discussion of ritual as mediator of memory and meaning, see the discussion of Macumba ritual by DeMarinis in "A Psychotherapeutic Exploration of Religious Ritual as Mediator of Memory and Meaning," this volume.

31. Other examples of this appear in older works of social anthropologists and classicists who have found that rites often are more stable than the myths on which they were presumed to be based. See David Stills, ed., *International Encyclopaedia of the Social Sciences* (New York: Macmillan and Free Press, 1968), s.v. "Ritual" by Edmund R. Leach. See also W. Robertson Smith, *The Religion of the Semites* (New York: Meridian, 1956), Chapters 6–11; Jane E. Harrison, *Ancient*

Art and Ritual, rev. ed. (New York: Oxford University Press, 1951). Harrison argues that the themes of religious art are intelligible only in light of the ritual acts that undergird them.

32. Sigmund Freud, *Moses and Monotheism* (New York: Vintage Books, 1939), p. 117.

33. Sigmund Freud, "Obsessive Actions and Religious Practices," in *Character and Culture,* Introduction by Philip Rieff (New York: Collier Books, Macmillan Publishing Co., 1963), pp. 17–26.

34. Gay, *Freud on Ritual: Reconstruction and Critique,* p. 6.

35. Ibid., p. 28.

36. See also V. Gay, "Ritual and Psychotherapy: Similarities and Differences" in this volume for a discussion of the ritual space provided by the priest or minister.

37. Carl Jung, "Archetypes of the Collective Unconscious," in *Archetypes of the Collective Unconscious,* Bollingen Series 20, trans. by R. F. C. Hull (New York: Bollingen Foundation, Inc., by Pantheon Books, 1959), p. 22.

38. Ibid.

39. Carl Jung, "Concerning Rebirth," in *Archetypes of the Collective Unconscious,* p. 118.

40. Carl Jung, "The Psychological Aspects of the Kore," in *Archetypes of the Collective Unconscious,* p. 188.

41. See also in this volume R. Slough's discussion on tacit knowing and ritual as strategic action.

42. Although my presence in the worshipping community no doubt contributed to its feeling "safe" for Joanne at least initially, her integration into the student-initiated and-administered program reflected her own growth and independence. The meaning of the community to her, independent of my involvement, probably is reflected by the fact that she did not inform me when she decided to leave the group. At a much later time she said in passing, "When I felt most of the students in the evening worship group were younger than me and I no longer shared many of their interests I thought I should move on." This move, however, was not a move away from religion. She was by this time involved in a nearby church. For a discussion of preenactment and mimesis in this volume see R. Payne, "Realizing Inherent Enlightenment."

43. Robert L. Moore, "Contemporary Psychotherapy as Ritual Process: An Initial Reconnaissance," *Zygon* 18, 3 (September 1983): pp. 292–293. See also Kenneth R. Mitchell, "Ritual in Pastoral Care," *The Journal of Pastoral Care* 43, 1 (Spring 1989): pp. 68–77.

44. See also W. Noonan, "Western Hospitalization for Surgery as 'Rite of Passage,'" this volume, for a discussion of the role and function of "liminality" in a hospital setting.

45. Sigmund Freud, *The Future of an Illusion*, trans. and ed. James Strachey, with a biographical introduction by Peter Gay (New York: W. W. Norton & Co., 1989), p. 69.

46. Arnold Van Gennep, *The Rites of Passage* (Chicago: University of Chicago Press, 1960), p. 191.

47. Victor Turner, "Betwixt and Between: The Liminal Period in Rites of Passage," in *Betwixt and Between: Patterns of Masculine and Feminine Initiation*, Louise Carus Mahdi, Steven Foster, and Meredith Little eds. (LaSalle, IL: Open Court, 1987), p. 5.

48. Ibid.

49. Ibid., p. 14.

50. Ibid. For a discussion of the mimetic quality of liminal space see Payne, "Realizing Inherent Enlightenment.

51. Moore, pp. 292–293.

52. These rules differ depending on one's therapeutic approach. Volney Gay, in a lecture at the Graduate Theological Union May 3, 1990, listed twelve rules that provide the frame for psychoanalytic approaches, e.g., time of appointment, length of appointment, empathic environment.

53. Moore, pp. 292–293.

54. In many situations a friend, relative, and/or coworker may provide the containment necessary to deal with an emotional issue. This is not the sole domain of professional therapists.

55. From the victim's point of view the ritual rape created psychic conflicts that required repression in order to maintain ego stability. It seems likely that without using the defense mechanism of repression Joanne's ego could not have sustained the sexual aggression of her grandfather. In such cases the repression serves an adaptive purpose.

56. For discussions in this volume of ritual as container see DeMarinis, Payne, and Noonan.

57. For a discussion in this volume of "gesture" as a nonverbal aspect of ritual, see J. H. Martin, "Bringing the Power of the Past into the Present."

58. Volney P. Gay, "Ritual and Self-Esteem in Victor Turner and Heinz Kohut," *Zygon* 18, (September 1983), p. 280. In this volume for a discussion of healing childhood trauma see Gay, "Ritual and Psychotherapy: Similarities and Differences."

59. Gay, "Ritual and Self Esteem," p. 278.

60. Ibid., p. 280.

61. For a discussion of meaning-creation and meaning-making in this volume see M. Aune, "The Subject of Ritual: Ideology and Experience in Action," and DeMarinis, "A Psychotherapeutic Exploration of Religious Ritual as Mediator of Memory and Meaning."

62. Joanne has for several years been in a committed, intimate relationship and has maintained a successful professional career.

10

Western Hospitalization for Surgery as "Rite of Passage"

WILLIAM R. NOONAN

INTRODUCTION

Much of the literature on rites of passage draws on anthropological interpretations of small-scale, "primitive" societies. There is a great deal of evidence of the rites' vitality in those societies, but doubt as to how rites of passage operate in modern Western society. There is even a question as to whether modern society has lost the ability to move its people through transitions.

The problem is compounded by the reality of pluralism found in multicultural societies such as in the United States. An effective social ritual depends on a sufficient degree of social cohesion and a common symbol system. The breakdown of social rituals, such as rites of passage, reflects a wholesale failure of meaning, but nevertheless it does create opportunities for nascent rituals to emerge from the creative energies of individuals stranded in life's transitions.[1]

Modern people still experience anxiety-provoking and traumatic experiences. Without the benefit of a social rite of passage, they must rely on their own resources and unconscious need to ritualize human affairs in order to cope with life's transitions. Along with divorce, career changes, and menopause, surgery can be a physical and symbolic transitional experience that challenges individuals to create personal rites of passage.

Anyone who has had to undergo surgery knows it is a traumatic, fearful experience. During the preoperative procedures, the anesthesiologist visits patients to explain the procedures and the possible risks that could result from being under anesthesia. While under anesthesia, patients are brought to a state of helplessness and dependence in order for a life saving operation to be performed. Often, a limb or organ must be removed in order to preserve human life. The term *go under* communicates the complete loss of control and memory on the part of the patient. The patient knows he or she will not emerge the same person as before, or fears that he or she will not survive at all. Yet, this is a necessary ordeal if the patient is to make the transition from illness to health.

The experience of surgery merits the need for a rite of passage to help patients cope with the predicament of surgery. Patients must face a situation where personal control is completely surrendered and where they are rendered helpless in order to undergo a potentially life-threatening situation. The situation resembles the conditions an initiate faces during a public rite of passage.

This paper will explore the commonalities the experience of surgery has with the phenomena usually associated with rites of passage, and will show how the procedures used in preparation for surgery ultimately fail in providing the benefits a rite of passage is designed to fulfill. Although surgery is clearly done to benefit the patient, it will be shown that hospital procedures surrounding the action of surgery fail to help patients cope with the experience of surgery. They do not yield the sufficient degree of psychological safety needed to contain the experience. Surgery remains a frightening experience unaided by rituals that might hold the promise of meaning and safety.

In the void created by the lack of a social rite of passage, I am proposing that individuals appropriate the highly repetitive procedures enacted in a hospital setting and use them as personal rituals to facilitate their experience of hospitalization. A case study is presented of a woman who ritualizes the hospital procedure of removing her clothes, storing them away, and receiving the hospital gown in order to protect herself from the clinical gaze of the medical establishment. After the ordeal of surgery, she uses personal mnemonic artifacts to recover her sense of self. Her ritual serves as a container for the stored memory of self, which allows her to make the transition through the ordeal of surgery and reclaim her identity on the other side of the surgical experience. Her experience provides some ritualistic clues and root metaphors for further reflection on ritual making in a hospital setting.

My proposal rests on two claims. First, human beings engage in ritualizing behavior in order to address their world in a meaningful fashion. Modern secularization has not eliminated the need for ritual, as much as the ritualistic need has been relocated to private expressions.[2] Second, rituals are culturally constructed and reflect the values, rules, and expectations of the society.[3] Since rituals were constructed before, it is possible that they can be recreated to attend to the important junctures in the human life cycle today. By analyzing the cultural matrix of a health care system, hospitals can design admission procedures and hospital policies to create an environment conducive to personal ritual making.

Hospital administrators, doctors, and staff are not likely to perceive their procedures as rituals, or as elements belonging to a rite of passage for the patient at this point in time. This insight is a labor borne from the anthropological perspective, which analyzes social action and its meanings. Anthropology has utilized a functional perspective to analyze rituals and social actions. By isolating the functional use of ritual, one can study how other social actions not commonly identified as rituals function in similar ways.[4]

The benefit that a functional perspective affords the health care field is an increase of awareness concerning the effects of its structures and procedures upon patients. For a system intent on promoting health, the greater the extent to which the health care field becomes aware of how its procedures function like rituals, the greater the potential there is for providing its members with the facility to maneuver through the most difficult transition of our human existence: suffering and death. The consequence of unawareness will deprive the individual of rich cultural resources available for making meaning of the illness experience.

THEORETICAL FRAMEWORK

I will build upon the tripartite structure of the rites of passage worked out by Arnold Van Gennep, together with Erving Goffman's analysis of the "stripping process" as a rite of separation. I will apply Victor Turner's concept of "liminality" and "reflexivity" to the transitional status of patient and hospitalization. These concepts are generally understood and applied to cultural groups acting in-a social context. I will be applying them to the individual, personal action of surgery, yet remain cognizant of the social dimensions that shape the clinical reality of surgery.

notes of passage

According to Van Gennep, the rites of passage have a fundamental tripartite structure: rites of separation, rites of transition, and rites of incorporation.[5] The initiate is separated from the preritual context and then enters a transitional period. This transition is a passageway toward a new social status. This period is referred to as the "betwixt and between or "limen," when reality is neither here nor there. Often the limen is represented by symbols of death. The final stage is the incorporation of the initiate into the new status. The newly initiated take their place as new members, and learn new information, behavior, and roles.

liminal

Victor Turner extended Van Gennep's concept through theories developed from his study of the transitional period. The liminal period is more than a mere intermediate phase. Turner emphasized the importance of disorientation at this stage as a prerequisite for transformation. The disorientation is caused by the separation of the initiates from their familiar surroundings and usual ways of comprehending the world. The disorientation is enhanced further when the initiates are brought to an unfamiliar location.

These shifts push the initiates to the edge of self-investigation. What counted as important before no longer does. Social values are inverted, boundaries are crossed, and a host of "playful," reflexive exercises of awareness are conducted within the safe confines of the ritual. This process that Turner refers to as "reflexivity" breaks new ground for learning. Although the rite creates anxiety as it explores the paradoxes inherent in the transition, it also alleviates it by providing the necessary information to manage the transition. During this time, culture passes on the values, norms, and patterns of behavior appropriate to the next stage of life or social position.[6]

Hospitalization for surgery can be a liminal experience and a transition to health. What a patient is incorporated into is the state of health determined by the social reality of the culture. The theories of Arthur Kleinman have defined the health related aspects of social reality as the clinical reality. Beliefs about sickness, illness behaviors, patient-doctor transactions and health care systems exist within the clinical reality. Arthur Kleinman's work on clinical and symbolic reality yields insights into the definition of health the patient is restored to by the dominating cultural model of health.[7]

The clinical reality that comprises the cultural context of illness, treatment, and health also includes a symbolic reality. The concept of symbolic reality refers to how people organize experience in a meaningful fashion, enabling them to relate to the social world around them and to the inner world within themselves. Individuals internalize what social reality offers through socialization and language acquisition. The personality is shaped according to the social and cultural environment. This process allows the individual to relate to the social world. Kleinman maintains that "the internalization of symbolic reality . . . also plays an essential role in the individual's orientation to his *[sic]* own inner world."[8] The symbolic meanings received from the culture affect an array of psychological processes and possibly also the physiological level. His claim is that culture determines what constitutes illness and healing. The concept of symbolic reality allows Kleinman to explain how symbolic meanings, grounded in the social reality, enter and influence illness and treatment outcomes. For the purposes of this essay, the concept of symbolic reality will explain how an individual constructs her or his own symbolic meanings around the clinical procedures used to prepare her or him for surgery.

RITES OF PASSAGE APPLIED TO HOSPITALIZATION FOR SURGERY

Although it is not intentionally designed to do so, I have proposed that the experience of hospitalization functions as a rite of passage from illness to health. Specifically, when surgery is to occur during a hospital stay, the procedures of admission and preparation for surgery operate as a rite of separation. The relinquishing of control and personal identity prepares the person to experience the ordeal of surgery. During the transitional period, the betwixt and between, the person is propelled across social boundaries into the role of patient. The surgery itself, waiting for test results, living in an unfamiliar environment, learning a new vocabulary, and receiving instructions from the medical authorities are a few experiences that compose the liminal situation of illness. The third phase, the rites of incorporation, takes place during the course of the hospitalization and beyond as patients enact their role and come into contact with the definition of health determined by the clinical and social reality of the health care system.

Medical procedures have been analyzed as rituals by adopting a functionalist perspective. Pearl Katz examines the medical procedures enacted around contaminated and sterile objects in the operating room.[9] Although they exist in a scientific context, the procedures exhibit symbolic and communicative functions characteristic of rituals. In a number of cases, the practicality of the procedures is dubious in the actual effect upon sterility. What is more apparent is the exaggeration of the definitions of contaminated and sterile objects that "serve to increase the autonomy of the participants by providing them with an unambiguous understanding of precisely which categories are operative at a certain time.[10] The ritualized procedures around contamination and sterility create boundaries that sanction appropriate behaviors, define space, and regulate the transmutation of "clean"and "dirty" states—all recognizable functions of ritual.

The overt reason for the existing series of stylized procedures for contamination/sterility is the protection of the patient from any danger of infection. Although presented under this benevolent guise, their covert symbolic functions serve to maximize the medical team's autonomy and effectiveness. "Rendering the patient unconscious deprives the patient of all autonomy, while increasing the autonomy of the staff."[11] The collection of ritualized procedures serves to support the surgical teamwork and to render the patient helpless and dependent.

The reductive nature of surgery allows the surgeon to perform a service for the benefit of the patient. Following Katz's analysis, the elaborate procedures act like rituals by establishing boundaries that ensure safe passage through the critical periods of surgery. Secure boundaries and a dispassionate manner are necessary to the successful completion of surgery. The medical staff rely on these highly elaborate, ritualized procedures in order to consciously perform the task required by the ordeal of surgery, namely, on face value, the act of supreme violence to a human body. In order to preserve safety and a single-minded focus, the ritualized procedures serve the needs of the medical staff. In this discussion about ritual and hospital procedures, is there room to respect the need for ritual for both the medical staff and the patient?

Whereas ritualized hospital procedures clearly benefit the medical team, usually no procedures are designed to help the patient cope with the predicament of surgery. Just the same, does the reality dictated by the physical action of surgery leave the patient with only a limited response to the experience of surgery? If so, the investigation continues along the lines of the possible ways a patient can prepare for and recover from surgery that give him or her the same benefits of safety afforded to the medical staff by their ritualized procedures. The insights gained from the work on the rites of passage offer some hope and ritualistic clues to this problem.

RITE OF SEPARATION: STRIPPING OF IDENTITY

From the point of view of the hospital administration, admission procedures are concerned with the effective management of patients' entrance into the hospital environment. Collecting information, securing proper authorization, and dispatching patients to their rooms are the main functions of an admission department. The admission department does occupy a unique position within the hospital, in that it represents the person's first experience of being inducted into the role of patient and initiated into the hospital's clinical reality.

Sociologist Erving Goffman has written on the admission of individuals into "total institutions" that use procedures and rituals designed to strip the person of autonomy, identity, and distinguishable separate status.[12] Initiates are required to submit personal information to the institution that is no longer accessible to them, and can be used against them. They are dispossessed of their property. Many personal items in which a person invests self-feeling, such as a wallet or photographs, are removed. Personal articles of clothing, which often represent a person's uniqueness, are shed and replaced with a uniform clearly marked as belonging to the institution. Usually a number is assigned to the person as the primary means of identification. Body space and personal boundaries are invaded by the authorities of the institution. Strip searches are conducted, privacy is eliminated, and daily schedules are predetermined by the institution. The newly initiated members into a total institution are isolated from their equals. Forming their own community is discouraged. They are kept dependent on the staff for information about the system. These procedures work to maintain dependency on the institution and clearly establish the lines of power between the members and staff.

In his book *Asylums*, Goffman does not include a medical hospital in his definition of "total institution." Although his list is not exhaustive, the general characteristics describe an institution where the barrier to outside social interaction is usually symbolically represented by a concrete wall, moat, or locked gates. His focus is mainly on prisons, mental asylums, and monasteries. A hospital does not fit the definition of a "total institution."

However, Goffman's analysis of the "stripping process" has been applied to the hospital setting. Hans Mauksch's description of the stripping process of the hospitalized patient judges this process as having a negative effect upon the patient, resulting in the total possession of the patient's life by the hospital.[13] I disagree. All institutions have the tendency to absorb the individual into their culture. A change of personal and social status occurs, although the result is not always the total possession of the individual by the institution. Rather than criticizing the "stripping process" as impersonal, is there a possibility that it is a realistic response to the ordeal of surgery?

Separation from a familiar environment, disclosing personal information, dispossession of personal property, the removal of civilian clothes, and wearing a hospital gown constitute a stripping process whereby a person assumes the status of patient. The critical difference between Goffman's analysis of the "stripping process" and what occurs in the admission of people into hospitals is the transitional nature of becoming a patient. In the total institution described by Goffman, an individual becomes an inmate, monk, or career mental patient. His or her social status exists over an extended period of time. The status of a hospitalized patient for surgery exists only for the duration of a hospital stay.

The transitional nature of surgery permits the "stripping process" to be temporary. Ideally, the stripping process prepares the patient for the inevitable relinquishing of personal control when he or she undergoes surgery. The process is contingent upon whether the clinical reality respects the transitional state of the patient.

THE RITE OF TRANSITION: THE LIMINALITY OF ILLNESS

Victor Turner widened the span of liminal situations to include periods of history, small nations, movements, and an assortment of marginal characters.[14] "Patient" is another liminal entity. The person entering the hospital faces the unknown. Surgery itself is a liminal period when, under the spell of anesthesia, the patient is truly neither here nor there, but held by technology between life and death.

The liminality of hospitalization is also experienced when the patient is undergoing tests, X-ray procedures, and workups. Each procedure probes the body for answers to illness and retrieves information from the body that will be factored into a life or death decision. Quite often a waiting period, a virtual limbo state, is endured by the patient. Answers to questions about longevity, death, and the quality of life are stalled during this period. The person can experience the entire gamut of fear from the uncertainty of not knowing what is wrong, to the possibility that death will be the only way to depart from the hospital. The person facing illness confronts liminal situations where the unknown exists and death is possible.

At this time there are no socially constructed rituals existing for preparing for surgery. There are no masks, costumes, or figures of death to enact the drama of the ordeal. The exercise of "reflexivity" during hospitalization is usually enacted privately. Individual patients may use a waiting period to ponder the quality of their lives; a life inventory may be conducted in preparation for surgery; or a nest of personal, symbolic objects may be constructed around the sickbed. These are all examples of "reflexivity" patients engage in on their own, apart from the support of social structures. Yet, the social situation casts them in the role of liminal entities.

Liminal entities are in "betwixt and between" social positions. The person is no longer a banker, teacher, or cook, but a patient. Patients are removed from their everyday world. For the first admission, the hospital is a strange, unknown place. Initial disorientation is common among patients when they try to find their room, labs, or doctor's office. Often they are unable to find their own way, but are transported there by orderlies. Patients rely on house staff for instructions, rules, and criteria for determining appropriate hospital behavior. The patient must quickly learn confusing medical terminology. They have to negotiate the complex network of relationships that exist within the hospital system.

Once again, patients are rendered dependent on the medical system. With rare exceptions, patients are not encouraged to seek medical knowledge independent from their physicians. There are no structured occasions for inpatients to gather and share with each other strategies for coping, information about managing the system, or hospital stories. The trend is toward brief hospital stays and more same-day surgeries, thus decreasing opportunities for patient-to-patient contact.

At spontaneous and random times, patients develop an intense interest in the stories of one another. They identify closely with one another and upon subsequent hospitalizations inquire about other patients they have met. Victor Turner observed that during the liminal phase, those deemed to be liminal entities form a feeling of solidarity. This unity, or what he refers to as "communitas" serves as antistructure.[15] The existence of communitas during the liminal phase is a potentially creative, imaginative opportunity to seek renewal, innovation, and genuine insight into the basic truths of the human condition.

Although patients qualify as liminal entities, the medical establishment has a vested interest in isolating the patients and not allowing the patients to become a multitude. The end effect of keeping the patient isolated is protecting immunity of the medical system from any criticism or change from its "weakest members." Rather than reaping the creative potential created within the liminal situation, the health care system truncates the experience by dominating the clinical reality with its scientific, materialistic definition of illness and health. What patients are incorporated into is the state of health so determined by the social reality of the health care system.

RITE OF INCORPORATION: THE CLINICAL
AND SYMBOLIC REALITY

The concept of initiation, specifically the rites of passage, has been applied to the hospital experience by John Katonah as a way to understand the crisis of hospitalization.[16] He designates the stripping process as the rite of separation. The liminal period takes place in the hospital. The final stage of incorporation, or what Katonah refers to as "transformation," does not occur in the hospital. For Katonah, the rite of passage experienced in a hospital is not an initiation of person to patient, but occurs on a spiritual level where the person experiences a deeper purpose for life.

Katonah transposes the concept of rite of passage onto the hospital experience from a theological framework. Since he writes for hospital chaplains, he sees the potential for pastoral care to facilitate the "creative possibility of new life through this rite of initiation known as hospitalization."[17] The difficulty with Katonah's application is that the rite of passage is not consummated. He admits that many people stay in the "betwixt and between" stage. The chaplain helps complete the process by being a maieutic ally for the patient.

Katonah has misunderstood the final phase of incorporation. He is correct in stating that patients are not incorporated into a state of health imbued with a deep spiritual purpose. This may be the state of health he would like to see them transformed into, but its absence does not negate the fact that patients are incorporated into *a state* of health.

According to the concept of the rite of passage set out by Van Gennep and Victor Turner, the rite is consummated when the initiate is returned to a relatively stable state. The state of health so determined by the clinical reality of the health care system is the final phase of incorporation. Clinical realities differ from culture to culture, and multiple ones can compete with each other in local societies. The point remains that in each health care system, there exists a clinical reality in which its patients are incorporated into a determined state of health.

The point to which I think Katonah is speaking is whether the medical model operative in our Western culture could fulfill the goals of a rite of passage. According to Turner, initiates are "ground down to a uniform condition to be fashioned anew and endowed with additional powers to enable them to cope with their new station in life."[18] This goal of transformation may be beyond the scope of the Western medical model. Regardless, the situation presents the opportunity for enhanced coping strategies to deal with surgery by the personal appropriation of ritual behavior.

Given the present clinical reality of Western medicine, how can patients utilize the existing hospital procedures or create their own rituals to maximize safety and return to health? Is it possible given the clinical reality of Western medicine? How do patients exit surgery and restabilize their identity so that their personal sense of control is restored? The presentation of a case study will illustrate one woman's meaningful assimilation of a hospital procedure and the creation of her own ritual to stabilize her identity after the event of surgery.

PRESENTATION OF CASE STUDY

M. is a woman in her early thirties. Her cultural heritage is Mexican American. She underwent major surgery to remove a growth on her right ovary. Before the surgery, there was uncertainty as to whether the ovary would be removed as well. She preregistered at the hospital two days prior to the surgery. She reported experiencing the preregistration as positive. "They went through the process to educate me as much as they could to prepare me." The night before the surgery, she and her husband picked out a photograph that had "fond memories for the two of us." She packed her favorite leisure clothes, a cartoon book, and a Forty-Niners football T-shirt. The next morning, she went to the hospital and was admitted directly to the surgical waiting room.

The surgical waiting room was a large room where all the morning surgery patients had gathered. They were separated and placed in curtained partitions. M. removed her street clothes, packed them carefully away in a bag she had brought with her, and put on a hospital gown. M. stayed there with her husband for approximately two hours while the staff took her vital signs, checked forms, and took a medical history, and the surgeon and anesthesiologist visited her.

During this time, M. began what she referred to as "my cocooning time."

"I was kind of wanting to be internally prepared, like cocooning. I understood it psychologically, and physically, but now I had to deal with the emotional component and was pulling in all of my energies to help go, 'This is it.'"

Previously, she had requested a spinal anesthetic so she could be alert during the time of the operation. While "cocooning," she decided against this procedure and opted for general anesthesia.

"During my cocooning I thought it was kind of an unusual kind of thing, why would I want to frighten myself more, and hear them talking, or doing something that you really don't want to see, so that's when I decided that I don't need to do this, I gave up and said to go with it. Give up the ounce of control that I wanted to keep. I gave myself permission to go through the whole thing asleep."

She describes a process of putting herself away in preparation for the surgery. She "stored" her identity through the action of packing her clothes away in a bag. The process is a gradual relinquishing of control, yet with limits. She sets up an internal time demarcation for the end of the surgery. "My limit was that I wanted to watch the Forty-Niners and they had to wake me up for that. The truth of the matter was that I had given myself, in my thought process, permission to do this. . . . I wanted it as a self-contained time." She asked the anesthesiologist to make sure she was awake by the time the Super Bowl game started. The start of the game would be the sign she had come through the surgery. Once on the other side, she could surround herself with her cherished belongings and watch the game.

On her own volition, she walked into the operating room and lay down on the table. She describes the experience as "getting swiped away by the event . . . it is like a current down a stream, it just keeps going, it is a process that is initiated, and engaged, it goes and takes you to, like a stream of water, through the doors and you go there and you've given up your control and they take over." Once on the table, she began to dissociate from what was happening. They had extended her arms and begun the IV lines. Her gown was pulled back and electrodes paced on her chest. These procedures ran counter to the inner direction of her "cocooning." "They had me extend my arms, which is not what I wanted to do, I just keep my body close, my arms close to myself, I remember having to make an effort to let my arm extend, because I didn't want to let it go." In hindsight, she wished she was put under anesthesia while in her "cocooning" phase.

After the surgery, she was informed that her right ovary had been removed. She was not surprised or shocked because she had inwardly prepared herself for this loss during her "cocooning." Her first request was to put on her Forty-Niner T-shirt and watch the game. Even though she couldn't remember much of the game, she knew the surgery was over. "That was the moment when I knew I had made it through and I was all right. It was like saying, 'OK guys, you've had enough, this is me now, I'm back.'"

DISCUSSION OF THE CASE

The Stripping Process

Does an orderly and informative set of admission procedures create an environment of safety and cognitive orientation, so that the patient can let go of personal control? The case of M. is evidence of a positive experience of admission procedures. Her admission experience serves as an example where order and education created an atmosphere of safety. M. reflected on her admission process, which occurred two days before her surgery.

> I think it starts around the point where preregistration happens, because it educates you on how you are going to become a patient. You go through the insurance kind of stuff and you are being processed into the system and getting your name into the computer, so you are getting introduced into the system as a member of the whole program, you get your computer ID number and that follows you the whole time you are there. Then you go for an interview before surgery and you talk about what to expect a little bit. What time you should be there, they go through the process with you, to educate you as much as they can to prepare you for the event. I found that the structure helped me because it defines for you what your role is going to be.

M. exhibits a high level of awareness around her admission into the hospital system. There is an exchange of information between M. and the hospital staff. She supplies personal information and, in turn, the hospital educates her about what to expect. The orderly setup and schedule of procedures communicated to her a structure of safety and security. A chaotic environment could have undermined her sense of the hospital's competence.

Her experience passes the point of safety when she lies down on the operating table and the surgical team begins the last-minute preparations for surgery. The immediacy of the event signaled by procedures that are dehumanizing (stripping off the hospital gown), highly technological (electrodes), and invasive (IV injection) prove to be too stressful and trigger dissociation. Her wish in hindsight to be put under general anesthesia before getting on the operating table is a clue to a line of demarcation.

The depersonalizing nature of the surgical procedures takes place well before M. enters the operating room. M. is clearly aware of how they affect her.

> It made me feel like it was depersonalizing me, as I was going through the process of removing my clothes and my self-identity, I was packing it away, not that my self-identity and clothes are in the bag, but because I was given the standard hospital gown, the standard issue . . . slippers, the standard

issue bag, the standard issue binder that goes into surgery,etc.
. . . there was nothing . . . even my hair was put into a hospital
beanie. So there was nothing, I felt like I was just being packed
away . . . because the clothes you pick are a part of you representing and expressing yourself through the colors and
clothes you are wearing, . . . that is not an option. You go in
with what they give you to take, so I thought it was a deper-
sonalization like a transitional phase where you are storing
away . . . and mentally I was putting away myself, getting
ready to accept this loss of control.

She converts the shedding of her clothes and assuming the impersonal,
standard hospital attire into a meaning-making activity imaged as
"storing." Taking off and putting on clothes becomes the central
means for constructing meaning in service of the preservation of memory, the safeguard of personal identity. Memory is a fund of mnemonic
contents that ensure the continuity of self through time. In the case of
modern surgery, there is an eclipse of memory. The patient awakens
from surgery remembering nothing of the event. "Storing" is a
metaphor descriptive of the transitional quality of liminality endemic
to the act of surgery. M.'s identity is not stripped permanently, but is
temporalily "stored."

M.'s metaphor of storing indicates a difference between the liminal quality found in the experience of modern surgery and the traditional rites of passage studied by anthropologists. Whereas traditional
rites of passage move the initiate into a new state or a transformed status, M.'s concern is more for the preservation of identity fortified by
surrounding herself with mnemonic artifacts. Because of the gap in
memory imposed upon the patient by the act of surgery, preservation
of self is more important than transformation.

Her case is an example of how, within her construction of symbolic reality, she is able to fashion a positive variance of meaning from
the ritualized procedure of shedding clothes. She sheds her personal
clothes, packs them away, and takes on the hospital gown as a way to
enter the liminal experience of surgery where no personal control
exists.

A crucial factor in her ability to let go of control and "store" her
identity was her trust in the health care system. Whether this trust is
warranted in every case is debatable, but what is of interest here is how
she experienced the environment so that she could place her trust in it.

The structure of the process helped me, it gave me something
to hang on, that there was a schedule of events and part of it

was that I had to take my clothes off and pack things away—
in that respect it helped me because it was very structured,
"This is now the time for you to assume the patient role". . .
when they come in and weigh you, take your temperature,
and pulse. Make sure the forms are there, take a quick medical history, and I think that all felt part of it because you
wouldn't normally take your temperature or blood pressure at
home, that is not a standard thing to do so that is already initiating you into that new role or that new phase. I think it prepares you in terms of "don't worry, when you give up your
control there is a system here that you can rely on."

Her description contains several characteristics of ritual behavior: the
structure provides a containment for the experience; the procedures
are sequenced toward the climactic event; and the activities are outside the normal sphere of everyday functioning. Each procedure takes
on additional meaning signifying another step towards the monumen-
tal event of surgery.

How could a person who did not have a trusting approach to the
clinical reality benefit from admission procedures designed to help
patients surrender personal control in a safe manner? M.'s positive
example is not meant solely to advocate a continuation of private
expression. Her experience reveals ritualistic clues to how admission
procedures could facilitate a safe passage through the experience of
surgery.

Liminality

After she had completed the rite of separation, the shedding of clothes,
M. moved into a liminal phase represented by symbols of death.

It was the first time that I felt the vulnerability of death. You
can't do anything about it. Even though culturally, I was
brought up to think that death is just another process, and we
celebrate death on the Day of the Dead . . . but it was the first
time I began to think about my own personal death, which
was kind of different . . . it could happen today, in a few hours
. . . it was something that I had to come to face with, and loss
of the organ. I was coming to grips with the fragility of oneself. Actually, I didn't start to think about death until after I
had put away all of my clothes in the bag, and things were
labeled.

The absence of socially provided rituals necessitates a reliance on custom-made, private constructions produced from the material of her symbolic reality. She engaged in a process of preparation she referred to as "cocooning" while in the surgical waiting space.

> I felt it was a nice quiet area. I was withdrawing into myself, my energy field . . . kind of weird . . . to have a battery pack ready . . . trying to bring into myself all of my energy and enclose into myself. D. was there, but at that point I almost didn't need him there. I was kind of wanting to be internally prepared, like cocooning. I understood it psychologically, and physically, but now I had to deal with the emotional component and I was pulling in all of my energies to help go, "This is it."

"Cocooning" is a personal image selected from M.'s symbolic reality that is linked to a culturally recognizable symbol of death. A cocoon is a dual image of grave and womb. The image offers the comfort of protection necessary to pass through surgery, as well as describes the transitional quality of the experience. Having packed away the exterior dimensions of her identity, she spun herself into a cocoon with the knowledge she would emerge a different person.

Incorporation

As in the analysis of the liminal quality of surgery, there is again a difference between the classical understanding of the rites of incorporation and M.'s particular case. Her need for a personalized ritual is generated out of an awareness that the hospital's clinical reality cannot provide the safety needed to psychologically endure the event of surgery. The clinical reality she is incorporated into by the medical institution is insufficient. The issue is not one of transformation, but of restoration of identity. Again, the role of mnemonic objects plays a crucial role in her recovery of self-identity.

She used personal items invested with self-feeling to locate her identity after the surgery.

> I packed them all away very neatly to help me to feel better about the whole thing. I picked them carefully to take them with me so that when I found them, they would be enriching me back with what I felt I had brought with me. I didn't know if I would be the same after I went through it all . . . at the time I didn't know what would be the full extent of the surgery.

Things [that she brought] were very important to me because they would help stabilize myself. They would ground me after the surgery, especially when you wake up in a room that you are not familiar with and people you are not familiar with. I needed these things to help me ground.

The items in her "symbolic nest" acted to "enrich" her back to the person she knew she was before the surgery. What was removed from her identity was restored. They anchored her back into the familiar. She also used the start of the Superbowl as the termination of the surgery. It formed a boundary line where she knew she had passed from the dangerous liminal area of surgery to the safety of postoperative recovery. Once she had on the Forty-Niners T-shirt and saw the game starting, she knew "this is me now, I'm back." In the same way that crossing the threshold of the operating room constituted a line of demarcation between preparation and the act of surgery, so, too, a boundary line needs to be established that marks the end of surgery.

Prescriptions for Nascent Rituals

A calm and orderly admission procedure could make the entrance into the liminal situation of hospitalization less frightening. Creating an environment in which the patient feels safe and trusting is a distinguishing feature that separates the hospital institution from the "total" institutions described by Goffman.

From the beginning, the procedures already working in admission and surgical departments function as rituals because of their orderly, stage-sequenced structure. Each procedure moves the patient along, closer to the event of surgery or hospitalization. The patients need order and security. Procedures carried out calmly and on time foster a professional attitude of competence and trustworthiness.

In the spatial zone of admissions or surgical waiting rooms, the clutter of papers, trays, carts, and a host of medical gear contribute to an environment of chaos and stress. Their elimination would dramatically quiet the atmosphere.

Following the thesis that the stripping process can be used positively to access the liminal phenomenon experienced during hospitalization, admission procedures need to be designed so that they deconstruct without dehumanizing. Personal information submitted by the patient should remain accessible throughout his or her stay. An item for redesign is the hospital gown. No one should be asked to walk down the hall clutching the back of the gown so as not to expose themselves.

The hospital could encourage the patient to bring in favorite clothes, as well as other personal, symbolic objects. These items could be handed over to a trusted friend or hospital personnel, who would assure the patient of their safekeeping and immediate return once the surgery has been completed.

The main point of the "stripping process" that occurs within the hospital setting is that it is transitional. Its purpose is to allow the person safe entry into the liminal phenomenon of hospitalization, especially surgery. It is successful when the person is not dehumanized in the process, but is instilled with a sense of trust and care, and feels ready to face safely the ordeal of surgery or hospitalization.

Given the radically depersonalizing nature of surgery, crossing the threshold of the operating room is the limit of safety for the patient. Once on the operating table, all last-minute preparations should be made to ease the patient into the sleep of anesthesia. As a part of their preparation for surgery, the staff should focus their attention on the patient: assurances can be given, relaxing music or videos played, or last minute requests from the patient heard. This effort honors the point of departure from the waking world to the liminal world of "under going" surgery. The depersonalizing nature of surgery should occur only after the general anesthesia has taken effect.

The "cocooning" metaphor has potential for creative thinking about the design of surgical waiting rooms. A ceiling duratrans (a large color transparency set in a light box) depicting comforting images of nature is conducive for mediation. These images can replace the bare, bright ceiling lights patients stare up at while lying on a gurney. Soft, gentle music can play in the background. The anxiety in a surgical waiting room can be reduced greatly through the incorporation of these various artistic media. A warm, darkened room sets the stage for patient "cocooning": weaving together memories capable of perserving identity.

The "reflexivity" fostered during the liminal "cocooning" stage could take place privately or in a shared context. The surgical waiting room should include comfortable furniture for family to wait with the patient. When it is medically safe, the hospital could encourage gatherings of patients. Volunteers who have experienced similar surgeries act as supportive guides. They could provide another source of knowledge, support, and power. These communities of patients would ease the isolation so often felt by patients, and reduce their dependency on the hospital and medical staff.

A privatized rite of passage for surgical patients is not only meant to encourage them to construct their own, but is also a challenge to hospital administrators to examine the shape of the hospital's clinical reality. Does its clinical reality allow for the restoration of personal control after a surgical procedure or, for that matter, when a patient begins to recover from the devastation of disease? Given the difficulty of creating a public rite of passage for the multicultural population found in Western hospitals, the best and most beneficial approach for hospital administrators to take might be to create environments where patients are encouraged to create personal rites of passage. The surgical staff can encourage patients to bring mnemonic objects endowed with special feelings. These objects will work to build a symbolic nest of safety and comfort in service of preserving the patient's self-identity.

The status of patient is meant to be transitional. The ritualistic clues gleaned from the clinical example of M. indicate a movement of stripping, storing, cocooning, and restoring. This drama can be played out in ritual form designed to facilitate the transitional nature of surgery. By encouraging ritualistic behavior on the part of the patient and medical staff, nascent rituals could emerge to the point where they are recognized as beneficial for all surgical patients and incorporated into the hospital's clinical reality.

CONCLUSION

Common characteristics of the rites of passage are shared by hospital admission procedures and preparations for surgery. They consist of repetitive, orderly, and predetermined procedures designed to bring the person into the hospital. These procedures have been described as a "stripping process" whereby there is a physical separation from the world of the familiar. Patients enter a realm in which prized or valuable possessions are not allowed; the medical staff has control over the daily schedule; and the duration of stay is determined by outside authorization.

In the liminal state, the patient is introduced to the new information, roles, and expectations of the hospital's social reality. The liminal state is marked by a period of "reflexivity" when the patient is exposed to questions and issues of ultimacy. The third phase of incorporation takes place during the course of the hospitalization and beyond when the patient enacts his or her new role. In the case of surgery, the experience is brief and transitional. The status of patient is not meant to be permanent. The need for ritual serves the purpose of restoration of identity, and not necessarily transformation.

Admission procedures and the preparations for surgery function as a ritual insofar as they transmit symbolic communications from the clinical reality to the patient. The symbolic meanings attached to hospital admission procedures are used to mark the patient's initiation into the hospital experience. In a ritualistic fashion, patients utilize the metaphorical communications contained in the procedures to orient their inner experience of being ill and in the hospital. As in the case of M., the removal of street clothes and adoption of the hospital attire assisted her to internally prepare for the ordeal of surgery.

By understanding the nature of rituals, specifically rites of passage, hospitals can increase their awareness as to the effect the procedures have on their patients. The metaphorical communication that takes place in the routinizing of its procedures needs to become conscious. Once surfaced, critical questions can be asked as to whether the procedures foster healthy, adaptive behaviors for dealing with illness. Do hospital procedures provide patients with practical strategies for coping with the change of self undergone while hospitalized? Does the hospital's clinical reality provide the patient with opportunities for the restoration of personal control during hospitalization? Does the physical environment communicate an orderly, calm atmosphere worthy of a patient's trust? By recognizing the existence of ritual activity, ritual studies offers a deeper critique on how these rituals operate in an environment concerned with illness and health.

NOTES

1. Ronald L. Grimes, "Defining Nascent Ritual," *The Journal of the American Academy of Religion* 50/4 (1982), pp. 539–555.

2. Robert Fuller, *Alternative Medicine and American Religious Life* (New York: Oxford University Press, 1989).

3. Victor Turner, *The Ritual Process: Structure and Anti-structure* (Chicago: Aldine Publishing, 1969); Victor Turner, *Dramas, Fields, and Metaphors* (Ithaca, NY: Cornell University Press, 1974; Clifford Geertz, "Religion as a Cultural System," *The Interpretation of Cultures* (New York: Basic Books, 1973), pp. 87–125.

4. I wish to acknowledge the limitations of the functional approach to ritual studies. Although commonalities between diverse and cross-cultural phenomena can be highlighted, unique differences, especially transcendent meanings, in Peter Berger's words, "flatten out" [Peter Berger, "Functionalist vs. Substantial Approaches to the Anthropology of Religion," *Journal for the Scientific Study of Religion* 13 (1974), pp. 225–134]. I accept Berger's cautionary advice that the

functional approach is a tool to be used sparingly. I will exercise this tool within the limits that Berger conceded as having a positive utility for certain types of inquiry, such as "investigations of social psychological mechanisms by which the world view is maintained as plausible in the mind of its adherents . . . [and also] when comprehensive world views legitimate social inequity."

5. Arnold Van Gennep, *The Rites of Passage*, trans. M. B. Vizedom and G. L. Caffee (Chicago: University of Chicago Press, 1960). Originally published in 1909.

6. Turner, *The Ritual Process*, pp. 128–29.

7. Arthur Kleinman, *Patients and Healers in the Context of Culture* (Berkeley, CA: University of California Press, 1980), pp. 35–41.

8. Ibid., p. 41.

9. Pearl Katz, "Ritual in the Operating Room," *Ethnology* 20/4 (October 1981), 335–350.

10. Ibid., p. 349.

11. Ibid., p. 348.

12. Erving Goffman, *Asylums: Essays on the Social Situation of Mental Patients and Other Inmates* (New York: Anchor Books, 1961).

13. Hans Mauksch, "The Organizational Context of Dying," *Death: The Final Stage of Growth*, ed. Elizabeth Kubler-Ross (Englewood Cliffs, NJ: Prentice Hall, 1975), pp. 7–24.

14. Victor Turner and Edith Turner, *Image and Pilgrimage in Christian Culture: Anthropological Perspectives* (New York: Columbia University Press, 1978).

15. Victor Turner, *The Ritual Process*, p. 96.

16. John Katonah, "Hospitalization: A Rite of Passage," *Hospital Ministry*, ed. Lawrence Holst (New York: Crossroad, 1985), pp. 55–67.

17. Ibid., p. 66.

18. Victor Turner, *The Ritual Process*, p. 95.

Contributors

John Hilary Martin, O.P. is Professor of History and History of Religions at the Dominican School of Philosophy and Theology, Berkeley, California. His recent publications include "The Land: who owns it?" published in *The Medieval World of Nature* (Garland Press, 1993).

Clare B. Fischer is Aurelia Henry Reinhardt Professor of Religion and Culture at Starr King School for the Ministry, Berkeley, California. She is the coeditor (with Richard Bell) of *Simone Weil's Philosophy of Culture* (Cambridge University Press, 1993).

Richard K. Payne is Associate Professor of Japanese Religion and Dean of the Institute for Buddhist Studies, Berkeley, California. He is the author of *Tantric Ritual of Japan: Feeding the Gods, The Shingon Fire Ritual* (New Delhi: International Academy of Indian Culture and Aditya Prakashan, 1991). He also serves as the Managing Editor for *Pacific World, Journal of the Institute of Buddhist Studies*.

Martha Ellen Stortz is Associate Professor of Historical Theology and Ethics at Pacific Lutheran Theological Seminary, Berkeley, California. She is the author of *Pastor Power* (Abingdon, 1993).

Michael B. Aune is Professor of Worship at Pacific Lutheran Theological Seminary, Berkeley, California. He is the author of *"To Move the Heart": Philip Melanchthon's Rhetorical View of Rite and Its Implications for Contemporary Ritual Theory* (Christian Universities Press, 1994).

Rebecca J. Slough is Assistant Professor of Ministry Studies and Director of Congregational and Field Education at Bethany Theological Seminary, Richmond, Indiana. She was the Managing Editor of

Hymnal: A Worship Book (Bretheren Press, Faith and Life Press, and Mennonite Publishing House, 1992).

Volney P. Gay is Professor of Religion, Psychiatry, Anthropology at Vanderbilt University, Nashville, Tennessee. He is the author of *Freud on Ritual* (Scholars Press, 1979) and *Understanding the Occult* (Fortress Press, 1989).

Valerie DeMarinis is Associate Professor in Psychology of Religion and Ritual Studies at Uppsala University, Sweden. She is the author of *Critical Caring: A Feminist Model for Pastoral Psychology* (Westminister/John Knox Press, 1993) and is the co-editor of *Clinical Psychology of Religion: European and American Interdisciplinary Explorations* (Swedish Research Council Publications FRN, 1995).

Joseph D. Driskill is Instructor of Spirituality and Assistant Dean, Disciples Seminary Foundation, Pacific School of Religion, Berkeley, California. His articles and reviews have appeared in *Pastoral Psychology* and *Critical Review of Books in Religion*.

William R. Noonan is the national Planetree consultant to the Arts and a freelance organizational development consultant. He is also an instructor at Marylhurst College, Lake Oswego, and the Columbia Gorge Community College, The Dalles, Oregon.

Index